The Next Place You Come To

A Historical Introduction To Communities In North America

Ruth E. Sutter

Diablo Valley College

Prentice-Hall, Inc., *Englewood Cliffs, New Jersey*

Library of Congress Cataloging in Publication Data

SUTTER, RUTH E
The next place you come to.

Includes bibliographical references.
1. Community. 2. Cities and towns—North
America. I. Title.
HT65.S9   301.34'097   72-4427
ISBN 0-13-622167-X
ISBN 0-13-622159-9 (pbk.)

© 1973 *by* Prentice-Hall, Inc., *Englewood Cliffs, New Jersey*

Printed in the United States of America

10   9   8   7   6   5   4   3   2   1

Prentice-Hall International, Inc., *London*
Prentice-Hall of Australia, Pty. Ltd., *Sydney*
Prentice-Hall of Canada, Ltd., *Toronto*
Prentice-Hall of India Private Limited, *New Delhi*
Prentice-Hall of Japan, Inc., *Tokyo*

To the memory of my parents,
Helen and George Sutter

Contents

v

Preface

A student in a social science class I was teaching last year commented one day that what was wrong with the college was that no one there had any "sense of community." It was hardly an original complaint; I had heard it elsewhere, had heard the president of the college himself call for a revival of community a few weeks earlier. And I had been reading about it ever since I started reading sociological literature. Feeling a little as though I was speaking memorized lines, I asked the student what he meant by "community." "I don't really know—a feeling you get about people, places. . . ." So, he had the same script by heart. Then he added, "I suppose you'll say there's no such thing, we're making it up, but that's the point. Maybe there never was any such thing in the past, and people just try to say there was. Maybe it's part of the future."

I would like to thank my students at Diablo Valley College for such expressions of vision and concern. They have provoked this study of people and places in the past and been good-natured about my trying out my ideas on them. Colleagues have been patient, encouraging, and helpful with source materials. Long-lasting acknowledgements are due also the late Robert Redfield, whose lectures at the University of Chicago first made me think about communities, and Earl S. Johnson, who taught there that the study of social relationships should always lead to bettering them, that social science is a way of informing oneself to act intelligently.

Ruth E. Sutter

1

"For Some, Places Mean Coming To Or Going From..."

At midcentury in the middle of the United States, some restless teenagers were exploring the backroads and the crossroads towns, maybe for want of better entertainment—I no longer remember why. My friends and I went nearly every weekend into some part of the countryside of eastern Nebraska, and sometimes we played a sort of *déjà vu* game: when we saw a small town in the distance we would stop and bet about the location of general store, post office, filling station, churches, and the look of the buildings. We knew where everything was; like Tolstoy's happy families, midwestern small towns were all alike. We must have been as often wrong as right, though. We began with an assumption of similarity, but none of us would ever have mistaken hometown for any other town. Hometown had its own identity.

Every town has its own identity for the people who live in it. Where the sense of "here" or of "home" comes from has been explored by novelists, by sociologists, by psychologists—perhaps by every human being in one way or another. This sense seems as close and as elusive as the sense of self. Sometimes a person will say, "My home is wherever I am." Yet there is ordinarily a definable place—if only a room—that is more known and felt than other places, a place that is not simply looked at, not simply noticed. In fact, it may be noticed hardly at all. It is recognized. Is this place contained only by familiar walls? As implied by Proust and Eugene O'Neill, are its boundaries made up only of memories of family? Or do other kinds of relationship produce similar recognitions? An image of a place often becomes part of a person's way of identifying himself and others: New Yorker, small-town boy, Westerner. When is it a primary source of identity, and when is it one among several?

There seem to have been changes in the nature and extent of areas that people recognize as essential to their lives, and of the places and groups they identify with. To take account of such changes is to take account of changing relationships, changing boundaries of relationships, changing horizons. History might indeed be thought of as a record of horizons, or of man's varying perceptions of them and identifications with them. The word *community* has sometimes been used for these perceptions and identifications. John Quincy Adams told the Massachusetts Historical Society in 1843 that "whatever in the transactions of associated man bears on the causes and motives of their congregation into communities, and on their corporate existence and well-being, assumes the character of a material for history."[1]

The present study is essentially a history, but it is a particular kind of history. With "community" as its theme, it can be classed with social histories or with sociological works, but the subject itself seems incapable of either historical or sociological definition, at least at the outset. Social scientists have developed and explored the concept of community. Particular communities and types of local community have been looked at, listened to, lived in, and described; by now a fairly long and many-faceted bibliography of community studies can be compiled. The most general classifications are *rural* and *urban*. Since the early part of the twentieth century, sociologists have made a distinction between "rural sociology" and "urban sociology," while they, along with political and economic historians, have worked to describe a shift in American society from the one to the other. History textbooks routinely include some local and many nonlocalized effects of and responses to industrialization. An even more persistent theme has been the development of nations and national identifications, sometimes referred to by the term *national community*. Generalizations from these studies, different as they are in scope and frame of reference, can be examined together, and perhaps some of them can be put together. For example, the usual statements about changes from a rural-agricultural to an urban-industrial orientation in the United States in the last third of the nineteenth century can be looked at from the point of view of diverse localities and regions as well as of nationally measured trends. For this kind of task, a perspective is required that would allow students of both Amer-

<hr>

[1] *The New England Confederacy of MDCXLIII* (Boston: Charles C. Little and James Brown, 1843), p. 4.

ican history and social organization and culture to see local and nonlocal patterns of change. Yet, assuming that such a perspective can be obtained, the problems of putting the whole picture together are immense. This, is, of course, one reason why the job has not yet been done, and why the present attempt does not pretend to be more than an outline, a suggestion or series of suggestions of what the necessary elements of the picture are.

One of the problems has to do with the time line. Although every identifiable place has its own chronological history, just as every person has, and every nation, and civilization, it takes much more than chronology to give order to a number of changes in a number of these entities at once. Referring to periods of time can simplify such a problem, but how should they be determined? The periods into which the history of North America is traditionally divided were not derived from studies of communities and might therefore mislead the historian who attempts to impose them. In any given period, local communities with different forms, functions, and futures have existed side by side. An appreciation of how each changed cannot be obtained by clustering events important to still another unit, the national, into periods. Some changes do stand out as significant on other than a local level, however, and they can be seen to affect different localities and groups within localities differently. Technological developments provide obvious examples. Electric power, for instance, created new local industries and nonlocal enterprise and yet did not affect some parts of the country until long after the rest. The preliminary problem, then, is to select the most significant kinds of change within local *and* nonlocal frameworks. It is change, and not time per se, that allows us to set up categories of time. And, as long as we are considering change, it should be noted that there is no such thing as a static community. If one appears not to be changing, it is probably because of the way it is being looked at. This is worth emphasizing if only because stasis is so much a part of the stereotype of rural communities in North America that even rural people have sometimes (superficially) held it. Sociological studies, too, have assumed a slowness of change in local relationships and in willingness to accept innovations. Yet there is change. It has only to be considered from the community's own perspective.

Another problem in this kind of study has to do with applying frames of reference and terminology of the social sciences to historical source materials. Social scientists have long made use of such materials—one of the founders of urban sociology, Robert Park, pointed out some fifty years ago that sociology had its origin in history, in attempts to explain historical facts by "exact methods"—but historians have only recently begun to work with concepts from the social sciences. For the most part the borrowed concepts are still applied nonanalytically, so that what results is simply terminology, a vocabulary expanded to include such terms as culture, community, social class, alienation, power structure. For a historian to reveal something new by his use of them, methods of study must also be changed or expanded. In general, however, training and experience in a special academic discipline—history, sociology, anthropology, or whatever—can be expected to promote special habits of thinking. Aside from the existence of "schools" of history, the techniques of study to which historians become committed have an integrity of their own, just as do those of the other social sciences.

Further, each disciplinary system develops its own set of questions about human behavior, or at least its own way of phrasing them. Lip service is often paid to "interdisciplinary" approaches, but that idea itself presumes separate disciplines. Yet there are questions that appear to cut across disciplines. Some do so because they relate to several aspects of behavior. Others have been asked over a long period of time and have become part of our way of trying to make sense of our lives. Thus, at the same time that professional specialization proceeds and each specialty develops its own set of questions and its own terminology, the academic disciplines are related to each other by common concerns that are part of a cultural heritage. As the culture changes, the concerns change, as well as the language used to describe them. We use present ideas to make sense of both the past and the present and to dream of the future, but we cannot escape the fact that the understanding we get is determined by the questions we ask. What community is, how it works and changes, what living place, life space, and social relationships have to do with ideas and actions —these are among the questions that appear to cut across disciplines. They do, however, have reference points in the development of ideas over time. For that matter, as I put together historical materials on the subject of community, I keep wondering if the questions they raise are themselves so tied to the past that they preclude recognition of what we ought to build or become. Is community itself an outmoded idea?

An idea, as such, has a history. About a century ago, that of community began to be used in an effort to understand social changes in the modern world. Social philosophers and social scientists developed it into a frame of reference within which a variety of social phenomena could be analyzed. It has constituted just one approach, of course, but it has been an influential one. Community studies are now an integral part of American sociological and anthropological inquiry. Methods of study may be criticized, evaluated, changed, and refined with increasingly sophisticated analytical techniques and devices, but the assumption that it is a worthwhile kind of study is seldom challenged. At the same time, and increasing in intensity through the fifties and sixties, comes the cry that we have lost community, that there is no community any more. As real and anguished as this cry may be, the meaning of the term is not always clear. Obviously it does not just refer to a place of residence. It may, however, be based on an ideal of community: small, relatively self-sufficient, the location of significant persons and experiences, or—a step removed—the sensation of belonging somewhere, treasuring certain relationships, recalling the experiences through which one's sense of identity has developed. This community may, in fact, be nothing that could be made fully conscious. It may even be a shortcut way to describe something that has been dreamed of or hoped for but never really thought out. The term is vulnerable by now, capable of being freely used with reference to all sorts of frustrations.

This is not to say that the search for community in the modern world is invalid. Aside from any theorizing, the search *is* being conducted, sometimes in a very practical way, by part of the present generation. It is, simply, that the pleas for a return to community, and also many of the community studies, have an underlying attitude which ought to be made explicit: Community, or the sense of community, holds a society together, even holds an individual together, and without it we are in trouble. I may be sidestepping the fundamental question of the importance of community when I speak in the present study of "places" and use the terms "community" and "place" almost interchangeably, but it is a deliberate sidestepping. I wish to discover something of people's relationships to places and to each other; as for the idea-ideal of community, its ambiguity at present is the clearest thing about it.

Past meanings of the term are easier to understand. The oldest one refers to a political or social unit with definite geographic and legal boundaries. In this sense, villages, towns, and cities are all communities. The second major meaning emphasizes commonality, whether or not it is related to a given place. A city would not necessarily be a community in this sense, since migrating residents might have little in common. Interestingly, both of these meanings are to be found in English usage by the seventeenth century, but though the first has been and still is the most commonly used, the second has received increasing emphasis as time has gone on.[2] To discover to what extent or how locality and commonality are interdependent has been the aim of many social scientists in the past century. John Dewey, for example, suggested that *community, communication*, and *in common* are inherently interdependent terms.

The idea of community has not been redefined, nor have people tried to understand it, apart from observable changes in communities. The most powerful force for such changes in the past two centuries has been the industrial revolution. It was in the context of industrialization, with the expansion of cities and the uprooting of people from villages and countrysides, and with the recognition that the most influential economic and political institutions existed above and beyond any local community, that

---

[2]E. C. Lindeman, in his essay "Community" in the first edition of the *Encyclopedia of the Social Sciences* (1931), IV, 102, describes concisely the change from a conception based on structure, or on institutions in a geographic area, to one based on process, or on psychological factors developing through interaction.

European social philosophers and sociologists began to examine and use the concept of community in new ways. Nisbet, tracing the "unit-ideas" of sociology, finds medieval society to be a source of inspiration for nineteenth-century critics of "modernism" in western Europe: "The rediscovery of medievalism—its institutions, values, themes, and structures—is one of the significant events in the intellectual history of the nineteenth century."[3] For founders of modern sociology, such as Comte, Le Play, Tönnies, and Durkheim, medieval society provided models for comparison. This was in terms mainly of family and local community relationships. The urban-industrial scene, of course, would show the greatest contrast, but at least some remnants of older social institutions could always be found in the midst of apparently normless, fragmented, mechanized, urban-industrial societies. Even in the United States, relatively new as communities were when, at the turn of the twentieth century, they were first closely looked at, greatly contrasting simple and complex communities could be found side by side. Their coexistence—their very need for each other—forms the subject of a later chapter. The point here is that, in the study of a society and its history, the models applied in one period of time are often drawn from another, or those used to analyze one social setting may actually have been developed from another. To decide whether this is a problem or a solution in the study of social institutions would carry us off the track at this point. We must, however, be aware of the possibility that when we are looking at one community we may be carrying in our minds the image or the model of a completely different community. It is partly to clarify the use of models that the present review of historical community types has been undertaken.

Of course the broadest of all problems in community studies (and also in this survey of them) is that of how one arrives at adequate generalizations. For example, to bring together the conclusions of some recent studies is to discover that urban life alienates, rural life constrains, and suburban life does both. Every type of community has been attacked at some time, from some point of view. A confusion of community models, as mentioned above, is sometimes involved. It may happen, too, that the image of one part of a place or of one aspect of life in it is applied to the whole. In this way late-nineteenth-century critics could identify industrial centers with the slum-tenements in their residential districts. Such confusions of image are, fundamentally, confusions about function. "Few communities were so frequently compared to hell" as Pittsburgh,[4] but its

---

[3]Robert A. Nisbet, *The Sociological Tradition* (New York: Basic Books, Inc., 1966), p. 14. See also his *The Quest for Community* (New York: Oxford University Press, 1953; republished as *Community and Power* in 1962), pp. 77–80.

[4]Roy Lubove, *Twentieth-Century Pittsburgh: Government, Business, and Environmental Change* (New York: John Wiley & Sons, Inc., 1969), p. 1.

industrial functions were essential to regional and national economic growth. It was one of the urban places raked over at the turn of the century. Several of those attacks were made by people who had grown up in small towns. Community-conscious suburban residential places have been studied just as devastatingly, and several times by people who grew up in multifunctional cities. At present, the virtues of small-town life are being revived in popular image. A television news feature-gatherer goes through a Maine fishing village on his vacation, notes friendly greetings on the street, and announces that something is left of old America—mentioning only in passing that, unfortunately, the fishermen are now hard put to make a living and are becoming increasingly dependent on summer visitors.

The image of a place as it once was may be held just as tenaciously, or even more so, by long-time residents as by nostalgic visitors. The image may, indeed, be important in maintaining attachments to a place and interest in its future, but it is often at the risk of obscuring the present realities of function and form, and what can or should be done about them. In a society made up of many types of community (as the modern industrial societies are), the risk is compounded by potentially conflicting images. This is a good part of what makes adequate generalizations—even about types of community—so hard to come by. It would be easier if, as in the heading to this chapter, we could simply assume that "places mean coming to or going from," if we didn't have to consider the identity and the image of a place among its residents and others, and if we didn't have to ask what the word "community" means and why it is so much used today.

This book represents, therefore, an exploring venture in mapped and unmapped regions of community. In some ways, it follows the more-or-less conventional itinerary of general historians. Pre-Columbian North America, European backgrounds, colonization, colonial struggles for independence and new nationhood, the westward movement, and so on are standard routes in American history. Taking the community theme along these routes requires that communities be considered not only in their function as local social units but also in changing contexts of translocal political and economic groupings and trends. Much of the story of North America is one of the building of new communities and the development of new kinds of community. In the establishment of colonial communities and in the settlement of frontier areas, it is sometimes assumed—as it was by some of the community builders, too—that what went on in a particular locality had its beginning and end in that locality. Such an assumption, however, makes it impossible to evaluate the effects of wider influences, which were often formative and then controlling in regard to local development and change. To show these contexts for community is to cover some of the ground of standard general histories, but I think it important to do so since change has occurred in the nature and impact of nonlocal influences as well as in local communities. Doing so suggests, in addition, factors in development of the nonlocal associations and identifications now often referred to as communities. It might also be pointed out here that aspects of community outside the present boundaries of the United States are included, partly because this is a survey of community, not of a nation as such, and partly to allow for more kinds of comparison than would otherwise be possible.

As for terminology used in this study, *community form* refers to those structures and features that seem significant to the life of the people in a locality. Their layout and use generally reveal patterns in work and social interaction. Thus, for example, a community may take the form of an agricultural village, with a cluster of houses surrounded by fields and other lands; or it may take the form of a market town, with trading, transportation, and administrative facilities, houses, and perhaps other structures arranged in a fairly compact way so that they are easily accessible to each other and to people from elsewhere. I use the term primarily to indicate that a community has a visible structure related to its functions (this does not, of course, take into account the existence of communities without localities). *Community identity* refers to what the patterns of work and social interaction, taken together, mean to the people involved in or aware of them. It is community identity when Sandburg calls Chicago "Hog Butcher for the World,/ Tool Maker, Stacker of Wheat,/ Player with Railroads and the Nations' Freight Handler"; he is citing functions, to be sure, but he personalizes and combines them into a unitary, unmistakable picture of that complex industrial city in the early twentieth century. It is easier to give words to community form than to community identity. Community identity is an essence, a distillation of essential features, but it must be remembered, essential features as they are perceived, not necessarily as they may be defined, measured, or examined in some objective fashion. This is a troublesome kind of concept for social scientists. Poets and painters have the advantage with it.

The term *urbanization* ought also to be considered at this point.[5] It is used in this book to refer to a set of processes, not a single process, say that of population concentration, as it is sometimes used. Population concentration is only part of the set. Concentration of functions—economic, political, religious, informational or educational, residential—is a second

---

[5]On methods of study and problems associated with this concept, see for example Eric E. Lampard, "American Historians and the Study of Urbanization," *American Historical Review*, 67 (October, 1961), 49–61, and Roy Lubove, "The Urbanization Process: An Approach to Historical Research," *Journal of the American Institute of Planners*, 33 (January, 1967), 33–39. The present study is not, of course, one of urbanization as such.

part; the division of labor and the specialization that are often cited as urban characteristics come under this heading. However, because community form, community identity, and expectations about a place are related to the particular functions concentrated in it, the general term *urban* is not as useful as those descriptive of types, such as *administrative center, commercial center, multifunctional center.* Interdependency of places, based on ties of transportation and communication lines, is a third part of the set of urban processes, and this has usually meant more than one kind of interdependency (not just economic, political, or administrative).

The last-named process makes it reasonable to speak of an urban or urbanized society, but only if the other two have also occurred. The three are not always discovered together, and where they are not, we should describe what is going on and not invoke urbanization, even if it does appear nearby or develops at some later time. For example, the Maya built *ceremonial centers* in which other than religious functions were probably concentrated, but most of the population lived in scattered hamlets and villages and the centers have not been shown to be interdependent. Thus, as defined above, there was no urbanization. The Aztecs, on the other hand, had in Tenochtitlan a large, multifunctional center of population from which political, military, and economic ties extended through most of central and southern Mexico. I would call that an example of urbanization and, though it was at first broken into, it was in the long run continued by the Spaniards. European towns in the early Middle Ages tended to be administrative and military centers only, with small populations; the trading towns that grew up in the late Middle Ages were economically influential but did not become multifunctional or populous until much later. Some of the colonial towns in North America had a similar development. By the middle of the nineteenth century, however, a sort of instant urbanization was occurring in parts of North America as places were dreamed up and built specifically to accommodate concentrated functions and population.

In general, three dimensions of community are explored in this study. Three questions are posed: How are people related to their surroundings? How are they related to each other? How or what do they think of themselves? In the terminology of the social sciences, the first question has to do with the *ecological system*; the second, *social organization*; and the third, *social* and *personal identity*. The context for study of them can also be posed as a question: How are these dimensions related? Yet, unlike the other three questions, it cannot be answered when communities are considered in isolation from each other. A history of communities in North America is more a story of connections between places, more a matter of "coming to and going from," than of the places themselves.

2

North American Settings

*"We have pounded our hands in despair
against the adobe walls,
for our inheritance, our city, is lost and dead. . ."*
—ELEGY FOR TENOCHTITLAN (1528)

If the Europeans who arrived in the New World after 1492 had occupied themselves with studies of community life, they might not have thought the Native Americans strange. They were leaving scattered homesteads, family communities, village communities, towns, brotherhoods, trading associations, cities, city-republics, duchies, religious organizations, principalities, and kingdoms; some of what they came to could have been compared, even though each place and group would have its own history and identity. That they did look for certain aspects of social and political organization among the peoples they met is a matter of record. Some seemed more important than others. Especially important were concepts of authority that they could readily understand and so make use of in dealing with the "Indians." For example, the Spaniards noted the distinctions and connections between religious and political authority among the Aztecs, and the English were so impressed with the confederation principle and the council of sachems among the Iroquois that they sought and encouraged similar arrangements among other groups. All, it might go without saying, were interested in military organization. They were not, however, looking for "community."

It is in some ways easy, in some ways hard, and in all ways risky to make comparisons of Native Americans and colonizing Europeans from this distance in time, although the impulse to do so seems unavoidable. The sources of information are different, and terms useful in analyzing one source may produce nonsense when applied to another. The main difference is that of written and unwritten records. Legal and political documents and literary evidence relating to community forms and social life are available for many centuries preceding the formative years of the European colonists. There is practically nothing of that sort for the Native Americans. Twentieth-century categories—archaeological, anthropological, sociological—may be imposed on the materials, but this does not necessarily mean that what they describe is comparable. Limitations must be recognized: the categories and concepts themselves; the nature of the materials, the different times, places, and ways of collecting and interpreting them; and the unverifiability of the self-views and world-views of the peoples who have left something of themselves for us to puzzle over. These limitations and the problems related to them should not be seen as barriers. They are given here only as warnings about overly general comparisons that one might be tempted into when making a survey of a complex subject over both time and space. They should be kept in mind as questions throughout this study. As such, they may open up areas that this brief study cannot cover.

European settlers often treated Indians as though they were part of the landscape, as though they could hurry across them, use them, try to refashion them in the European image. The first Americans were, in some sense, part of a landscape. They had worked out a long-lasting close relationship with their physical world. In legend, in song, in hunting and planting, they identified themselves with it or treated it as a neighbor, as kin, as god, and as itself, a world to talk to and to exchange things with. Yet they also changed that world, knowingly and unknowingly, as men everywhere, in building something, have had an effect on the setting they used. They established themselves in places, settled down, settled in, more than is usually recognized—and it may be added that Europeans had been moving about more than is usually emphasized.

American historians, generalizing about the earliest Americans from colonial and national references to them, have assisted nineteenth-century novelists and journalists and twentieth-century radio, television, and film writers in building an image of a nomad (with exceptions, the Aztecs, Mayas, and Incas, referred to in terms of "high civilization") whose social relationships were centered on the family and whose ability to make use of the land (which was presumably not private property) was as primitive as his knowledge of government (which, even if "democratic" in some sense, was presumably limited in scope). Since standard survey textbooks give so little space to Native Americans—from a paragraph to two or three pages, plus a few references to wars with them, especially on the Plains— their part in the image may derive from the generalization attendant on brevity. Sometimes, among the generalizations, note is taken of the diversity of pre-Columbian groups in North America, but the usual assumption is that, diverse as they may have been, Indians north of the Valley of Mexico can be combined and compared with what are referred to as "higher" or "more advanced" peoples there and in Yucatan and the central Andes. And that, finally, one can take all Indians and compare them with the still more advanced whites of western Europe and England. This is the historical tradition. Some historians try to get away from the European-centered value judgments inherent in it by showing only that, sooner or later, the Indians were conquered by the "superior" tools, techniques, and weapons of the whites. Physically conquered they were. However, many did resist invasion, and there were a few temporary successes; others were so "primitive" that they thought it was wrong to wage war.

Some students of Native American history and cultures, including archaeologists and anthropologists, have for at least a century been describing variety among the peoples of North America, variety in responses to the environment and in the effects of contact with European conquerors, tradesmen, and settlers. There were also a number of distinct community forms and ways in which localities were interrelated, and for this reason, a survey of pre-Columbian settings for community life can do more than set the stage for European newcomers; it can lead to some central questions about the nature of community.

To be outlined here are geographic settings, main subsistence bases found in them, and social and residential patterns as derived from archaeological, ethnographic, and, to a certain extent, historical accounts. The concept of *culture area* is fundamental to such an outline. First proposed around the turn of the century as a way of classifying museum collections, and then of categorizing types of North American Indian cultures in face of their diversity and the complexity of using such standard categories as language, it is by now widely accepted among anthropologists. It means, generally, that similar ways of life are to be found within identifiable geographic areas, that responses to a natural environment and the use of its resources become interrelated with social as well as economic organization, that people within such an area have more in common with each other than they do with people outside it. This is not, by the way, a species of simple environmental determinism; in the culture area concept man is seen as part, a dynamic part, of an ecological system.

The areas identified for North America differ somewhat in the different anthropological accounts, depending on which aspects of culture

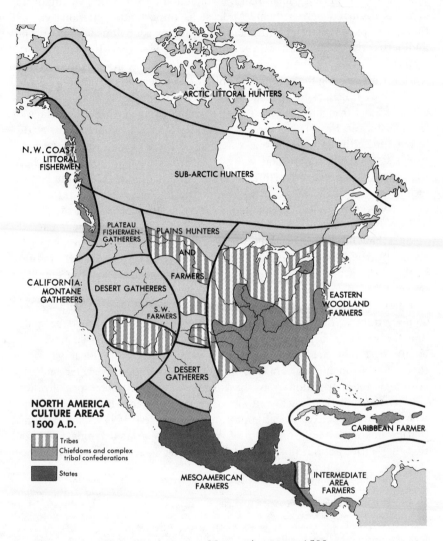

FIG. 2–1 CULTURE AREAS OF NORTH AMERICA, 1500 A.D.

Source: Reprinted, by permission, from William T. Sanders and Joseph Marino, *New World Prehistory: Archaeology of the American Indian.* (© 1970 by Prentice-Hall, Inc., Englewood Cliffs, N.J.)

are being emphasized.[1] Groups and traditions to be comprised within them changed over the thousands of years—perhaps thirty or forty thousand or more—during which man has inhabited North America. Important contacts occurred across them. At least as importantly, migrants carried their own special histories with them. That factor is obvious within Europe, and across the Atlantic after 1492; it should be assumed also within North America. In spite of these variables, the culture areas do provide a framework for assembling the components of North American community history.

By way of background, the first Americans probably came from Asia across a land bridge in the area of the Bering Strait during a late stage of the Pleistocene Era. There were several migrations, it would seem, at different times; the last major one was that of the Eskimo, who arrived between six and three thousand years ago. Projectile points that have been found in many parts of North and South America indicate that the earliest groups, those on the move at the end of the ice age, were big-game hunters. Around ten thousand years ago, as the glaciers receded and the climate and animal and plant life changed, other major traditions[2] began to develop: the Old Cordilleran in the Pacific Northwest, with a diversified economy dependent on both sea and land resources; the Desert tradition in the western and southwestern parts of the continent, with an emphasis on seed and plant collecting; and the Archaic tradition of the temperate, forested, and better-watered eastern part of the continent, with various combinations of hunting, fishing, and gathering foods. It should be added that the geographic and climatic conditions of North America have been about what they are today since 2500 B.C., aside from local variations (and aside from our current and incalculable pollution of water and air). Although these traditions may be taken as basic to later specializations within particular ecological settings, the social organization of the people who followed them can be little more than surmised. It is usually assumed that groups were small, made up of one or a few related family units, and that they moved about in search of food. There is archaeological evidence,

[1]Among the inclusive studies are H. E. Driver, *Indians of North America* (Chicago: University of Chicago Press, 1961); A. L. Kroeber, *Cultural and Natural Areas of Native North America* (Berkeley: University of California Press, 1939); and Robert F. Spencer et al., *The Native Americans: Prehistory and Ethnology of the North American Indians* (New York: Harper & Row, Publishers, 1965). Archaeological information specifically related to settlement forms is given in Gordon R. Willey, ed., *Prehistoric Settlement Patterns in the New World* (New York: Wenner-Gren Foundation for Anthropological Research, Incorporated, 1956). For archaeological backgrounds and relationships to major culture traditions, see also Gordon R. Willey, *An Introduction to American Archaeology: North and Middle America* (Englewood Cliffs, N.J.: Prentice-Hall, Inc., 1966).

[2]Archaeologists use this term both specifically and broadly to refer to characteristic tools and techniques that persist over time. See Gordon R. Willey and Philip Phillips, *Method and Theory in American Archaeology* (Chicago: University of Chicago Press, 1958).

supplemented by observation of post-Columbian peoples with similar economies, that such groups had campsites to which they returned regularly, often seasonally. Some of these sites, on rivers where fishing was good, for example, may have supported populations of several hundred at a time. And even before the spread of agriculture some sites (we might as well call them villages) were being maintained over long periods of time.

Survey of Culture Areas

ARCTIC

The Eskimo cultural tradition, beginning as a distinct tradition between 2000 and 1000 B.C., has been maintained by scattered groups across the Arctic from eastern Siberia to Greenland. Its strength across this length of time and breadth of space seems extraordinary, but there are variations in different parts of the Arctic. A variety of topographic and climatic conditions are found, along with the dominating features of indented coastlines, barren tundras, ice and snow, and seasonal contrasts in darkness and light. On the "Barren Ground" of the central part of the area are caribou hunters; to the east and west, along the many coasts, it is mainly the animal resources of the sea, especially the varieties of seal, that are depended on. People in the west have specialized further with the Pacific walrus and the whale.

Settlement patterns have varied too, though in general the Eskimo have been oriented toward the *nuclear family* unit—parents and children—in their social and residential relationships, as much as any society in North America and more so than most. This orientation may be related to the scarcity of food and difficulty of obtaining it. The people have known starvation, and larger economic groupings would increase the chances of it. The local grouping is not invariably a single family, however. The Eskimo of Alaska have established more or less permanent village communities for winter residence, with stone, sod, and wooden structures large enough to house several families, and the population of this region has tended to be larger than in other parts of the Arctic.[3] Throughout the Arctic area (at least until recent years), families have moved from camp to camp in summer and have not always returned to the same locality in winter. However, the most important ties are still kin-

[3]See Norman A. Chance, *The Eskimo of North Alaska* (New York: Holt, Rinehart and Winston, 1966), pp. 6–7. On settlement size, Driver writes: "Winter settlements averaged less than a hundred persons for the Eskimo as a whole, and less than fifty for those in the central regions" (*Indians of North America*, pp. 326–27).

ship ties. When other ties are formed, such as for work, the partners become like kin to each other. Travelers seek out their kindred; strangers in a community are looked on with suspicion until they can identify themselves satisfactorily with someone there. Yet hospitality is generally noted in studies of the Eskimo.

Contemporary changes instituted by United States and Canadian business enterprises and governments have begun to modify the old patterns for many residents of the far north. These changes have been a long time coming, when one considers that the Eskimo were probably the first North Americans to be contacted by transatlantic nomads. Norse seamen met them in Greenland in the ninth century, and then on the coast of Labrador, though the effects of these contacts cannot be discovered. European explorers and fishermen found them again in the sixteenth century, and Russian contact with western Eskimos occurred in the eighteenth century.

SUBARCTIC

The Indians of the area south of the tree line were also family-centered. Generally, this is a region of coniferous forests, with a few sections of treeless tundra, many rivers, lakes, and swamplands, and cold winters and warm summers. Life throughout the Subarctic, before European contact, depended on hunting and fishing, with shellfishing along the Gulf of St. Lawrence. Most of the people relied on the caribou and moose. Famines were common, especially in winter, and again the local group was small. The nuclear family was most important; an *extended family*, related families or kin up to three generations, sometimes banded together but membership in such a band was not fixed, for both individuals and nuclear families were free to come and go. Thus, the local community was as loose in the Subarctic as in the Arctic.

It was the Algonquians of the eastern part of the Subarctic who first had to deal with the French, early in the seventeenth century. These hunters and trappers set the scene for the fur trade, the initial economic base for French colonial development. If definite family territories had not already been established, they were then. In the northern tundra bands had mutually exclusive territories for caribou hunting within which the family units would sometimes split off to hunt smaller game when caribou were scarce. In forested regions, small families (6 to 15 persons) had their own hunting territories in winter but congregated for fishing in summer. By the nineteenth century, the bands were noted to have headmen who organized land use and trade, both among the Indians and with the Hudson's Bay Company. The headman's position was based on ability, not heredity, and he was sometimes assisted by an informal council.

NORTHWEST COAST

Among the nonagricultural peoples of North America, those of the Northwest Coast have been especially noted for their well-built villages, complex social structure, ceremonial life, and art forms. The area takes in the western slopes of the Coastal Range and the rivers, coasts, and islands of the Pacific between southeastern Alaska and northwestern California. Though it includes glaciers in the north and sandy beaches in the south, it is characterized by forests, many streams, and heavy rainfall. With the warming effects of the Japanese current, the climate is temperate even at high latitudes. The peoples of this area made use of all its sea resources, including sea mammals, and land animals, birds, waterfowl, and wild plants; salmon was the most important food source. Abundance of these resources permitted local population growth and leisure time for elaboration of the cultural heritage. According to Philip Drucker, "Even a large family group is unlikely to favor a nomadic way of life if they have half a ton of dried salmon to lug around with them."[4]

Structurally, the villages were made up of a row or rows of large plank houses fronted with carved or painted crests, or totem poles. A village usually housed related families; a single house would hold several nuclear families and in some instances apparently was regarded as a village in itself. Most often, the local group was, as a whole, a *lineage*—an extended family grouping in which the significant ties are genetic. With population growth and prosperity part of it would sometimes leave and form a new community. This "hiving-off" process always involved persons related to each other. The local lineages had their own names, chiefs, and territorial rights, combining at times for ceremonial or defense purposes. They shared language and other main cultural traits but did not form a nation in any precise sense; the local communities were politically autonomous, presided over by the man who ranked highest in terms of his wealth and heredity. Social ranking was an important part of one's identity. The villagers took their titles from their descent and their acquisitions (as revealed in the much-described displays of the potlatch ceremonies). The broadest distinctions were between "nobles," "commoners," and slaves (persons taken in war and, if not ransomed, held as chattels). Outside of the slave class, upward mobility in the system of ranking was possible through skill in the arts or crafts or in warfare, and also through charisma. Qualities of leadership were apparently most important among groups with fewer titles and opportunities for material acquisition.

---

[4] *Indians of the Northwest Coast* (New York: The American Museum of Natural History, 1955), p. 7.

Local and regional relationships were, of course, much modified by the arrival of European tradesmen. Several stopovers had been made by Russians and Spaniards in the eighteenth century, but these had little effect until Captain James Cook's stay in Nootka Sound in 1778, when trading for sea-otter skins was initiated. Subsequently, the English, Russians, Spaniards, and Americans made attempts to control trade in the area, and the Hudson's Bay Company succeeded in organizing it after 1821. Until this time population density in the area was second only to California and parts of Mesoamerica. Village size varied; early postcontract records show for the Haida, for example, a range from forty to several hundred persons, with thirty to forty in a single house and from one to a dozen houses in a locality. Population clustering seems to have increased, at least at trading centers, after European contact. For about a century, trade and new materials stimulated Northwestern arts and crafts, and then disease and economic dependency disrupted the local groupings and their culture.

Throughout the area a community had been a natural cooperative grouping in that one was born into a set of roles and relationships, worked with others in that place, and found status in their eyes. It was possible for a person to verify that these processes existed for others, in the same way, since villages were accessible to each other (mostly by sea) and within particular regions the language and heritage were shared. That most of these village communities were made up of related persons should not prevent us from seeing them as community groupings. The main characteristics of *family*, according to Driver, are (1) common residence, (2) economic cooperation, (3) reproduction, and (4) education of offspring.[5] Where related families have grouped together, as in the Northwest Coast culture area (and, if only sometimes or temporarily, in the Arctic and Subarctic), the lines of residence and of economic and educational responsibilities have varied. If we ignore for a moment the problematic concepts of family and community, we might see that the people of the Northwest Coast recognized a variety of relationships to be significant for existence, subsistence, and identity and that these were mostly localized but also crossed the village lines for mates, carriers of the cultural tradition (as in ceremonies), assistance (as in defense), and status (as in comparing wealth and achievements). Similar instances are to be found in other culture areas of North America.

INTERIOR PLATEAU

Geographically, the Interior Plateau comprises the Columbia and Fraser River systems between the Rockies and the Cascades and Coastal Range of the State of Washington and British Columbia. The northern

[5]*Indians of North America*, p. 285.

part is forested and cut by streams and rivers; toward the south, with the exception of river valleys, the climate becomes increasingly dry and the vegetation sparse. The rivers, with their rich supply of salmon, formed the focus of life for the peoples of this area, and western groups shared a number of cultural traits with the peoples of the Northwest Coast. Most supplemented fishing with the hunting of deer and other small game and the gathering of roots and berries. They would move to temporary camps for these purposes, but their villages were essentially river settlements. Their main attachment was to the local grouping. A village had its own territories for fishing, hunting, and gathering (though outsiders were not thereby excluded). It tended to be small, three to five families or thirty to forty persons for the Sanpoil, for example. Related persons usually had their own house: an earth lodge, a mat-covered lodge housing several nuclear families, or in some places, an extendable plank house similar to those of the Northwest Coast. There was no strict pattern of residence; the type of relationship in a given household varied from place to place and time to time, and kinship cut across village lines. Sometimes villages banded together, sharing their territories, but this did not mean a tribal identification. Leadership was based on ability and achievements; inheritable social rank occurred only among the western groups. A central group, the Sanpoil, has been noted for its emphasis on equality, principles of sharing, and dislike of conflict.[6]

The peoples of this area were indirectly affected by Europeans by the early eighteenth century, though direct contact probably did not occur before the expedition of Lewis and Clark (1804–1806). Then traders arrived. The population had been decimated by epidemics before prospective settlers were crowding the Oregon Trail in the 1840's. A series of small wars further reduced Indian numbers (though some groups insisted on neutrality); a final disruption followed the discovery of gold in Washington and British Columbia in 1857. Twenty years later, after lands had been "given" and taken away several times and the Indians had been unable to find a secure locality, Chief Joseph of the Nez Perce delivered his famous message of surrender, a message also of the agony of dispersal of family and community:

> Tell General Howard I know his heart. . . . My people, some of them, have run away to the hills, and have no blankets, no food; no one knows where they are—perhaps freezing to death. I want to have time to look for my children and see how many I can find. Maybe I shall find them among the dead. Hear me, my chiefs, I am tired; my heart is sick and sad. From where the sun now stands, I will fight no more forever.[7]

[6]V. F. Ray, *The Sanpoil and Nespelem: Salishan Peoples of Northeastern Washington*, University of Washington Publications in Anthropology, 5 (1932).

[7]Quoted in Ralph K. Andrist, *The Long Death: The Last Days of the Plains Indian* (New York: The Macmillan Company, 1964), p. 315.

CALIFORNIA

Studies of California Indians have shown a great range of community types. There appears to have been great diversity also in their origins and migrations, physical features, and languages. The landscape includes mountains and ocean, verdant valleys and deserts. In this area of contrasts, comprised roughly of all but the northwestern corner and southeastern parts of the present state of California, was the greatest density of population north of the valley of Mexico. Most of the people lived along the coast or lower river valleys, in regions of mild climate and varied food sources. Plant cultivation was not practiced beyond the southeastern fringes, but there was a plentiful supply of food in most localities, fish, shellfish, small game, and nuts (especially acorns). Gathering of wild foods was the predominant subsistence activity, common to the several hundred otherwise diverse, distinct, *independent villages*.[8]

For a few of the peoples, the immediate family was the only significant local unit; for others, several related or unrelated families together formed the social boundaries of an individual's experience. Kroeber's general characterization of California groups includes smallness (from twenty-some for the Achomawi to two or three hundred for most groups), "a sense of cohesion," autonomy, and recognized claims to ownership and use of a certain territory. Some groups, Pomo "tribelets" for example, had a principal settlement where the chief resided and smaller, outlying, sometimes temporarily occupied settlements. The Luiseño of southern California had a bond of locality but a more fundamental one of kinship, since villages were occupied by the families of a single lineage. In contrast, among the agricultural Mohave of the lower Colorado River valley the village seems to have been of much less significance than the small family and the individual's relation to the *tribal group* as a whole (but the only element of tribal government was the chieftainship). Homesteads were scattered, land was individually owned (and inherited through the male line), and there was enough vacant land for an individual to claim new plots when he wished.

An example of the extent to which a sense of wholeness with the group could pervade the culture of small communities is provided by Dorothy Lee's linguistic study of the Wintu (north-central region).

---

[8]See A. L. Kroeber, *Handbook of the Indians of California*, Bureau of American Ethnology, Bulletin 78 (1925), and "The Nature of Land-Holding Groups in Aboriginal California," in *Aboriginal California: Three Studies in Culture History*, published for the University of California Archaeological Research Facility (Berkeley: University of California, 1963), pp. 81–120. Jack D. Forbes uses the term *community-republic* in *Native Americans of California and Nevada* (Healdsburg, Calif.: Naturegraph Publishers, 1969), p. 139.

They say, "The chief *stood with* the people," which they have to translate into English as "the chief ruled the people." . . . There was such pervasive empathy among them that this, too, was expressed in the grammatical forms; if a boy was sick, the father used a special form of the verb phrase *to be sick*, and thus said, "I-am-sick-in-respect-of-my-son." . . . There is evidence that the Wintu Indians recognize or perceive first of all humanity, human-being-ness, and only secondarily the delimited person. . . . The Wintu language does not show the presence of a concept of an established separate self; but the Wintu can emphasize one "self," and through the use of grammatical devices he can distinguish an individual at will.[9]

This interpretation suggests that a sense of community among the Wintu was not simply recognition of one's relationship to the local group, but a perception of the wholeness of group and self. In Anglo-American culture such a perception would be thought of as a species of mysticism, even among those who adopt it, if only because they must do so deliberately and without benefit of a related framework of language and culture.

Wintu culture, along with many of the other pre-European cultures of California, by now lives only in a few records and memories. Beginning with Spanish mission-building in 1769, the Indian groups were regrouped, taught new patterns of life, subjected to new diseases. Once the Gold Rush was on it was only a matter of a few years before most of their territories were lost, and their ways of life along with their lives.

ARID AND OASIS AREAS OF WESTERN NORTH AMERICA

Parts of western North America provide both archaeological and contemporary ethnographic evidence for a more complete culture history than has been possible in any of the other areas so far described. A dry climate has preserved pre-European materials throughout the desert west. Written descriptions of some of the peoples of northern Mexico, Arizona, and New Mexico date from the first half of the sixteenth century. Subsequently, Spaniards, Anglo-Americans, the governments of Spain, Mexico, and the United States, politicians, tradesmen, and tourists—all come into the story, though with varying impact and implications. Opata Indians of Sonora adopted Spanish cultural elements within a short time of the establishment of missions among them. The Yaquis tightened their community ties and began to think of their towns as sacred when threatened by the political controls of the government of Mexico. Hopi fathers, in their ancestors' communities, still transmit the ancient history of the people.

[9]*Freedom and Culture* (Englewood Cliffs, N.J.: Prentice-Hall, Inc., 1959), pp. 8, 80, 128.

Western North America is a mostly arid region of mountains and plateaus, heights and lowlands. Because several ways of life were found in this area at and after the time of European conquest, it has been divided in most descriptions of it. The agricultural Southwest, centering in the present states of New Mexico and Arizona, is usually considered separately, since the peoples to the north and west were essentially food collectors (and supplies were poor) and those to the south, in northern Mexico, were either food collectors or part-time agriculturalists whose settlements were seasonal rather than year-round and permanent. The underlying tradition throughout the area, however, was the Desert tradition of seed collecting, seed grinding, and small-game hunting.

In the Great Basin, the interior-draining region between the Sierra Nevadas and the Rockies, the people became expert in the use of hundreds of species of plants, dozens of mammals and fish, and reptiles and insects too. When horses were acquired (after the arrival of the Spaniards), some groups in Wyoming and Idaho turned to bison hunting and, in addition to their increased mobility, began to emphasize aspects of personal wealth and political organization beyond local and family lines. Others had already established villages along streams where fishing was good, but these were mainly seasonal settlements of people who lived and worked most of the time as separate family units. Their poorer neighbors, and especially the people in the southern regions of the Great Basin, maintained a simpler pattern of individual families migrating from camp to camp, often isolated for long periods of time but sometimes joining other families to hunt rabbits or antelope or to share in a harvest of piñon nuts.

In the central Southwest and in parts of northern Mexico were settled village peoples whose history is quite different. Willey summarizes main changes in the Desert migratory and seed-collecting tradition: "Southwestern culture . . . appeared as a culmination of a series of events which had begun long before—the introduction of cultivated food plants from Mesoamerica, a gradual increase in community population size, more settled living, and, finally, the introduction of pottery."[10] Several distinct cultures have been traced by archaeologists. The Mogollan, beginning in eastern Arizona about 100 B.C., combined food collecting and small-game hunting elements of the Desert tradition with cultivation of maize, squash, and beans and year-round settlement in clusters of shallow pithouses. To

---

[10]Willey, *An Introduction to American Archaeology*, pp. 181–83. It is possible that previously "more settled" groups made the readiest transition from food-collecting to plant cultivation. For a number of interesting questions and information on such transitions in several parts of the world, see Robert J. Braidwood and Gordon R. Willey, eds., *Courses Toward Urban Life: Archaeological Considerations of Some Cultural Alternates* (Chicago: Aldine Publishing Company, 1962).

the west, in the Gila River valley, a similar development took place from the first century B.C. to about A.D. 1400. The people of this culture, known as Hohokam (a Pimo-Papago word meaning "the ancients"), relied at first on flood waters for irrigation; later, canals were dug to supply the maize and cotton fields. They had a number of traits in common with central and southern Mesoamericans, including the building of village compounds, platform mounds for ceremonial structures, and ball courts. A third major culture in the area was the Anasazi. It developed in northern New Mexico and Arizona and southern Colorado, probably with influence from the Southeast as well as from other parts of the Southwest and from Mesoamerica. By the twelfth century this had become the culture of the now-much-photographed cliff houses. The people had, over time, built many-roomed and sometimes several-storied structures, in the open and in cliff walls, usually to house the member families of a clan. These villages were scattered across the Colorado Plateau (Mesa Verde in Colorado is the best known) until the late thirteenth century and elsewhere in the area in the fourteenth and fifteenth centuries. They eventually were concentrated in the Rio Grande valley in central New Mexico and, to the west, at the still-maintained locations of Hopi and Zuñi. When Spanish explorers arrived, there were about eighty independent communities.

The Spaniards called these settlements *pueblos*, or towns, and the term has come to be applied to the people who lived there, though there are language and cultural distinctions among them. These villages varied from single apartment buildings to long rows of rooms. Each was politically autonomous, economically self-sufficient (though trading for ornamental and other specialized items went on everywhere), and the socially significant unit for residents. Their governments have been called theocracies, since priests of the several religious societies formed the village council and were responsible for legal and judicial as well as ceremonial concerns. The villagers had an influence on others in the area, especially the Navajo, who arrived from the north sometime after A.D. 1000 and adopted some of their farming techniques and built villages on the mesas. By the time of the Pueblo uprising against the Spaniards in 1680, they had several villages in northern and central New Mexico to which refugees appear to have gone. Others in the area, such as the Apache, were still following a mobile, independent way of life, ranging into the Plains and south into Mexico in loosely organized hunting and gathering bands made up of extended families.[11]

---

[11]For comparative effects of conquest on these different cultures, see Edward H. Spicer, *Cycles of Conquest: The Impact of Spain, Mexico, and the United States on the Indians of the Southwest, 1533–1960* (Tucson: The University of Arizona Press, 1962).

PLAINS

The popular image of Plains culture is of tipis, horses, bison herds, and wagon-train raiding; all mobile, none settled. But just as there is no such thing as an Indian in the general sense, there is no such thing as a Plains Indian. Though there were nomadic hunters on the Plains both before and during the period of conquest, they represented several different histories and cultures. In addition, agriculture and settled village life had spread through much of the eastern part of the area by the seventeenth century. It is this aspect of Plains life that is most often ignored, even though explorers and other travelers, from Coronado on, left written accounts of it.

Agriculture is not possible everywhere in this area. From central Alberta and Saskatchewan in the north to central Texas in the south, and from the western edges of Minnesota and Iowa to the Rockies, the climate is relatively dry, precipitation is irregular, and daily and seasonal changes in temperature are often extreme. The eastern part, however, is a prairie of taller grasses with heavier precipitation and it was here that maize, beans, and squash were grown by Native American settlers. Though non-Indian settlers were eventually to discover the agricultural potential of land beyond the Mississippi, Zebulon Pike and other early nineteenth-century explorers made it out to be a "Great American Desert": "The vast tract of untimbered country . . . may become in time equally celebrated as the sandy deserts of Africa. . . . Our citizens will through necessity . . . leave the prairies incapable of cultivation to the wandering and uncivilized aborigines."[12] Yet the trend among the native peoples had apparently been toward settled agricultural life well before Pike appeared.

Finds dated to before 500 B.C. include house clusters (perhaps for semipermanent residence) and maize. What has been called the "Plains Woodland" tradition was established by the early centuries A.D. and lasted to about 1000 A.D. This meant, on the Plains as in the Eastern Woodlands, a mixed hunting and farming economy and the construction of burial mounds and other earthworks for ceremonial purposes. Such works, anywhere, imply community organization. Settled village life became even more important in this area as newcomers came from the east. Probably by the eleventh century farming was being carried on in river valleys from North Dakota to central Oklahoma. Its importance to the groups that practiced it varied; all depended to some degree on bison hunting as well. The residential pattern in the villages of the northern and central Plains

---

[12]Quoted in Waldo R. Wedel, *Prehistoric Man on the Great Plains* (Norman: University of Oklahoma Press, 1961), p. 278.

seems to have been occupancy of a single house (an earth lodge) by an extended family. Women cared for the house and fields or gardens, while men were responsible for hunting and ceremonial activities. The men's work was usually organized on a clan or on a community-wide basis.

On the far western Plains, economic life was organized around bison hunts. The bands had their own territories and were basically autonomous, but they came together for ceremonial purposes and summer hunting was communal. In winter camps were made in stream valleys and other protected sites, and if water, wood, and forage for horses were plentiful enough they would be returned to year after year. Before the adoption of the horse for transport and for riding, these groups relied on the dog travois and on their own feet and backs. It is obvious that the horse would enable them to travel further than before. Just how much it changed the essential characteristics of their culture has been debated. Its effect on settled groups, however, and on the area as a whole, was immense. Sedentary agricultural villages, such as those of the Cheyenne on the Missouri River, were subject to raids by hunter-warriors of the area and to epidemic diseases introduced by whites; thus handicapped, the villagers turned to a nomadic way of life.[13]

EASTERN WOODLANDS

Included in this area are coasts, woodlands, the lower Great Lakes, the major river systems, and the eastern prairies. Inland climate is severe in the north, though tempered along the coasts by the Gulf Stream; it is subtropical in the south. The area is well watered and the soils generally fertile. Much of it is forested, and small game were at one time abundant. Food supplies were thus ample and varied. A division is sometimes made between the Southeast and the rest of the area, and even so, many different subareas can be identified in terms of environmental conditions and responses to them. Generally, however, the Archaic tradition underlay the various ways of life, and most of the people engaged in a mixed economy that included maize growing along with hunting, fishing, and wild-food gathering.

In the Southeast, not only crops and agricultural techniques but also some ceremonial and other cultural elements may have derived originally from Mesoamerica. Maize growing may have been introduced shortly after 1000 B.C., at which time large earthworks also were begun in the Ohio Valley. "Sacred circles," council houses, and elaborate burials have been

[13]See John C. Ewers, "The Horse in Blackfoot Indian Culture: With Comparative Material from Other Western Tribes," Bureau of American Ethnology, Bulletin 159 (1955), 331–39.

found, along with artifacts that indicate contacts with peoples over a widespread area. The village sites comprised several groups of two to five houses each. This Adena culture, as it is called, was followed by the Hopewell (around 300 B.C. to A.D. 500), with larger villages, more extensive earthworks, more specialized crafts, and trade items from as far away as the Rockies. The most important subsequent development was the Mississippi tradition, as identified at sites from northern Georgia to southern Illinois; its high point corresponds with the period of European contact— these were the cultures DeSoto found (1539–1542). Characteristic and impressive features of the Mississippi tradition were earth mounds, pyramidal in form and often arranged around an open plaza, used as platforms for religious and other public structures. The dwelling sites, some but not all of which were associated with the ceremonial centers, indicate a large, stable population. There is no question but that Mesoamerican artistic, religious, and community ideas influenced the people who established these places, though the means of transmission of such cultural elements are not known.

In their social organization, the peoples of the Mississippi tradition generally based relationships on the matrilineal, matrilocal family. Clans were important in a locality: In Creek villages each had its own place around the square, and Cherokees designated a particular place for each clan in the council house. They also helped to establish a tribal identification by promoting relationships beyond village lines. A head chief or an upper-class council had central political authority, and some villages dominated others, being able to exact tribute from them.[14]

The Iroquois of the northern part of the Eastern Woodlands resembled the peoples to the south to some extent, especially in their maize-growing plus hunting economy, compact villages, and matrilineal organization. Historians have given the Iroquois special attention, mainly because of their federation, the League of the Iroquois, which was once thought to be the only complex political organization among Indians north of Mexico. It was based on representation: The foundation was the family, with a woman at its head, and families were grouped and represented in clan and tribal councils; the fifty sachems who made up the council of the League were selected from particular families in the five tribes, and they also made up the tribal councils. Voting in the council was by tribe, each tribe having one vote, and decisions had to be unanimous. Unanimity was arrived at through persuasion, whatever the cost in time. The intent of the League was to keep the peace and regulate not tribal but external affairs.

[14]James B. Griffin, "Culture Periods in Eastern United States Archeology," in *Archeology of Eastern United States*, ed. by James B. Griffin (Chicago: University of Chicago Press, 1952), pp. 362–63.

In the course of wars for control of the fur trade after Europeans had arrived, it provided a sense of unity among the different communities and groups represented on the council. At one crucial time, however, allegiances were divided and a unanimous decision could not be reached: When the American Revolution began some members supported the American colonists and some the British.

The Iroquois village was a group of long, gabled, bark-covered structures that housed matrilineal, extended families. Villages were usually situated on terraces above a stream, river, or lake and fortified with log palisades. The maize fields were outside the village proper, in the surrounding woodlands. When, after a few years, fields became worn out, the village would move to new lands. In the course of an individual's lifetime several such moves might be made, but they were generally within a small, known territory. The women of the longhouse worked cooperatively at farming while the men worked cooperatively at hunting and fishing. In a sense, then, the women might be called the settled members of a community. In Wallace's description, "An Iroquois village might be regarded as a collection of strings, hundreds of years old, of successive generations of women, always domiciled in their longhouses near their cornfields in a clearing while their sons and husbands traveled in the forest on supportive errands of hunting and trapping, of trade, of war, and of diplomacy."[15] There were also trans-village obligations based on kinship. Tribal identification occurred through trans-village ties and was expressed in ceremonial ways.

The first contacts of Woodlands peoples with Europeans occurred during explorations into the southeastern interior and along coasts in the sixteenth century. Jesuit and, later, Franciscan missionaries organized a few missions in the southeast, and Spaniards also built military outposts. Direct contacts in the north were with the English, Dutch, and French. The fur trade and competition for it—first along the rivers and lakes of the north and then through the backcountry of the south—changed economic emphases and brought about new alliances and enmities that eventually destroyed some tribes and displaced or dispersed others. English settlements encroached on the villages and fields, and if these eastern groups did not then move their own communities (or, ultimately, even if they did) they were moved for them. The history of Indian removal, of boundary marking, and of reservation building begins at Chesapeake Bay in the early seventeenth century. Unlike the French, whose methods of religious and commercial conversion tended to bring peoples together, the English

---

[15]Anthony F. C. Wallace, *The Death and Rebirth of the Seneca* (New York: Alfred A. Knopf, 1970), pp. 28–29. This account of the Seneca during the late colonial and early national periods may be taken to illustrate changes in community life and identity.

engaged in little missionary activity and acted to increase separation as time went on. This purpose was the more easily accomplished as wars reduced the numbers of Native Americans. The segregated groups eventually became dependent on meager reservation resources but also, of necessity, on each other, and maintained their cultural identities through close community relationships even when they had been removed thousands of miles from their original lands.

CIRCUM-CARIBBEAN

The islands of the Caribbean were the location of the Spaniards' first contacts with New World peoples and the first Spanish attempts to develop viable communities among them. It was here that the term "Indian" was first misapplied; Columbus, as has been celebrated ever since, did not know where he was. Here also was the first anthropological research in the New World, carried out when Columbus, on his second voyage, commissioned an accompanying priest to discover something about Arawak religion. The western, mainland part of the area has been called an "Intermediate" area by virtue of its position between the influential Mesoamerican and Andean culture areas. It included the tropical coasts and highlands from the Maya frontier in Nicaragua to Equador and western Venezuela. The principal language group was Chibchan and the principal economic activity was maize growing. This was an area of small towns and chiefdoms, whose peoples have become known for their metal working (it was here that the myth of El Dorado had some foundation in fact: in coronation ceremonies a young chief would be covered with gold dust and placed in a boat filled with gold and emeralds for the gods). The Caribbean part of the area included eastern Venezuela, the islands off its eastern coasts, and the Lesser and Greater Antilles. Resident here at the time of Columbus were manioc- and maize-producing Arawak and Carib communities and a few hunting and fishing groups. The Spaniards described plazas and temples in their villages, though these have not survived. Living arrangements included the chief's "great house" and extended family households. While the communities were essentially autonomous, with the village the main governmental unit, there were also federations.[16]

The population in the Greater Antilles is thought, from Spanish records, to have been large and dense. Some villages may have had as many as four thousand residents. But the population was so reduced within two decades of the European discovery that the Spaniards had to make forays

---

[16]*Handbook of South American Indians*, ed. by J. H. Steward, Bureau of American Ethnology, Bulletin 143 (1948), 497–565. Special studies have been made by Irving Rouse; see, for example, "Prehistory of the West Indies," *Science*, 144 (May 1, 1964), 499–513.

to the mainland for a labor force for their mines and plantations. The Spanish crown made repeated attempts to develop a "humane" policy of religious conversion and regulation of labor, but disease, forced labor, warfare, and flight destroyed the island peoples and their cultures. Only some of the Caribs were able to survive, by withdrawing into the Venezuelan wilderness.

MESOAMERICA

Urbanization preceded the town-building Europeans in the New World by nearly two thousand years in the heart of Mexico, the valley Anahuac, and in parts of Central America, the Caribbean, northern South America, and the central Andes. The area of most intensive, long-lasting, and influential urbanism extends through tropical lowlands, the ridges and valleys of a volcanic area, and the high central plateau of Mexico. Mesoamerica, or Middle America, is characterized culturally by intensive agriculture, monumental architecture, long-distance trading, highly formalized religions, large territorial units with dominant religious and political centers, and special techniques of writing and computation of time.

The agriculturalists of this area were more numerous and densely settled than elsewhere in North America, and their public buildings were more elaborately planned and constructed. Temples, monuments, palaces, and various kinds of stone carving were the visible and tangible evidence of focusing community institutions. They appear early: the La Venta ceremonial center, an example of the so-called Olmec civilization, has been dated to 800–400 B.C. It was not "urban," in the sense of a multifunctional place with a concentration of population; it was a complex of courts, pyramid, earth mounds, and monumental stone sculptures on a small river island which could not have supported many people, perhaps only the persons directly responsible for the ceremonial functions indicated by its features. Yet the work represented there implies a large supporting population, probably residents of the surrounding regions. The Olmec "style," such as in uses of jade and the jaguar symbol, has been found at other sites in Mesoamerica, suggesting interconnections. One such place is in the highlands of central Oaxaca. The site known as Monte Alban dates from 500 B.C. and the surrounding valleys and slopes have been occupied almost continuously since then. Findings from the earliest period of occupation of the mountain spur on which the ceremonial center was constructed include large, flat-topped mounds, evidence of monumental art in relief carvings on stone slabs, Olmec-like pottery, hieroglyphics, numerals, and a calendar. Later, probably by the first century A.D., this ceremonial center was being developed by the ancestors of the Zapotecans who still live in the area. During the Classic Period, some of the most impressive building in Mesoamerica was being done here. Influences seem to have come from Maya places in Guatemala and from Teotihuacan, but the civilization at Monte Alban was essentially independent and had its own character. A hilltop was leveled for a great plaza, "one of the most beautiful open spaces ever conceived by man,"[17] which was surrounded by pyramids, temples, and a ball court. A number of small villages have been discovered in the valleys, and house sites extend up the slopes, but the center itself gives the impression of separateness, self-containment. Most of the people—perhaps a total of 250,000, including those at the center—lived in surrounding villages.

Monte Alban is like Classic Maya centers in this regard: The Maya built rectangular plazas enclosed on three or four sides by mounds; some are small, single focuses of attention in the landscape, but others are complexes of plazas, courtyards, religious structures, and palaces. Laid out in unique ways, they are all impressive in their surroundings. Scattered around them are clusters of house platforms, some more or less isolated, which made up the small hamlets and residences of the population that presumably supported the centers. The *city-state* concept has been proposed to describe these centers, each with "its special quality: the grandeur of Tikal, the Athenian classicism of Copán, the distinctive architecture and pure beauty of Palenque."[18] Although the concept derives from examples of forms in the history of Western Civilization, it is one way of identifying community form and interrelations, one way of distinguishing Maya from other patterns in North America. The government of each civic-religious center is thought to have been in the hands of a few priests and nobles, with the major centers being in a position of hegemony over minor ones and residential hamlets, and generally friendly relations between centers being maintained through the priesthood.

The first intensive urbanization in central Mexico was at Teotihuacan. Founded during the first century B.C., it lasted until about A.D. 800, with minor occupation afterward. It was built in a valley with a small stream and natural springs, and methods of irrigation may have been adopted during its early period of growth, as later, and perhaps even artificial islands (*chinampas*, or floating gardens) were built. The city spread beyond seven square miles in area, and its population may have reached 50,000 or more. It was made up of palacelike structures, compact residential units, and temples—the largest temples in the New World.

In the tenth century A.D., the Toltecs, migrants from the northwest,

---

[17]Jorge Hardoy, *Urban Planning in Pre-Columbian America* (New York: George Braziller, Inc., n.d.), p. 33.

[18]Willey, *An Introduction to American Archaeology*, p. 136. J. Eric S. Thompson's *The Rise and Fall of Maya Civilization*, 2nd ed. (Norman: University of Oklahoma Press, 1966) is an important work in which the city-state idea is fundamental.

built a city on a promontory overlooking the Tula River. The site had defensive advantages, and temple carvings were militaristic. The central zone comprised pyramids, platforms, and palaces around plazas, surrounded by residential structures. The population seems to have been mixed (that of Teotihuacan may also have been, with several cultural and linguistic groups living in and using the site) and included artisans brought to the capital as specialists.

The Aztec capital, Tenochtitlan, began as a village on the southwest shore of Lake Texcoco in 1325. The Aztecs were northmen too, who by the end of the fifteenth century had not only constructed a city but conquered most of their neighbors until they had an empire that stretched from coast to coast and from the valley of Anahuac to Guatemala. They depended on tribute and trade for their existence, not just on farming. The farming they did, however, seems to have been immensely productive. *Chinampas* were built out of the lake-water vegetation and silt. Such construction, and also the canals and causeways that allowed the city to expand across the waters, indicates an organized labor force. The layout of the city gives an outline of the social order, and Spanish records can be used to fill this outline in more fully than can be done for the earlier cities.[19] Spaniards noted, for example, that houses at the outskirts and among the *chinampas* were simpler than those in the city proper. The city, in the form of a square covering about twenty-five hundred acres, was divided into four districts, which the conquerors retained throughout the colonial period. A further subdivision was into wards or districts—the Spaniards called them *barrios*—of the *calpulli*, a landholding group of households often referred to as a clan, of which there were apparently twenty. Each of these had its own temple, market, and school; the districts had more important ceremonial sites and markets. Also, the *calpulli* had an elected head, while the district had an appointed military chief. Houses stood on stone-faced platforms along the streets and canals, with their rooms arranged around a courtyard. Most were flat-roofed, single-story structures, but they became more luxurious toward the center of the city where the high officials lived. The emperor's palace was just outside the central sacred precinct, with its great square and twin-temple pyramid. The social classes of the city included the royal lineage from which the emperor was selected, the high priests and aristocratic families, commoners, and serfs or bondsmen (probably drawn from subjugated peoples); there was also a military class and the specialized occupations of artisan and merchant.

The Spaniards noted the buzz and traffic of city life along the streets

---

[19]One of Cortés' soldiers wrote, many years after the event, a lively description of the city and its conquest: Bernal Díaz, *The Conquest of New Spain*, tr. by J. M. Cohen (Penguin Books, 1963). See also Jacques Soustelle, *The Daily Life of the Aztecs* (Pelican Books, 1964).

and canals and in the markets. Merchants and craftsmen had warehouses and stalls along some streets, and boats went back and forth along the canals and in the lake. The marketplace of Tlatelolco, apparently a merchandising district north of Tenochtitlan, is said to have drawn twenty to twenty-five thousand buyers and sellers every day and forty or fifty thousand every fifth day. As for the total population, estimates vary widely. The conquerors' records give figures of 60,000 to 120,000 inhabited houses. Willey suggests 300,000 persons for the "full zone" of this urban place; Soustelle, more than 500,000 and less than one million for Tenochtitlan-Tlatelolco; Hardoy, 65,000 for the capital, on the basis of the land area (750 hectares, or 1,852 acres, 75 percent of which were *chinampas*).

Like earlier cities in central Mexico, Tenochtitlan was conquered and destroyed. Unlike them, it happened abruptly and at the hands of a few hundred soldiers who, in Soustelle's analysis, acted according to a concept of war quite different from that of the Aztecs. The Aztecs had waged wars of religion and of conquest but had allied the vanquished tribes to them. "The Spaniards, for their part, were making 'total' war; there was only one possible state for them, the monarchy of Charles V, and only one possible religion. The clash of arms was nothing to the clash of ideologies."[20] And in that sense, the clash resounded far beyond the community whose members lamented, "Our inheritance, our city, is lost and dead."

General Questions of Community in Pre-Columbian America

Sources of information about pre-Columbian peoples use the term community on occasion but not analytically. The point of pre-Columbian culture histories has been to gather information about cultures and not about community per se. Therefore, to look for community in them is to look deliberately for certain aspects of ecological and social organization. Other students might make other choices than the ones made here as to what is important in regard to community. It is obvious, too, that more detailed studies would be needed to show correspondences or constants across time. Yet this survey of pre-Columbian settings for community raises some generally applicable questions. They are listed here and discussed with reference to Native Americans; they can be asked of other groups as well.

ECOLOGICAL SYSTEM

1. To what extent is community form a response to the physical setting and the subsistence or productive activities possible within it?

[20]Soustelle, *The Daily Life of the Aztecs*, p. 217.

2. How is community size related to the subsistence base?
3. How are patterns of migration and of settlement related to physiographic conditions and subsistence activities?

Beyond such basic matters as choice of site and materials for shelter, communities have taken many different forms. It is not only that some have been dispersed and others compact. Some of each kind have had a center or focus (religious, for example); others have not appeared to. Some groups dispersed and recongregated periodically. As for size, the local group seems to have remained small if the food supply was uncertain, but periodic recongregations might be considered to have increased the number and kind of associations significant to a particular person. Generally speaking, there was greater population density and more instances of population concentration among the peoples who cultivated plants than among those who did not. Further, those who had engineered an irrigation system clustered more and for longer times than those who depended on natural sources of moisture.

Plant cultivation is usually taken to be a prerequisite to settled village life. Certainly the history of the development and spread of cultivation in North America, as in other parts of the world, is also a history of the growth of relatively permanent communities. Yet not all of the peoples who have lived in long-lasting communities have relied upon the growing of crops; some combined it with other activities that affected community form, size, and permanence. Some, in fact—the most striking example comes from the Northwest Coast—have not cultivated plants at all. It should also be noticed that regular planting and harvesting have not led to a particular pattern of community life. The crops, the soil, the amount of arable land available, the source of moisture, and the climate influence the daily, seasonal, and yearly cycles—such factors, along with methods of cultivation, affect also the amount of work the people must do to support themselves and the size of the group that can be supported. The group's history is important, too, in the nature of the community that develops. Social definitions of who customarily does what, who decides what, who is responsible for whom, who lives next door or in the next valley influence the community whatever the subsistence base. Finally, the idea of permanence is open to question. Is the permanent community to be identified in terms of an ongoing group or an ongoing place? For most of the modern world, such a distinction may seem beside the point; in pre-Columbian America, whole villages sometimes picked up and moved when the soil wore out or when they felt threatened by other groups, and their sites might then be occupied by a new group. Short of complete moves, groups moved their fields, parts of groups "hived off" to new localities and yet stayed emotionally and socially close to the old group; individual families spent part of a year with the main group and part of the year by themselves; and in some places community buildings were maintained "permanently" though they were occupied only periodically or seasonally. Irrigation systems that permitted more intensive farming on less land were developed in Mexico and Central America, the Southwest, and parts of the Caribbean, and it is in these areas that structural permanence is most impressive. Through the innovations related to plant cultivation, human communities were inventing their own landscapes.

SOCIAL ORGANIZATION

4. Should a local grouping organized primarily along kinship lines be called a community? What kinds of translocal ties are important enough to be included in the identification of a community?

5. What role do religious and ceremonial customs play in keeping a local group intact, and perhaps in identifying a group as a community?

6. How is the division of labor related to the social structure of the community?

7. How are decision-making roles related to the social structure?

8. Under what conditions do territorial claims, or boundary lines, appear?

Representations of the community as family have been made both by Europeans and by non-European Americans. The idea of chief or king as father antedated Freud, and from King James I to Sir Henry Maine to contemporary communalists, community members have been likened to family members. The Iroquois compared their confederation to a "longhouse" compartmented by tribes. The languages that refer to the earth as feminine or mother suggest a relation between the world as perceived and the generation of perception and feeling for others. Such images should be taken seriously. They convey at least a hope that the affective and effective contents of local relationships can be compared. Yet kinship has variable boundaries. The villages of the Northwest Coast can be called kinship communities, but the same local groupings are not found in other North American cultures with similar kinship structure. Although kinship may bind a village, it does not make a community nor is the presence of particular kin required to maintain it. In other words, the kin group is important, and so is the local group, but there are many combinations of the two.

When a community has a definite structural center there is less ambiguity. A religious shrine, a plaza that could serve as a marketplace, a head man's residence indicate a center, especially when such structures are next to each other. Public works imply a means of organizing people for construction and maintenance and, with other evidence, suggest political and/or religious authority. But they do not necessarily mean a division of labor in the contemporary sense of specialization. In the Maya region, for example, work on public buildings appears to have been done by men drawn periodically from the general farming population.

Claims to land and the maintaining of territorial boundaries are difficult to generalize about for pre-Columbian America. Among nonagricultural peoples territorial rights seem to have been important in areas of abundant food sources (such as California). Among agricultural peoples they were related to the settlement pattern, but farmlands tended to be held by a group, sometimes the community as a whole, and not by individuals (though tenure with regard to particular house sites, gardens, and fields would be allotted to a family head or some larger kin group). Among the part-time farmers of the Eastern Woodlands, the female head of a kin group often held the right to a particular plot; when the village moved to new lands, these would be apportioned among the households as represented by their female heads. In the southeast, there were also town fields, worked by everyone under the direction of the chief, the produce of which was stored for emergencies—for guests as well as for local crop failures. In the southwest, property was often assigned to a kinship group headed by a woman, but the men were the farmers.[21] For the Aztecs, the land belonged ultimately to the state but was divided among political subunits and then among families, with nominal ownership by the male head; there were also special lands worked by citizens and slaves for the benefit of political and religious personnel. Of course the lands used or available do not by themselves identify a community. As the Aztec state expanded, it may be that particular community boundaries disappeared, were overlaid by other kinds of group boundaries. A state may develop from a community, but in pre-Columbian America a state is not the same as a community.

---

[21]According to Driver, "The sexual division of labor for farming activities presents a clear picture. . . . To sum up, in the areas most intensively farmed, Oasis and Meso-America, men were the principal farmers. In areas where farming was secondary in importance to some other subsistence activity, women were the principal farmers. The East superficially appears to be an exception to this rule, but we must remember that although farming seems to have dominated subsistence, it is problematical whether it provided over half the total food supply in this area. Therefore, we may say that for North America as a whole there is a positive correlation between the importance of farm products in the dietary and the amount of time men devote to farming" (*Indians of North America*, pp. 53–54). Lewis Mumford's generalization on the subject of women's responsibilities for subsistence in early cultures is provocative, to say the least: "House and village, eventually the town itself, are woman writ large" (*The City in History: Its Origins, Its Transformations, and Its Prospects* [New York: Harcourt, Brace & World, Inc., 1961], p. 12).

IDENTITY

9. Where and how does a group place its members so that the members recognize their relation to the group?

10. What associations are likely to be most influential (if not essential) in formation of the individual's concept of who he is? What sort of nonlocalized self-identity is expected?

11. What is the effect of translocal identification, as in tribalism and nationalism, on a locality and local relationships?

12. What aspects of community life persist longest (that is, across several generations)? What most commonly makes for disruption?

Public works and other physical features, such as location of households or kin groups, allow for speculation about roles and associations even in the absence of directly applicable records. Distinctions between priestly and noble classes and commoners allow for further speculation on identity as related to social role. But the records do not answer such questions as the ones listed above; individual statements—better, life histories—would help. Postcontact records do give some idea of the attachment of the Native American to his world, however. For example, Chief Seathl told the governor of Oregon Territory in 1855:

> To us the ashes of our ancestors are sacred and their resting place is hallowed ground. You wander far from the graves of your ancestors and seemingly without regret. . . . We may be brothers after all. We will see. . . . When the last Red Man shall have perished, and the memory of my tribe shall have become a myth among the White Men, these shores will swarm with the invisible dead of my tribe, and when your children's children think themselves alone in the field, the store, the shop, upon the highway, or in the silence of the pathless woods, they will not be alone. . . . At night when the streets of your cities and villages are silent and you think them deserted, they will throng with the returning hosts that once filled and still love this beautiful land. The White Man will never be alone. Let him be just and deal kindly with my people, for the dead are not powerless. Dead, did I say? There is no death, only a change of worlds.

3

European
Settings

"Then I did dream a marvelous dream:
that I was in a wilderness—where, I did not know;
and as I looked toward the east, aloft to the sun,
I saw a tower on a hillock most splendidly built,
and a deep dale beneath, with a dungeon therein,
with deep ditches and dark—a dreadful sight.
A fair field full of folk I saw lying between,
with all manner of men, the humble and the rich,

—PIERS PLOWMAN (c. 1375)

Immigrants to North America over the past four centuries left dispersed farms, compact villages, and urban places, each with its own traditions and identity. Sometimes they tried deliberately to re-create them in the New World. Of many of these efforts little remains but the name of the place: New Glarus, New Ulm. Others tried just as deliberately to realize an ideal of community, as formulated before they came or on arrival. Thus there would be a Bethlehem, a Harmonie and New Harmony, an Icaria. Many, of course, made no conscious attempt at community creation or re-creation, yet they often expected things of family and locality that indicate the influence of community relationships in the Old World. Old World settings must, therefore, be looked at here.

The basis for community life throughout western Europe before the sixteenth century was agricultural. As in "pre-Columbian" North America, agricultural communities took a number of different forms and changed over time. A good deal of what is now known about "pre-Columbian" Europe has been searched out since the mid-nineteenth century, when interest in local communities and the nature of community began to develop in western Europe. Earlier historians were interested in the Western "great tradition" or "universalist" themes of Church and State. Social histories now give attention to the village folk, the masses and social classes, everyday life—however the chapter headings read—and try to explain social change through as much of the society as there are records or imagination for rather than simply through documents of political and legal forms and events. The histories of the Old and New Worlds have thus been brought conceptually closer than they once were. A recent suggestion that the culture-area concept be applied in the Old World as well as the New may bring them even closer.

Culture Areas

Arensberg's tentative "Old World culture area"[1] differentiates land use and livelihoods of Europe and the Middle East from those of East Asia, Africa beyond the Sahara, and India. Its "distinctive and organizing culture complex" is based on a mixed agriculture—hard grains, with plowed and winter fallowed fields, and domesticated hoofed animals—and a diet of bread, meat, and milk. Within the regions of this area communities took several forms.

Around the Atlantic fringes of Europe, from Finland to parts of the Iberian peninsula, the traditional settlement pattern was one of single-family and more or less self-sufficient farms. Homesteads were dispersed, and a sense of neighborhood was probably maintained through kinship, trading associations, crossroads fairs, religious gatherings, and rural courts.

These *open-country neighborhoods* were scattered elsewhere in Europe too, but through much of England and transalpine Europe the community took the form of a *compact village*, a cluster of households separate from fields. This agricultural village community has been studied in detail most often as part of the manorial system between the ninth and fifteenth centuries, but the type may have predated and certainly existed outside manorial Europe.[2] It was small enough to involve all the villagers with each other's lives; population ranged from perhaps fifty to five hundred.[3] Types

[1]Conrad M. Arensberg, "The Old World Peoples: The Place of European Cultures in World Ethnography," *Anthropological Quarterly*, 36 (1963), 75–99.

[2]The general category is that of "corporate community," which has become linked to analyses of peasant life. Eric R. Wolf discusses it in such a context in *Peasants* (Englewood Cliffs, N.J.: Prentice-Hall, Inc., 1966), pp. 84–86, 89–90. Other terms for it are "nucleated," "open-field," and "wheat village" community. An important sociological study is George C. Homans, *English Villagers of the Thirteenth Century* (New York: Russell and Russell, 1960).

[3]G. G. Coulton, *Medieval Village, Manor, and Monastery* (New York: Harper & Row, Publishers, 1960), p. 65.

of land tenure differed from place to place, but agricultural tasks were usually carried out cooperatively. A cooperative system of some sort was made more likely in the early medieval period by adoption of the heavy wheeled-plow that required four to six oxen (later, horses) to pull it and, since individual cultivators seldom had that many, led to pooling such resources. The farmers worked large open fields and together maintained the fallow for grazing. Decisions about land use were made either by the community as a whole or by a village council. Depending on size and relation to a parish, many such villages supported a church, which would also bring the villagers together as a social unit.

In the valleys and cleared uplands of the major rivers, an area of intensive mixed agriculture which Arensberg calls the "Alpine Climax," there appears to have been no characteristic settlement pattern. Dispersed neighborhoods, compact villages, long rows of households, and independent large landholders were all to be found. Among them, methods of farming developed that produced a surplus to support an increasingly diverse economy, population growth, and, eventually, urbanization. Essentially, these methods involved livestock raising with field grazing and fertilization to increase crop production. An impetus was provided by commerce in the late medieval period.

The lands and islands of the Mediterranean form a distinct region with its own community characteristics. From ancient centers of civilization to modern urban places, town life has been culturally more important than in transalpine regions. Farmers have lived in or closely around the military, commercial, and industrial centers, and the peasant proprietors and the landless—rural or urban—have been less distinguishable than in other parts of Europe. Early development of a light scratch-plow that was sufficient for the soils of the area, the raising of small livestock, and the commercialization of specialized crops (such as olives and grapes) helped make for independent rather than cooperative cultivation. Also, the landholding nobility of the Mediterranean area were more urban than their counterparts in northern Europe, participating more in town life and government even when they lived on estates outside of town.

Towns and Population Movement

Roman towns in western Europe were military and administrative centers, bases for ruling the provinces of the empire. To secure long-term control over conquered areas, Roman emperors attempted to extend the Mediterranean city-state system. Places established as provincial centers remained, however, relatively small. The towns of the Carolingian empire were mostly administrative centers too, and the fortified places created by kings and nobles in the ninth and tenth centuries were not towns as such.

European society between the fourth and eleventh or twelfth centuries was a rural society, however much the villages may look like towns to Americans used to dispersed settlement in agricultural areas. The many points of small population concentration were, if not entirely isolated and self-sufficient, at least not greatly dependent on outside sources for food-stuffs and manufactures; most of what was needed was grown or made locally, and the weekly market and annual fair in various regions provided the rest.

Trade by sea and land increased after the eleventh century, and new trading centers developed along the routes. Northern Italian city-states—Venice, Genoa, Pisa—were the first to prosper with this revival of commerce, and their influence extended into Europe as well as through the Mediterranean where, as part of their activity in helping the crusaders, they were able to establish commercial colonies. In northwestern Europe, Flanders became a center for main trade routes and such places as Paris and London began to grow.

Townsmen north of the Mediterranean area had to contend with the traditional powers of large landholders. The growth of a market at a castle site, the settlement of merchants at or near an old Roman town, the concentration of population around a cathedral or abbey—how impor-tant these became depended not only on the advantages of the place for trade but also on the achievement of liberties and rights of self-government for the townsmen. By the twelfth century many places were being granted charters, whereby town dwellers were assured such privileges as free land tenure, freedom from servile and manorial obligations, exemptions from or limitations on manorial tolls, and trading monopolies. Free status for the burgher was perhaps the most important development; peasants at this time were considered servile or semiservile in status. "Town air brings freedom," it was said, for a serf who managed to live in a town for a year and a day was accounted free.[4]

[4]"The development of autonomy [of towns] occurred simultaneously with the transition from the personal to the territorial principle in law. No longer were old relationships of a personal nature to decide the legal standing of the individual, but the judicial area of the place he was living in.... After 1100 the free status of the burgher upper class was no longer in doubt. It was on this account that the demand for general freedom of the urban population became an internal necessity.... It laid the basis for their subsequent designation of the proper relationship of the individual as 'citizen of the state, not a subject' " (Fritz Rörig, *The Medieval Town*, trans. D. J. A. Matthew [Berkeley: University of California Press, 1967], pp. 27–28; see also Carl Stephenson, *Borough and Town: A Study of Urban Origins in England* [Cambridge, Mass.: The Medieval Academy of America, 1933], pp. 44–45). The classic statement of change in the nature of relationships is in Sir Henry Maine's *Ancient Law* (London: John Murray, 1861): "The movement of the progressive soci-eties has been uniform in one respect. Through all its course it has been distin-guished by the gradual dissolution of family dependency and the growth of individ-ual obligation in its place.... We may say that the movement of the progressive societies has hitherto been a movement *from Status to Contract*" (pp. 168–70).

Castle towns, new towns planned by princes or kings to take advantage of the new prosperity, and cities with their own governments, such as Venice, were the main types of urban places in the late Middle Ages. From rule of the local aristocracy, a system of elected magistrates developed and often the citizens—nobles and commoners—formed a league for the advancement of their common interests. Eventually a kind of mayoralty came into being, or leadership vested in one person with assistance by a council. Town self-government developed throughout northern Italy, parts of Spain, and southern France, and then in northern Europe too. Sometimes, in Lombardy and Picardy, for example, the changeover occurred through revolutionary means. Even after the granting of liberties the townspeople were prepared to take up arms.

In northern Europe, the institution of the guild merchant became powerful in municipal government. It included all local traders and thus assured controls over local business. Some nonlocal federations were also established within the same trade. A sort of federation, or at least an alliance of towns, developed along with commercial activity in the Baltic; this was the Hanseatic League, which was organized to obtain trading concessions in the northern countries. It maintained trading establishments at commercial centers (Novgorod, Bruges, Bergen, London) and held a monopoly on many Baltic products. First composed of towns around Lübeck, by the early fourteenth century membership had been extended to German colonial towns along the eastern coasts of the Baltic.

Colonization within Europe during the late Middle Ages was important to both agriculture and commerce. Beginning in the twelfth century, German burghers established colonies to the east, in thinly populated areas; places built on the German urban model included Berlin, Wroclaw, and Leipzig. There were also new mining towns in Saxony, Bohemia, and Hungary. By the thirteenth century colonization efforts were widespread. New areas were opened to agriculture in both eastern and western Europe. The abbey was one of the most important agents for agricultural colonization, especially in the Cistercian order, which sent groups into new lands in Brandenburg, Pomerania, Poland, Bohemia, Hungary, and elsewhere during and after the twelfth century. Flemish and German peasants were brought east of the Elbe River to improve and settle swampy and wooded areas along the Baltic; they helped reclaim the lands around the North Sea. There were frontiers also in western and northern parts of the British Isles. The peasant colonists were exempted from most servile obligations. They had rent to pay, but could work for wages and buy and sell on a cash market. They were also more free to move than persons of servile status. Such opportunities may have tied in with the decline of the manor system; as serfs moved to towns or joined a colonizing group, lords of manors began to remove obligations and grant new kinds of tenure, often based on cash or rent, in order to keep them on the land.

Spanish, French, and English
Backgrounds to Transatlantic Colonization

In the Iberian peninsula, as elsewhere, new settlements were established and old towns obtained new freedoms during the medieval period, but here these changes took place under the conditions of the Christian Reconquest. As territories were gained from the Moslems, the practices and institutions eventually to be carried to the New World were developed. For example, in newly conquered areas on the Moslem "frontier" an office of military and civil governorship was used that carried with it extensive rights over land and people. It was often a reward for military service. The title was *adelantado*, and it implied almost royal powers, for its holder had charge of extensive territories, with powers of judicial review and tax collection, and was treated as the direct representative of the crown. Another practice with origins in the Reconquest that was to be revived during the colonization of the Americas was the *encomienda*. The term refers to the protection a feudal lord owed his serfs, and it came to be applied to the apportioning of Indians to landholders for purposes of work (see Chapter 4). Cities and towns in Spain, as elsewhere during the medieval period, received charters or *fueros* that granted them a number of local controls, including the election of a council or *cabildo*, with representation in the *cortes*, the royal council.

The twenty years or so that preceded the expansion of Spanish power beyond Europe was a time of change in the Spanish kingdoms. The marriage of Ferdinand and Isabella, heirs respectively to the kingdoms of Aragon and Castile, occurred in 1469. When they received their crowns a few years later, their kingdoms could be united in foreign relations. Internally and historically, however, there were great differences between Aragon and Castile, and what happened in Castile was to have the most effect on policies in the New World. Briefly, while Aragon had a limited monarchy, town autonomy, and a relatively strong *cortes*, Castile had been subject to conflict between nobility, towns, and crown, the outcome of which was the assumption of absolute authority by the crown. This absolutism, as it turned out, could be imposed more easily on distant, new colonies than on areas close to home that had their own traditions of feudal and municipal rights—even though they too were finally made subservient to the royal will. Moreover, political unity and religious unity reinforced each other. The Inquisition was established in Castile in 1477 as an instrument of the crown, with papal confirmation in 1483. The Catholic Church was to be purified; heretics or aliens were to be executed or expelled, as though they were traitors to the nation. The year 1492 was not only the year of Columbus' adventure. At the beginning of that year, the Moslems were defeated in Granada, ending their power in the Iberian peninsula, and shortly before Columbus sailed the Jews were forced to leave.

In France, royal authority grew gradually until, at about the beginning of the major French colonization effort (1660's), Louis XIV is supposed to have said, "l'Etat, c'est moi!"—and the assertion that the state was embodied in the king was not inappropriate to French government in the second half of the seventeenth century. The legal side of the idea had its basis in Roman law as revived in the twelfth and thirteenth centuries, in, for example, the dictum, "The king's will has the force of law." The royal domain had been quite small up to this time, that is, until Philip Augustus (ruled 1180–1223) and subsequent kings began to acquire surrounding counties and duchies. By the fourteenth century feudal courts were disappearing, though some aspects of seigneurial jurisdiction, such as in cases of misdemeanors, remained—in theory as concessions by the crown—and were to be carried to New France. A *parlement* sat as a regular court of justice, and no law could be put into effect that was not registered by it. A royal council came into being also, with administrative and governmental functions; its members were drawn from the clergy, the nobility, and state office-holders. The fourteenth and fifteenth centuries are sometimes referred to as a period of limited monarchy; tendencies both of local authority and representation and of royal centralization were present. During the fifteenth century representative bodies began to be suppressed, and when a colonial government came to be established in Canada no such institution was considered. At the same time, centralization proceeded along several lines. The crown was reannexing fiefholds; eventually, when Richelieu (chief minister of Louis XIII [1624–1642]) was in power, the medieval castles would be ordered torn down, as if to destroy the physical evidence of local authority. Provincial provosts, military governors, administrators, and royal inspectors were appointed who had authority over the countryside and in the towns. Once supported and protected by the crown, the towns and the business conducted in them now came under its control.

While Spaniards were finding and mining the riches of the Aztecs and Incas, the French were occupied with their frontiers, adventures for political power in Italy, and religious conflict. With districts depopulated and devastated by wars, France was in no condition to share in New World discoveries or their early benefits. By the time a certain amount of economic recovery had taken place, the country was caught up in a series of religious wars. Protestantism took form as a political party—the Huguenots—in the 1550's, partly as a popular urban movement but with most support coming from the nobility (it has been estimated that close to half the nobility in France was at one time Protestant). In its political aspects, the basic question was one of control of royal authority. Protestants were not necessarily opposed to the principle of the divine right of kings, for at the prospect of accession to the throne by Henry of Navarre, who was sympathetic to the Protestant cause, they supported that idea while Catholics spoke of sovereignty of the people and the right of election. The Edict of Nantes (1598) was a compromise agreement in which Protestants were limited in public worship but were assured of liberty of conscience, state payment of ministers, admission to all employments, and certain political privileges. Until Henry's assassination in 1610, Protestants could therefore participate in French ventures to the New World, but subsequently it was feared that they would obtain a hold on America and they were excluded (1627). It was the Catholicism of the French Counter-Reformation that was carried to New France.

In England, the small Anglo-Saxon kingdoms had been consolidated in the ninth century. There were shifts, however, in actual power within the central government and in the extent to which its activities affected localities. At the time of the Norman Conquest the country was composed of a half dozen earldoms, one of them the king's. The Conquest transferred lands to Norman barons, but their holdings tended to be scattered and royal authority as represented by sheriffs and commissioners could hold sway in the shires or counties. The Domesday survey (1086) considered all villages and lands within shires to belong to manor lords, making the manor the elemental unit for taxation. Also basic was its private (manorial) court. In the second half of the twelfth century Henry II increased the powers of the judicial committees of his council—the early king's courts—and a "common law" began to replace the diverse local customs. The royal judges were students of Roman civil law and the canon law of the Church, but they built up a body of case law that, with the king's writs and assizes, and later statutes, developed into a peculiarly English law, superseding feudal and ecclesiastical courts and being self-perpetuating instead of subject to the king's will. In addition, trial by jury was instituted, a jury of witnesses to the facts presented and not of hearers of evidence (this jury of witnesses was to be carried into Virginia in the seventeenth century, an interesting example of maintaining a custom that draws on people's direct knowledge of each other rather than on objectivity or impartiality). In the thirteenth century assemblies began to be called that included knights elected from the shire courts and representatives of the chartered boroughs. This was less a deliberate creation of a parliament or any new government agency than it was a further means for the central government and the localities to do business with each other that they had previously done locally or individually. That persons from many localities could now deliberate together over petitions and royal assessments did, of course, carry potential for political change. The medieval English Parliament had financial and judicial functions and gradually acquired the right to introduce legislation. Many judges, lawyers, and members of Parliament regarded the king as subject to the law, not originator of it (the thirteenth-century jurist Bracton wrote, "The King is under God and the Law"). This view alone did not limit royal authority or power. The king summoned Parliament, and appointed administrative servants. Lords had to contend with him, and the House of Commons (distinct before the sixteenth century as a body drawn from the lesser nobility, rural landholders, and burghers) with both lords and king. Some kings asserted their centrality in government; others did not. Under the Tudors the Privy Council, inner council of ministers and others of the upper house, formed into a decision-making body for the crown, but the older institutions of Parliament, law courts, circuit courts of assize, and county justices of the peace were also royal agencies.

The *county* was the significant unit of local administration, and the office of justice of the peace (established during the reign of Edward III [1327–1377]), was becoming the more important link between the central authority and the county. Justices were men of property and social position; many held other local offices in the course of their lives or went on to sit in Parliament. Within the county, political subdivisions were the *hundred*, an ancient, mainly judicial unit that was disappearing by the time of colonization; the *manor*; the *town* or *township* (both terms used variously for a village and its lands, and "town" sometimes for an incorporated urban place); and the *parish*, originally an ecclesiastical unit. The landholders and householders of a parish assembled from time to time as a vestry, important as a unit of local self-government insofar as it made its decisions binding on local officials and residents.

The Tudor monarchs of the sixteenth century drew local institutions more definitely than before into the circle of central authority. Parish officers were called on to carry out new laws and royal orders, including ones previously decided on by local guilds, towns, nobles, and church officials, such as poor relief and apprenticeship regulations. Henry VIII disestablished the Church of Rome in England and had himself proclaimed Supreme Head of the Church and Clergy of England, and Elizabeth completed the reconstitution of religion in a Church of State. The Thirty-Nine Articles of 1563 were expected to be acceptable to the diversely committed and uncommitted subjects of the realm and thus, somehow, to unite them. They were not and did not; in fact, after their promulgation the dissenting positions stood out more clearly, until at the end of Elizabeth's reign (1603) dissenters could not simply be lumped together as "Romanists" or "Papists" and "Puritans" (first used in the 1560's as a derogatory term for persons opposed to official policy). By the early seventeenth century the distinct ideas about church organization, ideas with political implications, were developing that were later to be known as Presbyterianism, Congregationalism, and, along with the latter, Separatism or Brownism.

Separatist congregations were few and small, but they are of special interest because of their attempts at local autonomy. For that matter, congregationalists were by definition concerned with the integrity of local groupings, and this in a period of extension of royal sovereignty. As Puritan causes gained sympathy in the House of Commons the Puritan movement developed more of a national orientation, partly by proselytizing among people of all classes throughout the realm and partly by being supported in cloth-producing and market towns where people had other kinds of nonlocal interests. Yet it did not succeed in taking over the Church of England. The idea of church government by the laity went counter to the inclusive rule of both church and state. It was not democratic in the more recent meaning of the term—seventeenth-century sermons in England (and in America) referred to properly "aristocratical" forms of church and community government[5]—but it did imply a diffusion of authority.

Physical relocation, migration to Holland and then America, was the outcome for a few; others sought to relocate national political authority, to transfer it from king to Parliament. At the same time the Stuart kings were claiming divine right to rule, members of Parliament were drawing up statements of their rights. In 1604 James I announced his supremacy to his first Parliament with familial, personal, and rural images: "I am the husband and all the whole isle is my lawful wife. I am the head and it is my body. I am the shepherd and it is my flock."[6] The members' claims were legalistic, based on ancient statutes and rights. In 1604 some of them said that the House of Commons represented the nation, or "commonwealth," and in the petitions of 1610, 1621, and 1628 it was argued that the Commons was the rightful place to debate such matters as the king's revenues, foreign affairs, and the nature of the Church of England.

The tension between these opposing claims to authority was increased by awareness of social and economic problems. Enclosure, the consolidation of village open fields or "champion" into compact farms and large estates, had meant evictions, dismissal of tenants, and forced sales from the fifteenth century on. Traditional subsistence farming as a community base was giving way to individually capitalized sheep raising and food production for a national market. The clergy, members of Parliament, and other

---

[5]"So then for *popular government*, we hold it not, we approue it not, for if the multitude gouern, then who shalbe gouerned?" asked Henry Ainsworth, who has been called the Separatists' "ablest spokesman"; and John Robinson, pastor of the migrant church at Leyden, Holland, which was later to send forth the Pilgrims, wrote that "it behooves the elders to govern the people, even in their voting, in just liberty, given by Christ whatsoever. Let the elders publicly propound, and order all things in the church . . . let the people of faith give their assent to their elders' holy and lawful administration" (quoted in Perry Miller, *Errand into the Wilderness* [Cambridge, Mass.: Harvard University Press, 1956], p. 22).

[6]Quoted in Edward Potts Cheyney, *European Background of American History: 1300–1600* (New York: Collier Books, 1961), p. 145.

observers were concerned—with reason—about unemployment and depopulation of the countryside. In Sir Thomas More's *Utopia* (first published in 1515), one cause of stealing is said to be the sheep, for these once meek and tame animals have become "so wylde . . . they consume, destroye, and devoure whole fields, howses, and cities." Attempts to control enclosure by legislation did not work; as time went on more and more people came to see it as a means toward agricultural efficiency. The agrarian poet Thomas Tusser wrote in the mid-sixteenth century:

> *"More profit is quieter found*
> *(Where pastures in severall be)*
> *Of one seelie aker of ground,*
> *Than champion maketh of three,*
> *Againe, what a joie is it knowne*
> *When men may be bold of their owne!"*

Rebellions occurred in several localities; in 1607 an armed revolt spread throughout the midlands, where the peasants filled the ditches and levelled the hedges that set off property (from such action came the name "Levellers," applied to an egalitarian party during the Civil Wars of the 1640's). The Privy Council set up commissions of inquiry. Lands continued to be enclosed.[7] Bridenbaugh describes people in the late sixteenth and early seventeenth centuries as "cut adrift" from occupations, families, and old loyalties and says that the woes of the average man were mounting, especially after 1620. These included crop failures, disease, economic depressions, and wars, as well as dislocations as a result of enclosures, and the fear of all of these.[8]

There was fear also of social unrest. During a depression in the early 1620's in the eastern-country cloth centers, the poor were ordered kept in their parishes, to prevent a new surge of vagabondage, new crowds of sturdy beggars who might turn out to be rogues and ruffians. The parish had been considered the accountable unit for purposes of social responsi-

---

[7]The open-field village did not disappear before regrets and idealization had begun to maintain some of its traditions. For example, in 1635: "How much and so many pleasant and commodious habitations for men, are tragically turned into rude and ruinous heapes, and the many delicate and delightful fields, plentifully abounding formerly with folds and flockes, with rich and rejoicing fruits; deformed and defaced, laid languishing like deplored and desolate desarts, haunted and inhabited onely by bruit beast and a few solitary mansions remaining where there is little help in time of necessity, comfort in time of doubt, or society in time of peace" (Joseph Bentham, quoted in W. E. Tate, *The English Village Community and the Enclosure Movements* [London: Victor Gollancz Ltd., 1967], p. 169). The best-known regret is Oliver Goldsmith's "The Deserted Village," written in 1770, after much more land had been enclosed.

[8]*Vexed and Troubled Englishmen, 1590–1642* (New York: Oxford University Press, 1968).

bility. From the time of the Elizabethan Poor Laws, however, church-wardens had been shuttling the poor between parishes. The poor, in effect, were outside any community. One theologian said as much: "Rogues, beggars, vagabonds . . . commonly are of no civil society or corporation"; "they join not themselves to any settled congregation for the obtaining of God's kingdom."[9] Yet the poor increased in the countryside and in the towns, and moved from the countryside to the towns. They engaged in food riots on occasion, and, as Bridenbaugh has pointed out, there was an invisible poverty of humble families in addition to the visible poverty of people on the move, totaling, he says, "almost half of the population."[10]

At the same time, local government became more and more the province of the "better sort." In the countryside this meant landholding families, and in the towns, men of reputation and wealth. New opportunities for investment, especially in foreign trade, helped create new fortunes that were used sometimes in urban opulence, sometimes on country estates, sometimes also in the capitalization of joint-stock company ventures. The House of Commons was made up mainly and persistently of landholders, even though commerce was becoming increasingly important to the nation.[11] But commercial regulations (import-export licenses, patents, and the like) as well as grants of property, revenues, and privileges to courtiers and to merchant oligarchies were among the recurrent issues that excited the gentry, lawyers, and townsmen of the Commons. Although the wealth of the country seems to have increased, as did the number of lesser gentry, between Elizabeth's reign (1558–1603) and the deposing of Charles I (beheaded 1649), royal revenue getting and the distribution of royal favors were arbitrary and members of Parliament together became acutely aware of it.

It may be going too far to say the seventeenth-century struggle between crown and Commons was for the control of a new national community. That was the outcome in modern terms, but in the seventeenth century the English were still a disparate and mainly locality-minded people, of whom a small proportion had formed a special and perhaps specialized political community, Parliament, which members insisted represented the rest. It was during this period, too, that some of the English began reaching beyond national boundaries. For a century there had been jealousy of Spain's claims in the New World, expressed, if in no other way, in piracy

----

[9]William Perkins, influential Calvinist at Cambridge in the late sixteenth century, quoted in Christopher Hill, *Society and Puritanism in Pre-Revolutionary England*, 2nd ed. (New York: Schocken Books, 1967) p. 283.

[10]*Vexed and Troubled Englishmen*, p. 375.

[11]"The proportion of merchants and urban officials in the Commons was a mere 12 per cent in 1584 and was still the same in 1640" (Lawrence Stone, *The Crisis of the Aristocracy, 1558–1641* [London: Oxford University Press, 1965], p. 31).

and privateering. By the early seventeenth century a combination of explicit national and private interests, quite different from traditional, implicit community concerns, turned attention to the benefits of colonization.

The first official steps were taken in Ireland. Attempts to possess the land and subdue its inhabitants had been made from the twelfth century on, but they were military attempts. The idea of settling English families there as a means of conquest was not promoted until the second half of the sixteenth century, when it was decided to garrison the most rebellious areas and turn the others into colonies. Ireland seemed attractive during the Tudor period because it was fertile, undeveloped, and close. The land was not fully farmed; part of Ireland's relatively small and scattered population followed a pastoral way of life, with a tribal social structure that was strange to the English. Furthermore, the Irish were Catholic at a time when English Protestants were interested in proselytizing—at least arguments for settling in Ireland included an appeal to the missionary spirit. English settlers might help convert the Irish, and incidentally maintain law and order out of an interest in preserving their own property. In 1556 the Earl of Sussex was authorized to establish a plantation, and his instructions specified restrictions on Irish landholding. A few years later, small grants were being made to both English and Irish tenants, but the Irish who were ejected from their lands in the process turned to guerrilla tactics. Defeated rebels had to forfeit their lands to the crown, which were then granted to Englishmen on seigniorial terms. Often the men who received such grants failed to settle either themselves or other Englishmen on them. Irish attacks continued, and after a full-scale rebellion in 1598 a policy of resettlement was introduced: Rebels and their supporters were transplanted to remote districts, a prelude to the removal acts with which Native Americans would later be cleared from desired lands.

After the accession of James I the occupation of Ireland proceeded more systematically than before. Shires were organized along English lines, and commissioners were sent to advance the undertaking for several successive years. The "flight of Earls" from Ulster in 1607 freed more lands, and new forfeitures were declared until all of northern Ulster could be parcelled out among English and Scottish settlers (with a few portions reserved for the natives). The Privy Council decided that the support of London companies was needed to promote emigration, as the Virginia Company was doing with regard to America at the same time, and to develop the area. Accordingly, the Irish Society was set up by the Common Council of the City of London to coordinate the job. It reserved the sites of Derry and Coleraine for itself and enlisted other companies to undertake the development of other sites. In the Articles drawn up between the Privy Council and the Common Council in 1609, the latter was to spend £20,000 in building two hundred houses in Derry and be prepared to provide three hundred more. The town plan subsequently adopted was for a central square with market, prison, and town hall in one structure and streets laid out in a gridiron pattern with uniform rows of attached houses along those leading to the square. Other new towns took this regular form of clustering or followed a linear pattern of building along a road.[12] Sir Francis Bacon was among those who advised compact settlements, but that was hardly enough to make the Irish content with imposed arrangements. In a poem of the time is this lament: "We have lived to see (affliction heavy!) the tribal convention places emptied; the wealth perished away in the stream: dark thickets of the chase turned into streets . . . the mountain all in fenced fields . . . the green is crossed by girdles of twisting fences."[13] Not all the settlers were happy either; the diplomat Sir George Carew reported in 1611 that with the conquered living side by side with the conquerors there would be a new rebellion. Settlement did, however, proceed more rapidly than in America, especially on the lands in Ulster that James I granted to selected Scotsmen. The Scottish tenants were, of course, the ancestors of the Scots-Irish or Ulster Scots who emigrated again, to America, in the colonial period.

Howard Mumford Jones has suggested that knowledge of English procedures in Ireland and attitudes toward the Irish is basic to understanding the English in America. "The doctrine that a plantation had to be, in its origins, a military establishment, and the excuse that native sloth made invasion and settlement necessary were, in addition to the misinterpretation of the 'wild' inhabitants, the most important notions developed by the Irish experience and transferred to the New World. Equally important was the idea that the subjugation of, or through, a colony implied a system of feudal tenure."[14] Encouragement of compact villages may have been related to the agricultural tradition in parts of England, or to concern over defense and social control under colonial conditions, or to both—it is hard to tell from the records—but similar plans were made by American colonizers. Encouragement of town building derived from considerations of marketing and trade as well as that of clustering. The urge to keep natives and occupiers separate appeared first in Ireland; removal of previous inhabitants would make more room (or land) for newcomers and also increase the chances of homogeneity in the new communities. Physical separation of conquered from conquerors became one of the principles in maintaining conquest across the Atlantic.

    [12]Described in John W. Reps, *Town Planning in Frontier America* (Princeton, N.J.: Princeton University Press, 1969), pp. 20–22.
    [13]In Constantia Maxwell, *Irish History from Contemporary Sources (1509–1610)*, (London: George Allen & Unwin Ltd., 1923), pp. 290–291.
    [14]*O Strange New World: American Culture, the Formative Years* (New York: The Viking Press, 1952), pp. 174–175.

Governmental provisions for Ireland also anticipated those for America. The Privy Council was the decisive body; the Irish Parliament had to go through an Irish Privy Council, viceroy, king, and English Privy Council in order to get anything done, and, aside from that, the English Parliament was more important in passing statutes for Ireland than the Irish Parliament. In the early eighteenth century the English Parliament announced its supremacy in so many words: "The English Parliament had, hath, and of right ought to have full power and authority to make laws and statutes of sufficient force and validity to bind the people of Ireland" —a statement of portent, Cheyney points out, for the American colonies later in the century.[15]

Problems of Change

This sketch of local and translocal aspects of the European settings for community is meant only to suggest traditions. In point of fact, the kinds of studies available for the period just preceding overseas expansion provoke more ideas about change than about tradition.

For one thing, there was a good deal of population mobility as well as stability in the European background to colonization. Stability, however, is most often inferred from special studies of agricultural communities, the more so the further back in time one looks. Such communities are thought to have lasted over many generations by means of family and other local transmission of cultural elements. Yet major migrations were being made in Europe well into the medieval period, and minor ones occurred thereafter in the crusades, in rural-to-urban shifting with the growth of commercial towns and new towns, and in colonization projects on Europe's frontiers. Exact figures for migration are not known, but its occurrence should not be ignored. Most often neglected in descriptions of the "expansion" of Europe are the early colonizing ventures; such movement is assumed to be overseas. The discovery of the New World did, of course, add a different dimension to it, especially because of promotion by increasingly powerful national governments. Earlier settlements and occupations (except in Ireland) were not "national."

There was also small-scale migration of families from place to place and of family members from household to household and locality to locality. In a study of the concept of family in western Europe, Philippe Ariès describes changes in significance of the parent-child relationship between the thirteenth and seventeenth centuries, suggesting that the nuclear family took on functions once located in a wider community or a number of

[15]*European Background of American History*, pp. 149–150.

households. A household was not limited to a conjugal family; children from other families might be there for some part of their education or training or as servants; and for that matter childhood was not considered to be a distinct and long phase of the life cycle as it has now come to be. Gradually, the conjugal family especially of the middle class set itself apart and special attention was given to the raising and educating of children within it. It might be said that "community," during this period, was on its way to becoming a collection of separate nuclear-family-centered households with some separate supportive institutions, such as the school, after having itself been an extended household. Along with this reduction to small family units came a new spatial differentiation of the social classes. Ariès' general conclusion:

> It was all as if a rigid, polymorphous social body had broken up and had been replaced by a host of little societies, the families, and by a few massive groups, the classes; families and classes brought together individuals related to one another by their moral resemblance and by the identity of their way of life, whereas the old unique social body embraced the greatest possible variety of ages and classes. . . . [The middle class] seceded: it withdrew from the vast polymorphous society to organize itself separately, in a homogeneous environment, among its families, in homes designed for privacy, in new districts kept free from all lower-class contamination.[16]

Manners, dress and appearance, and language had marked off social distances between people of different statuses who were in close and constant proximity; by the seventeenth century homes were providing more physical distance than before, for more people. Lewis Mumford says that building for privacy was "the first radical change" in the medieval house, and that ultimately it ended the reciprocal relations between the ranks of society which had been maintained through face-to-face contact. "The desire for privacy marked the beginning of that new alignment of classes which was to usher in the merciless class competition and individual self-assertion of a later day: for once consciences become tender, it is easier to practice inhumanity upon those you do not see."[17] It should be added, however, that separation of classes by districts in a town was not an innovation of the period. Administrative and commercial centers had always had districts or quarters related to status and occupation and sometimes lineage and ethnicity, and often a wall had drawn the line against outsid-

---

[16]*Centuries of Childhood: A Social History of Family Life*, trans. Robert Baldick (London: Jonathan Cape Ltd., 1962), pp. 414–15.
[17]*The City in History: Its Origins, Its Transformations, and Its Prospects* (New York: Harcourt, Brace & World, Inc., 1961), p. 285.

ers, including the poor.[18] It was mainly the middle-class residential area that expanded and increased its homogeneity and exclusiveness.

Since this was also the period in which centralized political institutions and their jurisdictions were displacing older local customs and authorities, some synthesis of these complex changes is tempting. For one: as the modern nation-state came into being, with support now from landholders, now from burghers, life in both urban and nonurban localities became more atomized, individualized. Or, we could speak of a gradual shift in socioeconomic importance from the local community to the national community—an easy, neat, but unverifiable generalization. The nation-state that had come into being by the seventeenth century in western Europe was a central government to which localities and regions were not evenly attached (nor are they today). Political and economic centers were indeed important, but it is worth remembering that " 'all roads lead to Rome,' not to any outlying village."[19] Probably few of the outlying villages, however, were ever isolated and self-contained communities. They were more likely points in a network of kinship, religious associations, economic interdependency, and political ties, networks of varying extents,[20] differing from place to place. But where you were from still mattered, wherever it was you were going.

As for colonists, they took with them their perceptions of what was changing at home, or what ought to change and of what ought not to change. The nature of local authority was an implicit and sometimes an explicit concern of theirs, but in the New World nonlocal authorities established its terms. Status in the old agricultural localities had been based on landholding, and work had been to some extent cooperative, but could proprietorship and cooperation be coordinated in new colonial settings? The old village communities had visible institutions, structural centers

---

[18]See Gideon Sjoberg, *The Preindustrial City: Past and Present* (New York: The Free Press, 1960), pp. 91–103. This is a cross-cultural, general study, with a few examples from preindustrial Europe. Mumford notes districts—and community focuses—in European cities, but also quite generally (*The City in History*, pp. 305–11).

[19]Sjoberg, *The Preindustrial City*, p. 115.

[20]Robert Redfield has described the peasant society as a "part-society" (*Peasant Society and Culture* [Chicago: University Press, 1956]). The work summarized and suggested by Peter Laslett in *The World We Have Lost* (London: Methuen & Co., Ltd., 1965) is to the point with regard to preindustrial England. He says: "The very large numbers of small settlements in which so many of the population lived were in fact all connected by the local rural centres. They were independent as communities, but their independence implied the existence of communities larger than themselves. Though these larger villages and towns turned out to be so small as compared with the provincial cities of the rest of Western Europe, they were nevertheless differently constituted from the others because they were centres of exchange as well as of communication. The whole pattern must therefore be thought of as a reticulation rather than as a particulation" (p. 57).

(church and manor house stand out), but the church and aristocracy had in many places been called into question by the time colonists set out. In the port towns and cities, where wealth was accumulating as a result of the activities of newly powerful commercial groups, there were several possible frameworks for community, and perhaps some choice between them; which of these should be taken to the colonies?

Tensions were evident, especially in England, between old and new community forms and relationships. The Separatists and Puritans who migrated tried to covenant their way into community, voluntarily, but a community that rests on traditional associations and traditionally shared assumptions about associations could not be reached that way. "Working and wandering as the world required of them," ever farther afield, they were more conscious than before of the problems of structuring community groupings. But if they sought a traditional community, the search itself precluded finding it. The sense of change that they carried with them was, on the whole, different from that which stayed at home. Those who left in the 1620's and 1630's by no means demanded the kind of community that some of the men in Cromwell's army were proposing in the 1640's. If there were Levellers and Diggers in the American settlements, they left no mark on them. It was in England that they sang:

> *The Poore long*
> *Have suffered wrong,*
> *By the gentry of this Nation,*
> *The Clergy they*
> *Have bore a great sway*
> *By their base insultation.*
> *But they shall*
> *Lye levell with all[,]*
> *They have corrupted our Fountains;*
> *And then we shall see*
> *Brave Community*
> *When Vallies lye levell with Mountains.*[21]

[21]From Robert Coster, "A Mite cast into the common Treasury. . ." (1649), quoted by Eduard Bernstein in *Cromwell & Communism: Socialism and Democracy in the Great English Revolution* (New York: Schocken Books, 1963; first published 1895), pp. 112–113.

4

Planting
And Transplanting
Communities

*"The way to prosper and achieve good success is
to make yourselves all of one mind for the good
of your country and your own."*
—ADVICE OF HIS MAJESTY'S COUNCIL FOR VIRGINIA
(1607)

Columbus' first camp and Oglethorpe's preplanned Savannah, and all the new places built in between, had one feature in common, as important as it is obvious: people a long way from home. In most settlements ties with the home country (if not with home) were maintained. A few independent settlements were tried, some of them by people leaving the sponsored settlements, but sooner or later they would have to deal with someone else's jurisdictional claims. Sponsored settlements, too, were affected by conflicting claims. The small forts and villages of the Swedes and the Finns on the Delaware, for example, were lost to the Dutch in less than a generation, and then New Netherland, in turn, was taken over by the English. The presence of French Huguenots in Florida brought Spaniards in force to defend their northern frontier, partly by building a new fortified settlement. Early settlements often showed in their shape the expectation of conflict, if not with some other national group then with Indians. Where no conflict occurred, communities still changed rapidly in the early years of settlement when newcomers had to be accommodated, when groups took themselves off to "plant" elsewhere, when nearby settlements expanded. Thus, though ideas of the form communities should take

55

can be discovered, not all of them had a chance to be influential. Those of African peoples had even less chance than others, since most were brought to North America as slaves, but in the Caribbean and elsewhere in Spanish and Portuguese colonies groups of escaped slaves set up *palenques*, palisaded agricultural villages that formed bases for attack against the plantations as well as places of refuge for fugitives, many of which survived and prospered over long periods.

Colonial communities lend themselves to the study of community because origins, form, and function may be made to stand out relatively clearly. They are tangibly communities-in-the-forming. However, by definition a colony exists in relation to a sponsor, a nation or group which decides it should exist, and so it cannot answer the question of how a community grows and changes on its own terms. Colonial communities have sometimes been described as though they were a sort of laboratory for community development. Some of the colonists themselves thought of their new places as models for others to use. These places do and did offer chances to see how human beings act when relocating themselves. They cannot and could not be controlled like animals in an experiment. They escape the tests, turn about and study themselves to the confusion of the researcher, threaten in a moment to transform themselves into another species. Origins can be identified easily enough, but what made them change? Perhaps something in their origins, perhaps a push or a pull from outside them, perhaps a predictable process of community change, or perhaps some combination of these factors (always safe to say).

Chronologically, nearly a third of Euro-American history and about half of Anglo-American history is colonial history. Migrants came from all parts of Europe; they came as community groups, as groups under contract, as diverse persons brought together for a particular venture, as shipmates, and as individuals. Advance planning was sometimes significant, sometimes not. From the great number of diverse settlements established in the three centuries between discovery and demands for independence, five broad types stand out. As types, they might be used to characterize the colonial period. Criteria for selecting them are viability and influence. They are identified, in other words, through a number of instances in which distinctive community forms, focuses, and social patterns lasted across several generations, and through evidence of being important not only to a particular locality but to a number of places established over a period of time. The Spanish *pueblo*, the French *rang* (row village) *and parish*, the *plantation and county unit* in the English South Atlantic seaboard colonies, the *village and township* in New England, and the *open-country neighborhoods* in the Middle Atlantic colonies fulfill these criteria. The full story of how they developed is too long and complex for this survey, but descriptions of each type must include steps taken by the

Spanish, the French, and the English to establish colonial communities. Some of these steps are familiar to students of American history; they are reviewed here for purposes of considering their influence on the places that came into being and lasted. Colonial administrative measures laid the foundations of form, government, social structure, and means of expansion for New World settlements. To begin this account with them is to give point to the significance of nonlocal and translocal frameworks for community building. Many of these measures were, however, modified by nonadministrative conditions, and the interaction of externally imposed measures with local conditions is also a continuing story.

These and Those Kingdoms

Estos y esos reinos, as Spanish monarchs referred to their holdings, implies not colonialism but equal status. However important this fiction of equality may have been to Spaniards of "those kingdoms," their communities were colonial in two senses of the term: separate territories being held in a political relationship to a nation through settlement of some of its subjects in them, and economic resources being exploited for national purposes distinct from those of the localities so used.

The Spanish monarchs did not envision colonies at first. The goal of their support of exploration was to find a sea route to trading centers of the Orient. When it became clear that there were unknown but exploitable lands in the way, Spanish policy-makers had to decide whether to settle them, to continue the search for a trade route, or—as was hoped for a time —to do both. The first settlement resulted from an accident: the *Santa Maria* was wrecked off the north shore of the island Columbus called Hispañola, and its crew had to be left behind when he returned to Spain. A fortress was built and the place was called La Navidad. It was destroyed before he returned the following autumn; the men, a local Arawak chief reported, had too actively demanded gold and women. With Columbus on his second voyage were some 1,500 men, for his reports and his samples of exotic plants and people had attracted popular as well as royal attention. Ferdinand and Isabella had provided more funds, and the expedition was supposed to establish a permanent base, keep foreigners out, find gold, convert Indians, and look further for the way to the Orient. It was not specified that the soldiers, nobles, a few artisans, and five priests who formed the group would have to make the discovery also of how to get along with each other and the natives of the West Indies. But tools, livestock, and seeds were shipped with them, and Columbus ordered the building of a town, Isabella. Peter Martyr, first historian of the early explorations, wrote that a site was selected near a harbor (to the east of La

Navidad) and that houses and a church were built within a few days. The event, the achievement of a new community, was marked by the celebration of the Holy Sacrifice on the Feast of the Three Kings. There seems subsequently to have been little to celebrate in Isabella. Disease, hunger, and dispute were not so eventful.

A constant source of dispute was the question of who was to do the work of the colony. The group was composed mostly of "gentlemen," not accustomed to building and farming, though energetic enough otherwise. They demanded labor in the fields and mines and food as well from the Arawak tribes, who then went hungry themselves. Columbus had not initially allotted lands to individuals, and this may have added to the ambiguity of their position, since landholding had been the source of local status in Spain. In 1497, before his third voyage, Columbus was given authority to assign freeholds on condition that they would be occupied for four years, but the labor problem remained. Indians who did not die from new diseases or the conditions of forced labor ran away.

No single labor policy was ever instituted by Spain, but in general three ways of organizing labor developed as the conquest spread through the islands and across the mainland, all of which affected both Indian and Spanish community life: the *repartimiento*, the *encomienda*, and slavery. After an Indian uprising during Columbus' governorship, the practice was begun of dividing up the local Indians for specific jobs, private and public, in lieu of their paying tribute. As developed in the sixteenth century, *repartimientos* often involved the moving of villages, in part or in whole, from place to place for work in mines, on estates, on roads and other public projects. Always a form of forced labor, it was variously limited by the crown and a wage was required as for free persons. For, beginning with Isabella's troubled conscience, there was a concern for the welfare of the new subjects, at least for purposes of leading them to salvation. This is emphasized in royal instructions on the *encomienda*, which differed from the *repartimiento* in that Indian villages and villagers were assigned to individuals who in turn had the obligation of protecting them and instructing them in Christianity.[1] Since the Indians were technically free, the uses to which they were put by these individuals, the *encomenderos*, disturbed some of the Spaniards. Notably, Bartolomé de las Casas renounced his own *encomienda* and took holy orders in 1510, and spent the rest of his life arguing in the West Indies and in Spain that the enslavement of Indians, by whatever name it was called, was a great evil. At one time he thought enslavement of Africans would be preferable—an idea of which he later repented. In fact, the African slave trade had already begun. The Portuguese had helped finance their ventures around Africa toward India

[1]See Lesley Byrd Simpson, *The Encomienda in New Spain: The Beginning of Spanish Mexico* (Berkeley: University of California Press, 1950).

by taking slaves to sell in Europe, and a few had been brought to Hispañola to work at mining. Spanish officials for a time refused to allow the colonies to participate in the trade, but by the middle of the sixteenth century it was flourishing. It was especially important in providing labor for the developing sugar plantations of the West Indies, because Indians, free or not, were rapidly disappearing from the islands.

As for colonists, emigration from Spain was restricted to orthodox Christians. Persons taking ship for the New World had to have a royal license and be registered with the Casa de Contratación (board of trade, established in 1503). Few women migrated to the Spanish colonies, and proportionately fewer families than was the case in other colonizing nations. Marriage with Indian women was correspondingly more frequent, and it was encouraged by governmental and religious authorities. Although Spaniards of all classes did not immediately rush to the new discoveries, Spain was second to England in numbers of colonists sent out, and they were a diverse lot. The town of Sevilla was filled with restless persons: soldiers and sailors; younger sons of noble families who would not be able to inherit the family lands; merchants and artisans who imagined better social and economic chances in lands less peopled with competitors; people who saw themselves as "outsiders" and hoped to find a way into society or up in society through achievements and possessions in a new world; and people whose restlessness seems like an inborn trait. Many also had religious aspirations, to win souls or even to establish pure Christian communities. The latter included most obviously the missionaries, who spread throughout the lands Spain claimed.

By 1507 there were fourteen settlements with a total of 12,000 settlers on the island of Hispañola; Santo Domingo was the largest and the seat of government. The following year the first formal occupation of mainland territory was proposed. Though royal agreement was sooner or later imperative in every case, private enterprise was most important in extending the conquest on the mainland. Individuals would contract with the crown for rights in a new territory, and the agreement constituted a kind of charter for a new government. The cost of the expedition was then borne by the person or persons who organized it, who in turn expected rewards as founder and governor. A number of such persons in the sixteenth century received the title of *adelantado*, and along with it proprietary rights, revenues, tax exemptions, powers of nomination to municipal and ecclesiastical offices, and the privilege of distributing land, labor, and water rights. They were often required to establish a certain number of settlers on the land, to bring priests or friars to it, and to build towns or forts within a specified time. When such terms had been fulfilled, however, their powers were soon limited; royally appointed officials were sent out and jurisdictions reorganized. The powers themselves changed over time, mostly being reduced. The first governors acted as chief justices, were responsible for tax collection, could make a number of appointments, and authorized land grants. As the conquest expanded, specialized agencies were called into being and the governor became more of an administrator. Decision making was increasingly reserved to the king and the Council of the Indies. The Council, in fact, came to hold nearly absolute power in the legislative, judicial, financial, commercial, military, and ecclesiastical affairs of the colonies. Its members made important appointments and proclaimed policies, from censorship to town building to the establishment of new viceroyalties.

By the time the French and English were settling in North America, the Spanish frontier had been extended up the southeastern Atlantic coast and through northern Mexico, and an outpost was being established at Santa Fe. Frontier regions were held not so much by colonization as by military and missionary activity, but town building was expected to follow. Town planning, moreover, was based on predetermined specifications that were expected to be generally applicable, rather than on the needs of particular localities.

Royal regulations set the patterns of settlement, government, and economic development much more precisely for Spanish than for other colonies of the New World, though many of them seem simply experimental. When, in 1509, Columbus' son Diego, his bride (a cousin of King Ferdinand), and their retinue of relatives and friends and plumed horses arrived at the muddy collection of huts called Santo Domingo, there was no standard plan for community building. Like others who came to the colonies with high position, they wished immediately to establish some evidence of their status as they perceived it—in short, a court. But "spontaneity and independence" in community development were not long permitted in the Spanish colonies[2]; specific instructions were given to later governors and other officials. Rulings were made also in response to immediate problems, and the result was a maze of sometimes contradictory orders. First in 1523 and again in 1573, attempts were made to systematize the various regulations for colonial settlements, which numbered about a hundred in Central and North America by the latter date. Very nearly the same rules and regulations reappear in the Laws of the Indies of 1681, and these seem to have been binding for the rest of the colonial period. They also had some influence on the Mexican government in the development of frontier areas after independence from Spain had been achieved.

The *pueblo* was to be the basic unit of local government. It was not a town in the ordinary meaning of the term but rather a jurisdiction over

---

[2]See C. H. Haring's comparison of Spanish with English community building, in *The Spanish Empire in America* (New York: Harcourt, Brace & World, Inc., 1947), pp. 147–49.

an area with an administrative and marketing center. If these functions are considered to be "urban," it could be defined as an urban-rural unit. It was through it that Spanish traditions of local form and function were transplanted to the New World. Through it, too, cultural change occurred, since it set the scene for contact between Indian and Spanish populations.

The regulations of 1573 specified desirable kinds of sites: "The chosen site shall be on an elevation; healthful; with means of fortification; fertile and with plenty of land for farming and pasturage; fuel and timber; fresh water, a native population, commodiousness; resources and of convenient access and egress."[3] Layout was prescribed too, with differences (mostly for purposes of defense) depending on whether it was located on a seacoast or inland. The basic form was gridiron or quadrangular. The first concern of the founder was to measure a main square and streets "by cord and ruler," with provision for arcades "for those who resort thither for trade." Then building lots next to the square, or plaza, were designated for church, royal and town council house, customhouse, arsenal, and hospital. The main lots closest to the plaza went to principal citizens. After lots were distributed among the first settlers, leftovers were held for grants to people coming later. Land was also reserved for common pasturage and woodland, for recreation, and for municipal uses. The rest of the land was divided into plots for cultivation, irrigable land going to the first settlers. Even house plans were regulated, to the degree of situating houses so "that in the living rooms one can enjoy air from the south and from the north, which are the best." Mediterranean traditions were followed: low, flat-roofed structures with a portal opening onto the interior and rooms grouped around one or more courtyards or patios. These houses were built with several generations in mind. They had rooms also for servants. As specified in the regulations of 1573, the house area included corrals for horses and other domestic animals. Some of these structures survive, evidence of the patriarchal and extended nature of the colonial family, in which close and home-based relations could be extended even to cousins several degrees removed. But their spaciousness and grandeur contrasts with the closely-packed, poorly ventilated structures, huts or little more, in sections of the *pueblo*. These too were provided for by Spanish officials.

Indians were kept from the area during the building period, and were subsequently allowed to live only in special sections outside the main part. From these sections the Spanish residents could draw their domestic and other workers. Provisions regarding local peoples were as follows:

136. If the natives should wish to oppose the establishment of a

[3]The regulations quoted here and in the next few paragraphs may be found in "Royal Ordinances Concerning the Laying Out of New Towns," trans. Zelia Nuttall, *Hispanic American Historical Review*, 5 (May, 1922), 249–54.

settlement they are to be given to understand that the settlers desire to build a town there not in order to deprive them of their property but for the purpose of being on friendly terms with them; of teaching them to know God and His law by means of which they shall be saved. This shall be explained to them by the friars and clergy and persons deputied by the governor, by means of good interpreters. Attempts are to be made by all fair means to establish the settlement peaceably and with the consent of the natives. If, after many different attempts have been made to gain their consent, the natives still withhold it then the settlers are to proceed to establish their own but are not to take any of the personal belongings of the Indians or to do them more hurt than what may be necessary in order to protect the settlers and enable them to build without interference.

137. While the new town is being built the settlers, as far as possible, shall try to avoid communication and intercourse with the Indians and are not to go to their villages or amuse themselves or disperse themselves over the country. Nor are the Indians to enter the circuit of the settlement until the latter is complete and in condition for defense and the houses built, so that when the Indians see them they will be filled with wonder and will realize that the Spaniards are settling there permanently and not temporarily. They will consequently fear the Spaniards so much that they will not dare to offend them and will respect them and desire their friendship. When the settlers begin to construct the town the governor is to appoint someone to take charge of the sowing and cultivating of wheat and vegetables so that the settlers can immediately employ these for their maintenance. The cattle are to graze and be tended in a safe place where they can do no injury to the cultivated lands or anything else belonging to the Indians. . . .

As early as 1503, Isabella, in a royal edict in response to problems of the governor of Hispañola, advised bringing native peoples together into towns. From that time on, their concentration or "congregation" was royal policy, formulated and reformulated throughout the century and after. One aspect of this was resettlement, the moving of already "civilized" Indians to new towns. Tlaxcalans, Aztecs, and others were transported from earlier conquered areas to help indoctrinate and acculturate the "barbarians" as well as to provide an immediately usable labor force. Thus the native peoples were expected to (and did) have new effects on each other, although historians traditionally give almost exclusive emphasis to European elements. If we look at the political scene and the structure whereby Spain administered her colonies, then, clearly, we will find the Spanish culture. If we look at the *barrios* and the Indian villages—if we could look fully at them, of course, in the relative absence of records of them for this period—we might find traditional Indian families and Indian patterns of authority and a wide range of customs from the Indian cultures.

Another aspect of the policy of congregating the Indians was the creation of villages on the basic model of the Spanish *pueblo*. The village forms were strictly specified. The church was to be the heart of the community. There were similar public officers, including one or more magistrates and councilmen elected yearly. There were similar provisions for communal lands, and by a law of 1546 Indian lands were not to be alienated—though much was, later, especially in the last part of the nineteenth century. Once settled in their villages, the Indians were not supposed to move. Moreover, through the sixteenth and seventeenth centuries particular groups were gradually excluded from them by law, so that finally few non-Indians were allowed. The crown's segregation policy had several implications. It was, in a sense, contradictory to the aim of acculturation into Spanish ways, but its purpose was to protect the Indians from abuses. Missionaries in particular were worried about harmful influences of outsiders that would affect their work. As a policy, it failed. It reflects, however, at least one aspect of the stratification system that existed in Spanish America: a sense of the necessity of a hierarchy. This sense is explicit in a report to the crown by the Council of the Indies in 1806:

> If it is impossible to deny that the different hierarchies and strata are of the greatest value to the monarchical state because their gradual and connected links of subordination and dependence support and substantiate the obedience and respect of the lowest vassal towards the King, this system is required for many more reasons in America. This is so, not only because of the greater distance from the Throne but because of the great number of people who by their vicious origin and nature cannot be compared with simple people in Spain and do constitute a very inferior species. It would be utterly reprehensible if those known to be sons and descendants of slaves sat down with those who derive from the first conquistadores or families that are noble, legitimate, white and free from any ugly stain.[4]

The larger towns were the places in which the stratification could most readily be seen. Wealth and prestige were based on landholding, but landowners lived in the towns where they could receive the satisfactions of having their status recognized. The landowning aristocracy of Spanish America had some complaints during the colonial period, for the top positions—administrative, religious, and economic—were reserved for *peninsulares*, persons born in Spain. Because of royal privilege, an unbridgeable gap existed between them and the next social class, the *criollos*. Legally, "creoles" were not disadvantaged, but as persons of Spanish descent who could not manage to be born in Spain, they could not hope to receive the highest royal appointments. Many tried, therefore, to maintain status by appearances (dress, carriages, furnishing of the town house, support of the arts). They sent their daughters to Spain, if they could, for purposes of marriage and childbearing. They were also careful in distinguishing among

---

[4]Quoted in Magnus Mörner, *Race Mixture in the History of Latin America* (Boston: Little, Brown and Company, 1967), p. 48. See his discussion of "the racial separation policy," pp. 45–48.

the social classes below them. The race-class nomenclature ran to dozens of terms. It varied from country to country and region to region in Spanish America, but everywhere it revealed the heterogeneity of the population, particularly in the towns. There the *castas*, persons of mixed blood (mestizo, mulatto, zambo), formed a large part of the artisan and laboring classes. There, too, some opportunities of advancement through economic means were available. Otherwise, the military was an avenue for social mobility, for creoles as well as for the castes.

Creoles did fill some positions in the church, the universities, the professions, and the trades and commerce. A wealthy merchant class came into being in the towns favored by Spain's trading regulations. Also, positions in local government were open to them. To structure local authority, the *cabildo* had been established early in the colonial period. The founder of a *pueblo* usually chose the first council members and magistrates. An ordinance of 1523 had the local property owners electing council members, but the provincial governor and even the king sometimes chose them. Officials—magistrates, constables, clerks, and others—were gradually added to the government, and all places did not have the same complement of them. The number of councilors depended on the size of the town; there were four to six in the smaller towns, twelve or more in the capital. By the beginning of the seventeenth century the general practice was for the provincial governor to nominate them, often on the recommendation of retiring councilmen, and less initiative on their part in local affairs was expected as time went on. As with other administrative and economic matters, local affairs became more and more subject, as time went on, to a chain of command that originated in Spain. However, while the authority of local offices may have decreased, they still carried prestige and they were still the local ear for local problems. It was through the *cabildos*, and through the town meetings that they could call, that independence movements were organized in Latin America in the early nineteenth century.

Religion was everywhere prominent, beginning with early instructions to build the main church of a town where it would stand out. Emphasis on ritual and ceremonial life can be seen as a constant source of community identity. Streets of cities and towns bore the names of saints or commemorated some part of Christian history. There were religious brotherhoods, the *hermandades*, to honor particular sacred images. In every city and region the church was a major landholder.[5] The clergy was re-

---

[5]In 1578 the *cabildo* of Mexico City complained to the king that religious orders possessed the largest and best part of the property in the city, and in 1790, of the 3,387 houses in Mexico City, 1,935 belonged to the church, according to J. Lloyd Mecham, "The Church in Colonial Spanish America," in *Colonial Hispanic America*, ed. A. C. Wilgus (Washington, D.C.: The George Washington University Press, 1936), p. 227.

sponsible for schools and charitable institutions, and local *curas* or *doctrineros* were expected to instruct the Indians in or near a given town. (The clergy tended to cluster, however, in major cities, and were scarce in some outlying regions that were no longer under missionary control.) That a local priest sometimes had considerable local influence is shown in the way Mexico's war for independence began: an uprising of Indians and the poor led by the priest Hidalgo. There were, of course, other factors in that uprising, but the readiness with which village people grouped themselves and acted under Hidalgo's protective authority suggests a common identity that, under stress, could be called forth.

New France

Spain's discovery of ready riches attracted people to the port at Sevilla, but not to it alone. Seamen from all parts of Europe and around the Mediterranean made their way to share—illegally—in the Spanish take. Beginning in 1522, when a collection of Aztecan treasures was captured by a French corsair, French pirates were a threat to Spanish claims. Their most permanent settlements were perhaps on board ship, for they did little to develop the harbors and coasts where they camped or lay in wait for Spanish ships, but their activities might have served to warn the Spaniards that the Americas would not forever be Spanish property.

Also attractive to the French and to other Europeans was fishing in the North Atlantic. The fishermen's communities were built no more solidly than those of the pirates, but over time fishing did have an effect on colonization. Fishing trips helped to build knowledge of western routes and areas not controlled by Spain, and in some instances fishing provided an economic base for settlement. Moreover, it was among the fishermen that the fur trade began, which attracted others to the North Atlantic lands in the seventeenth century.

There are records, vague enough to puzzle over but not so vague as to discount out of hand, of settlement attempts early in the sixteenth century: sandy and inhospitable Sable Island, for example, where cattle were taken about 1518 to supply the fishermen, and Cape Breton a couple of years later. An expedition to the St. Lawrence in 1541 is interesting because those who backed it expected to act out a dream of a northern Mexico replete with metal wealth. Jacques Cartier had gone "to the New lands to discover certain islands and countries where it is said that he should find great quantity of gold and other valuable things."[6] Two Huron princes

---

[6]Quoted in John Bartlett Brebner, *The Explorers of North America, 1492–1806* (Cleveland: The World Publishing Company, 1964), p. 98.

whom he took back to France with him, to learn the language for purposes of interpreting, spoke of kingdoms: their own, Hochelaga, in the environs of the island of Montreal; Saguenay, on a river that descends from Lake St. John to the St. Lawrence; and Canada, around the island of Orleans, with a village called Stadacona. On the next trip, however, the Huron seemed reluctant to take Cartier to Hochelaga; the village might not meet his expectations. The kingdom of Saguenay then became the goal—an equally elusive one. Theoretically, the territory was Spain's. But the French monarch, Francis I, said of the Papal Bulls of 1493 and the Treaty of Tordesillas of 1494, which had in effect divided the world between Spain and Portugal: "The sun shines for me as well as for others. I should very much like to see the clause in Adam's will that excludes me from a share of the world." He decided to help outfit ten ships, provisioned for two years, to conquer Saguenay and settle the area. In charge were Cartier in a military position and the Sieur de Roberval in a governmental position. Roberval had some trouble locating volunteer colonists, and the crew of soldiers, sailors, well-born adventurers, and craftsmen was supplemented with convicts released for the purpose and a few women, it is said, of ill repute. Cartier set out ahead of them in 1541. He fortified a place up-river from Stadacona, which he hoped was on the way to Saguenay, and put some men to work planting a garden. They stayed the winter, found some pretty but worthless metals and rocks, and then started back to France, meeting Roberval on the way. Cartier displayed the treasures to him and then, according to Roberval, crept away in the middle of the night in order to have all the glory, leaving him to stay for a winter in turn without finding anything to keep him longer. Roberval's chief pilot later insisted that the northern kingdoms were connected both to Peru and to the Orient, but by then no one was listening.

It was not until the end of the century that further colonization attempts were made. The compromises built into the Edict of Nantes provided an opening, though a temporary one, for Huguenot commercial ventures. By this time it was clear that profits could be made from furs, especially beaver skins, obtained in northern North America. It was individual merchants and explorers who were at first most interested in French expansion in North America, for Henry IV was concerned with reconstruction in France and his chief minister, the Duc de Sully, thought the French character was not suited to overseas colonization. He also disapproved of the means to finance it that were being tried. A partnership or company would request a charter for a monopoly of the fur trade, agreeing in return to various conditions, including taking a certain number of colonists per year to the New World. They had trouble fulfilling the conditions, and traders who had been excluded complained. Without government support colonization did not, in fact, proceed well. The first settler to come to the

St. Lawrence valley with his family for the purpose of clearing land and farming, Louis Hébert, a retired pharmacist from Paris, arrived as late as 1617. In 1627, the year the Company of One Hundred Associates was created by Louis XIII's chief minister, Cardinal Richelieu, and the Huguenots were barred from New France, there were fewer than 100 French settlers in northeastern North America, and in 1663, when colonial organization became royal business, there were about 2,000.

Samuel de Champlain, a Catholic associate of some Huguenots who had monopoly trading rights, was responsible for the first lasting settlements in Canada. He went to North America as a geographer, not particularly interested in either trade or colonization. The expeditions he accompanied in 1603 and 1604 were aimed at exploration and established Port Royal (1605) on the western coast of Nova Scotia mainly as a base of operations. There were forty-five settlers, however, who built their houses around a square, planted crops, and even organized a social club, The Order of Good Cheer. One wonders what their last meeting was like, for within two years the grantee, the Sieur de Monts, had lost his charter and most of the settlers returned to France. In 1608, De Monts obtained a new grant of a one-year monopoly of the fur trade, and Champlain turned toward the St. Lawrence valley. This time he decided that a securely based settlement would be advantageous both for trade and for further exploration. He began building his "Habitation" on the old site of Stadacona, which had by then been abandoned by the Indians. The river narrowed here—the Indians called the place Quebec, "the closed-up place"—and a bend in the river where the island of Orleans is situated helped to form a deep and protected harbor. Toward the end of the first year, before help arrived, Champlain noted that only eight were left of the twenty-eight who had begun the settlement, "and half of these were ailing." Yet Quebec was to become the capital of a new province for France. In the 1620's, when Richelieu was thinking that colonial development would increase French power in Europe, most of the French in North America were using Quebec as a home base, but only two families could be considered to have settled there permanently when English privateers attacked the town in 1629; the others—officials, traders, monks—were temporary or transient residents. Nor was the town to grow much in the next thirty years, though the number of missionaries increased. Champlain had gained the enmity of the Iroquois while attempting to maintain the friendship of fur-supplying Hurons, and Iroquois-Huron wars kept the area in turmoil. Moreover, settlers would clear the woodlands, and the fur trade depended on the original ecological conditions.

Government was a matter of company rule until 1647, when a colonial council was established to assist an appointed governor. Then, in 1663, the colony was turned into a royal province by Louis XIV and his finance minister, Colbert. Its form was similar to that of the centrally administered provinces in old France. Three main officials were appointed: governor, bishop, and *intendant*. The governorship was primarily a military position, though some who held it assumed or tried to assume wider authority. With the first governor, the Sieur de Courcelles, who arrived in 1665, came the Carignan-Salières regiment, the colony's first regular troops, who pushed the Iroquois back from French settlements (and destroyed a number of Iroquois settlements). As for the bishop, François de Laval had already been appointed (in 1658), though a separate diocese was not formally set up until 1674. It might also be noted that its area corresponded to that of the administrative district, a departure from the practice in France. Laval's personality and beliefs are said to have been at the heart of the development of the Catholic Church in Canada. He was appointed through the influence of Jesuits, and he represented the ultramontane view of church-state relations, holding to the absolute supremacy of the Pope and insisting on church participation in state affairs. One of his earliest acts was to institute a seminary for training clergy locally. The position of *intendant* was perhaps the most important in breadth of powers, involving supervision of the administration of justice, law enforcement, provisioning of military forces, income and expenditures in the colony, and allocations of land. The first *intendant* was Jean Talon, who arrived in the colony in 1665 and returned to France in 1672 after a brief but intensive period of encouragement of immigration, exploration, new settlements, and diversification of the economy. Governor, bishop, and *intendant* headed a Sovereign Council that included from five to twelve citizens appointed on a yearly basis, an attorney general, and a registrar. This Council acted mainly as a court, though executive, administrative, and judicial functions were not differentiated. The king could, of course, act independently of his colonial officials. It was under him that the Ministry of the Marine had responsibility for colonial affairs. The king's will and Roman law were basic in colonial justice, although that body of law known as the Custom of Paris was also introduced (in 1637, and officially established in 1663), and a kind of common law developed out of the decisions of the Sovereign Council.

It is often emphasized that French Canadian law had its sources in feudal, rural society, and retained its older characteristics even when law more amenable to commercial activity had developed in France. Certainly the seigneurial system of land tenure provided a basic organizing principle for French Canadian society, at least in theory. However, French feudalism could not be exactly transplanted, for in Canada there was plenty of land and a royal administrative system to perform legal tasks that otherwise might have been the *seigneurs'* to do. It was, of course, suited to providing for local government and defense in the wilderness. According to the feudal system, the *seigneur* owed judicial and military duties to his tenants and they, in turn, obedience and armed support to him.

Because the Canadian Indian population was not large and could not be organized for the French government's purposes as it was for Spain's in parts of Mexico and South America, the persons and religious orders with grants of land were required to bring settlers from France. They did not do so consistently or persistently, but with royal encouragement the population did increase. Talon's census of 1666 gave a total of 3,215, nearly two-thirds of which were males. One of his measures, therefore, for increasing the population was to have shiploads of girls—*filles du roi* ("king's daughters")—sent out for wives for the colony's bachelors. Many of them came from Normandy, and people were also recruited from the rural districts around Paris, Rouen, and La Rochelle. Other measures included bounties for families of more than ten children; payments for marriage before sixteen years of age for girls and twenty for boys; and fines for fathers whose children were still single when they reached these ages. The population did more than double during Talon's intendancy, and the census of 1681 showed a total of 9,677. Then immigration fell off again and most of the later increase was the result of a high birth rate.

The grants made to *seigneurs* fronted the rivers and extended inland. Grants to their *habitants*, the tenant settlers, also began with river frontage and ran in strips back through meadows and often to wooded slopes. The settlement pattern that resulted was one of fairly close-set farmhouses along the "road" of the river with fields and forest behind. With growth, a new *rang*, or row, of holdings would be established in back of the first, with a road parallel to the river and farmers' strips of land perpendicular to it. A parish came into being when a church could be built and included the people who supported it. At first a seigneury constituted a parish, but those in which population increased greatly were eventually divided into several parishes. "Parishes always tend to be convenience areas and, therefore, to be limited topographically," Horace Miner says in his study of the parish of St. Denis. "People at an inconvenient distance from the church will try to separate themselves as a new parish. To do this they must be sufficiently numerous to support a new church; therefore population distribution is an obvious factor" in parish building.[7]

The information Miner gives on the settlement of the area where the Rivière Ouelle empties into the St. Lawrence is interesting as background to the development of the community of *rang* and parish. In 1672 Jean-Baptiste Deschamps, a young officer in the Carignan-Salières regiment, married a Canadian-born girl and was granted a seigneurial fief by the

[7]Horace Miner, *St. Denis: A French-Canadian Parish* (Chicago: The University of Chicago Press, 1939), p. 44.

intendant Talon. It had two leagues of frontage on the St. Lawrence and was one and a half leagues in depth. Deschamps brought two carpenters, two masons, and four laborers from France, and other settlers from around Quebec joined them; nine years later eleven families had settled on this land and the population had reached sixty-two. Whatever special skills the settlers had, they also farmed and fished in these early years. By way of evidence for there having been little social distinction between *seigneur* and *habitants*, Miner notes that the *seigneur* had one servant boy, twelve head of cattle, fifteen *arpents* of land, and three guns, while one of the *habitants* had three servants, sixteen head of cattle, fifty *arpents* of land, and fourteen guns. (The average household had a 12-*arpent* frontage, or about 500 acres.) When other seigneurial grants had been made in the area, a country *curé* was appointed to make the rounds of the new settlements, covering a distance of seventy miles. The *seigneur's* house was used for masses and prayers at first, both during and between the *cure's* visits. If the *seigneur* was not resident in the community, as was the case in the St. Denis grant, the house of one of the *habitants* was used. In 1685 the *seigneur* of Rivière Ouelle donated land for a chapel. A Recollet missionary from France was the first to settle there; in 1690 a Canadian-trained priest was sent to the parish. During the eighteenth century the *habitants* of St. Denis went either to this church or to the one in the parish on the other side of them. Not until the 1830's was their settlement designated a parish. The new parish appears to have made togopraphical sense, since there was a natural barrier to travel and "no continuum of habitation from one parish to the next along the main road."[8]

Once established as a religious unit, the parish would become a civil unit as well. Frontenac, during his first governorship (1672–1682), instituted the office of *captaine de milice*, to see that parish men and boys were trained in musketry. The appointed (and unpaid) captains of militia gradually took on other local tasks and roles—superintendent of roads, official host to guests, recorder—and became the main liaison between parish and central government. The parish church itself had functions that today would be called civil: maintaining records of births, marriages, and deaths, and conveying public proclamations to the community. *Curés* were early given the right to tithe parishioners to one twenty-sixth of their grain harvest, and for a time the tithes were the only taxes paid by the *habitants*. The church was thus the focus of a community that was at once territorial, religious, civil, and social in its nature. The *curé* would necessarily have

---

[8]Miner, *St. Denis*, p. 21. (The course of events has been summarized from pp. 8–15.) With population growth south toward the mountains, two other parishes were later split off, though such splitting was resisted—as it had been in the case of St. Denis to begin with—because it reduced numbers and thus increased the burden of supporting the parish for those who remained.

a great effect on the community. He was present at the most important occasions in community members' lives, those that represented the cherished beliefs. Baptism, first communion, marriage, death—these were also occasions for gatherings and for discussion of community problems, and the priest often took a crucial part in proposing solutions. He had control over education and was influential in public opinion.

The *seigneur's* role was also important, representing prestige and social status,[9] and perhaps reminding the new Canadians of traditional social organization. The role did not necessarily represent wealth. Many *seigneurs* were not materially better off than their *habitants*. *Seigneurs'* duties to tenants in the wilderness were, in fact, real burdens to some of them, such as when they had to feed them on their work days.[10] Mostly, relations between *seigneur* and *habitant* were closer than in old France. One way in which some of them showed special status was, as in the Spanish colonies, by living in town (Montreal, Quebec, or Trois Rivières) part of the time. This alone would set them apart in the eyes of their *habitants*, although they were then faced with the problem of establishing and maintaining a position in town society.[11]

The closest relationships were those of the *rang*, of *habitants* living near each other along a road. One road of a parish might provide easy access to one trading center, another to another center. The parish would not thereby be divided, but, as might be expected, there would be various degrees of familiarity within it. Trading centers were simply the location of those who became in time nonfarming specialists—tradesmen, craftsmen, and the like. By the time Miner was studying St. Denis (the 1930's), its center was a close cluster of houses, without farmlands, at an intersection. Early land divisions for inheritance brought residents even closer

[9] W. J. Eccles, *Canadian Society During the French Regime* (Montreal: Harvest House Ltd., 1968), pp. 22–24.

[10] The *corvée* of feudal tradition, limited as it was in Canada to six days a year, and apparently not a burden. See G. M. Wrong, *The Rise and Fall of New France*, 2 vols. (New York: The Macmillan Company, 1928), I, 406–407. Arthur R. M. Lower says that in French Canada today the word refers to a "general community effort and get-together for a specific job in neighbourly spirit, sufficient commentary on the onerousness of the original obligation" (*Colony to Nation: A History of Canada*, 4th ed. rev. [Don Mills, Ont.: Longmans Canada Limited, 1964], p. 42).

[11] Its demands could be rigorous: "The more well-to-do entertained in their homes and custom demanded that a social call be returned the following day, even though this might require paying a dozen such calls in an afternoon. Dinner parties and balls were frequent and the fare provided was usually lavish. Mme. Bégon commented, in December 1748, that at a ball at Mme Verchères' the guests had danced all night. The following night there was another ball at the Lavaltrie's and the night after that at Mme Bragelogne's. A few weeks later, after a dinner party at the Lantagnac's, the guests worked up a fresh appetite dancing the minuet so went to Deschambault's for onion soup and wine. Messieurs de Noyan and St. Luc emptied five bottles between them and had to be carted home *en paquet* in a sleigh" (Eccles, *Canadian Society*, p. 65).

than they had been at first settlement (and intermarriage within a parish and between contiguous parishes kept families in contact). The Canadian historian Lower cites a story of a great elm tree that supposedly came to shade the frontages of three farms.[12]

A general equality and ease of life was often remarked by Canadians and by visitors in the seventeenth and eighteenth centuries. In 1684 the Baron de Lahontan, who had just come to Canada as an officer of the Marines, wrote back to France:

> As soon as we landed last year, Mr. *de la Barre* lodg'd our three Companies in some Cantons or Quarters in the Neighborhood of Quebec. The Planters call these places *Cotes*, which in *France* signifies no more than the Sea-Coast; tho' in this Country where the names of *Town* and *Village* are unknown, that word is made use of to express a Seignory or Manour, the Houses of which lie at the distance of two or three hundred Paces from one another, and are seated on the brink of the River of St. *Lawrence*. In earnest, Sir, the Boors of those Manors live with more ease and conveniency, than an infinity of the Gentlemen in *France*. . . . The poorest of them have four *Arpents* of Ground in front, and thirty or forty in depth. . . .
>
> Most of the inhabitants are a free sort of People that remov'd hither from *France*, and brought with 'em but little Money to set up withal: The rest are those who were Soldiers . . . and they exchang'd a Military Post, for the Trade of *Agriculture*. . . .
>
> In this Country everyone lives in a good and a well furnish'd House; and most of the Houses are of Wood, and two Stories high.[13]

French-Canadian agriculture was mostly of the subsistence sort, with wheat the main crop, and evidently the farmers did not extend themselves to produce a surplus for export. Yet visitors kept being impressed with how much better off the Canadian was than his counterpart in Europe. He was never hungry, they said, and if winters were long and cold he had plenty of fuel. From a picture of *habitant* life first published in 1810:

> The Habitans have almost every resource within their own families. . . . They build their own houses, barns, stables, and ovens; make their own carts, wheels, ploughs, harrows, and canoes. In short, their ingenuity, prompted as much by parsimony as the isolated situation in which they live, has provided them with every article of utility and every necessary of life. A Canadian will seldom or never purchase that which he can make himself; and I am of opinion that it is this saving spirit of frugality alone, which has induced them to follow the footsteps of their fathers, and which has prevented them from profiting by the modern improvements in husbandry, and the new implements of agriculture introduced by the English Settlers. . . .

[12]Lower, *Colony to Nation*, p. 44.
[13]*New Voyages to North-America by the Baron de Lahontan*, ed. R. G. Thwaites, 2 vols. (Chicago: A. C. McClurg & Co., 1905), I, 34–38.

They live on good terms with each other; parents and children to the third generation residing frequently in one house. The farm is divided as long as there is an acre to divide; and their desire of living together is a proof that they live happily, otherwise they would be anxious to part.[14]

Charters and Covenants

The French settled along the St. Lawrence until by the mid-eighteenth century English invaders thought the river looked like one continuous village street. They developed Montreal and Quebec into lively administrative centers. They traveled the major waterways of North America, stopping over in Indian villages, building fur-trading posts and forts at key junctions, until they were scattered through the continent up to the Spanish borders. La Salle's expeditions toward the end of the seventeenth century worried Spain into new fort-building and town-building projects on its northern frontier. But in 1699 the Sieur d'Iberville, who had been sent to found a buffer colony on the Gulf Coast, wrote of another threat, one deriving from "the spirit of colonization." The English would finally chase all other nations out of America, he said, for "however much they enrich themselves [they] do not return to England but stay and will flourish by their riches and their great efforts; while the French abandon them and retire as soon as they have gained a little wealth."[15]

"The spirit of colonization"—it would be hard to define it. What d'Iberville saw was a steady expansion of English settlements along the Atlantic seaboard and of trade with Indians inland. First colonial efforts were superficially alike for Spain, France, and England: abortive post building, wide-ranging exploration including feats with no practical outcome, infighting among the earliest settlers, searches for mineral wealth and then for profitable staple crops or other exports, and large land grants to proprietary persons who expected to have their lands worked by farmers in a position of dependency. But by 1700 the English had not only a strong mercantile potential but also colonial communities that appeared to be self-perpetuating, subject to England's laws but not in need of its material or moral sustenance. One of the differences lay in the use the English sponsors of colonies made of their charter. Another lay in the use some of the migrants made of the church covenant.

[14]John Lambert, *Travels Through Canada and the United States of North America, in the Years 1806, 1807, & 1808*, excerpted in *Early Travellers in the Canadas: 1791–1867*, ed. Gerald M. Craig (Toronto: The Macmillan Company of Canada Limited, 1955), pp. 30–31.

[15]Charles Upson Clark, ed., *Voyageurs, robes noires, et coureurs de bois* (New York: Publications of the Institute of French Studies, Inc., Columbia University, 1934), p. 297 (trans. by author).

Sir Walter Raleigh's ventures mark the beginning of English hopes for community building in America. His plan for the colony of Roanoke (the famous lost one) was to establish a city and fort as a nucleus for a seignory. Far greater visions are in his later book, *The Discoverie of Guiana*: gold, empire, cities and people. He himself was never involved in the perhaps tedious round of building houses, clearing land, fishing or planting and harvesting, and shipping of goods that constituted life in a new colony in the early seventeenth century. But the publicity that surrounded him was publicity also for colonial enterprise. He reinforced popular sentiment against Spain and helped build English confidence about competing with the nation that had found mines, and his promotion of a Virginia colony was promotion also of the idea that permanent settlement was possible and desirable.

One man, or a few men and families, could not finance, organize, and manage a distant colony. Nor would the crown, at this time, take direct responsibility. The first English settlements that lasted were sponsored by companies. The merchant companies of this period were indirect descendants of medieval guilds; they sought means of controlling trade in a locality and of protecting their members. In the joint-stock system just then developing, a number of individuals would contribute toward an enterprise that required a large amount of capital. A council would make the decisions, and though subscribers could attend a "general court" for the discussion of business, they took little part at first. Some of these companies were incorporated by royal charter, and some were more like voluntary associations, often subchartered by an incorporated group. All ultimately derived their privileges from the national government, requiring its protection and sometimes its support. Merchants often invested in more than one company. This was the case when the first colonies were established. In the early seventeenth century some who had been engaged in enterprises in Russia, Europe, and the Levant turned to New World prospects and joined in two Virginia Companies, of London and of Plymouth, for which a royal patent was granted in 1606. The charter identified large, overlapping areas within which each group was to "begin their said first Plantation and Habitation," and called for a company-appointed resident council in each colony and a superior royally-appointed council in England. The latter was to maintain governmental control while the companies carried out their business of settlement, mining, trading, and keeping others away. Later charters distributed authority more widely within the London Company, but at the same time, in the settlements themselves, attempts were being made to keep order by limiting authority to specific leadership roles: governor and minister. Unincorporated associations were also common in the colonial period, for through them merchants could make investments without undergoing the expense of incorporation. One such group helped the Pilgrims deal with the Virginia Company. Finally, company structure was the basis for a number of colonial governments.

PLANTATION AND COUNTY

The plans of the London Company were to locate and export raw materials (if not gold then forest products), to settle people in compact villages, and to foster the growth of a few commercial centers. The settlement pattern that eventuated was quite different from the plan, as it was also in the neighboring colonies, though they were organized as proprietorships and theoretically had other opportunities to implement their plans. In Virginia, the company had begun settlement as a corporate venture which carried with it a kind of communal organization in the sense that equipment, supplies, and produce went into a common store from which settlers could in turn draw, and that land and stock were not to be divided for seven years. The main settlement, Jamestown, was begun in 1607 with great hopes. It was to be "a great cittie," according to John Smith. But there was trouble from the start, including a status and labor problem like Spain's on Hispañola. Smith, in charge the winter of 1608–1609, wrote to the sponsors:

> When you send againe I intreat you rather send but thirty Carpenters, husbandmen, gardiners, fisher men, blacksmiths, masons, and diggers up of trees, roots, well provided; then a tousaud of such as we haue: for except wee be able both to lodge them, and feed them, the most will consume with want of necessaries before they can be made good for anything.[16]

They did seek skilled persons, and tried to attract more colonists by offering shares in the company in exchange for work, the implication being that individuals could thereby advance their status in society.[17] People did not rush to apply, however, and the company cast about for ways of shoring itself up. Various land offers were tried, including the "headright" system: fifty acres for every person sent to the colony. In 1619, new "Orders and Constitutions" spelled out a land system that included public estates, which were intended to pay for public services so as "to Ease all the In-

---

[16]Included in Smith's *The Generall Historie of Virginia, New-England, and the Summer Isles* (Ann Arbor: University Microfilms, Inc., 1966; first printed in London, 1624), p. 72.

[17]See Sigmund Diamond, "From Organization to Society: Virginia in the Seventeenth Century," *The American Journal of Sociology*, 63 (March, 1958), 457–75, for the implications of status, and Edmund S. Morgan, "The Labor Problem at Jamestown, 1607–18," *The American Historical Review*, 76, No. 3 (June, 1971), 595–611, for suggestions on the transatlantic migration of attitudes toward work.

habitants of Virginia forever of all taxes and public burthens as much as may be."[18] Four boroughs were projected on the model of the English municipality, and the colonial assembly established at this time took its name from the new way of organizing local administration: the House of Burgesses. Craven suggests that this institution, customarily called the beginning of representative government in America, was introduced to maintain unity of the colony when new proprietary ventures were bringing in "a diversity of interest and a dispersal of settlement unknown in the primitive and relatively compact community of earlier years," that its sponsors sought to balance "the requirements of local particularism and the necessities of an essential union."[19]

Financial trouble in the company led to its investigation by Parliament and its dissolution five years later. At that point Virginia became a royal colony, but without benefit of any long-range plan for its growth. Settlement proceeded through individual land acquisition and the importation of people to work the land. In 1705 the Virginia historian Robert Beverley wrote that, after the establishment of royal government,

> People flock'd over thither apace; every one took up Land by Patent to his Liking; and, not minding any thing but to be Masters of great Tracts of Land, they planted themselves separately on their several Plantations. . . . This Liberty of taking up Land, and the Ambition each Man had of being Lord of a vast, tho' unimprov'd Territory, together with the Advantage of the many Rivers, which afforded a commodious Road for Shipping at every Man's Door, has made the Country fall into such an unhappy Settlement and Course of Trade; that to this Day they have not any one Place of Cohabitation among them, that may reasonably bear the Name of a Town.[20]

Another early eighteenth-century analysis of the town problem was that the assemblies tried to set up too many towns in relation to local conditions,

> . . . for every Man desiring the Town to be as near as is possible to his own Door, and the Burgesses setting up every one of them for his own County, they have commonly contrived a Town for every County, which might be reasonable enough hereafter, when the Country comes to be

[18]W. F. Craven, *The Southern Colonies in the Seventeenth Century, 1607–1689* (Baton Rouge: Louisiana State University Press, 1949), p. 129.

[19]*The Southern Colonies*, pp. 134–135.

[20]*The History and Present State of Virginia*, ed. Louis B. Wright (Chapel Hill: The University of North Carolina Press, 1947), pp. 57–58. Thomas Jefferson, in his *Notes on the State of Virginia* written in the 1780's, also emphasized the role of rivers: "We have no townships. Our country being much intersected with navigable waters, and trade brought generally to our doors, instead of our being obliged to go in quest of it, has probably been one of the causes why we have no towns of any consequence" (ed. William Peden [Chapel Hill: The University of North Carolina Press, 1954], p. 108).

well peopled, but at present is utterly impractical for want of People to inhabit them, and Money to build them.[21]

Land had been taken up along rivers when it was discovered that tobacco could be grown for English and European markets. With a convenient anchorage and a planter's willingness to build his own docks, the need for commercial centers was bypassed. When lands wore out, new lands were sought, dispersing the population. Land speculators helped. Then, when the government ordered the building of port towns (1662, 1680, 1691, 1705, to solve the problem of collecting customs and to centralize and diversify the economy), the planters resisted or, once they were built, failed to use them.

Expansion of settlement along the southern Atlantic seaboard took place under comparable conditions: navigable streams and rivers and staple crops for export, grown most profitably when large amounts of land and a stable labor force were available. The men who had proprietary grants of land in these regions also started out with ideas of compact settlements, but went on to make it possible for individuals to acquire large amounts of land. The Maryland grant of 1632 gave the Baltimores near-autonomy. Cecilius Lord Baltimore's instructions to the first colonists specified a town, St. Mary's, with houses to be built "neere adjoyning one to an other" along streets and "divisions of Land to be made adjoyning on the back sides of their houses and to be assigned unto them for gardens and such uses according to the proportion of every ones building and adventure and as the conveniency of the place will afford."[22] That the settlers did not behave as though they were bound by these instructions is suggested by reports later in the century that the town had only about thirty small and scattered houses. The land of the grant had been laid out along seignorial and manorial lines: six-thousand-acre tracts for members of the proprietary family, up to three thousand acres for others. To encourage town life, the early land allotments included parcels at St. Mary's even when the receiver had his main acreage elsewhere. Yet while the colony expanded, St. Mary's grew little. It was the governor's residence and assemblies of leading colonists were called there, and thus it was tech-

[21]Henry Hartwell, James Blair, and Edward Chilton, *The Present State of Virginia, and the College*, excerpted in Aubrey C. Land, *The Bases of Plantation Society* (New York: Harper & Row, Publishers, 1969), p. 26. A thorough local history is C. Malcolm Watkins, *The Cultural History of Marlborough, Virginia: An Archeological and Historical Investigation of the Port Town for Stafford County and the Plantation of John Mercer* (Washington, D.C.: Smithsonian Institution Press, 1968).

[22]"Instructions to the Colonists by Lord Baltimore, 1633," in *Narratives of Early Maryland, 1633–1684*, ed. Clayton Colman Hall, Original Narratives of Early American History (New York: Charles Scribner's Sons, 1910; reprinted by Barnes & Noble, Inc., 1959), p. 22.

nically an administrative center, but like Jamestown it failed to provide a focus for a colony made up of large estates. The estates, the manors, were more important as administrative units in the early years of settlement; later, the hundred and the county with their regular courts and appointed officials took their place.

In the central section of the Carolina grant of 1663, town life did develop, along with large plantations. Charleston was intended to be an administrative center, and it turned into the most important commercial center south of Philadelphia during the colonial period. The proprietors had hoped for compact settlement; Lord Ashley wrote that the "Cheife thing that hath given New England soe much the advantage over Virginia" was settlement in townships, and that Carolinians should avoid the "Inconvenience and Barbarisme of scattered Dwellings."[23] But when, beginning in the 1690's, marshes and swamps were turned into rice fields, the plantation system took hold. Charleston, meanwhile, grew first as a trans-shipment depot for furs from the south and west and then as a rice-exporting center. It profited also from fear of the Spaniards and Indians, which kept the planters close to the town for many years. As early as 1700 it was being described as a "Metropolis":

> . . . [It] stands on a Point very convenient for Trade, being seated between two pleasant and navigable Rivers. The Town has very regular and fair Streets, in which are good buildings of Brick and Wood, and since my coming thence, has had great Additions of beautiful, large Brick-buildings, besides a strong Fort, and regular Fortifications made to defend the Town. . . . They have a considerable Trade both to *Europe*, and the *West Indies*, whereby they become rich, and are supply'd with all Things necessary for Trade, and genteel Living, which several other Places fall short of. Their co-habiting in a Town, has drawn to them ingenious People of most Sciences, whereby they have Tutors amongst them that educate their Youth a-la-mode.[24]

The grant of the southern, and so-far unsettled part of Carolina in 1732 involved detailed prior planning both for a town and for estates. Reformers headed by James Oglethorpe wished their "Georgia" to be a place for "the poor, whether subjects or foreigners" (referring to persecuted Protestants from Salzburg, Germany) and especially for jailed debtors. Because settlement of this area might buffer the other colonies against the Spanish in Florida and the French in Louisiana, Parliament for the first time voted appropriations to maintain a colony. Oglethorpe's plan

---

[23]Quoted in M. Eugene Sirmans, *Colonial South Carolina: A Political History, 1663–1763* (Chapel Hill: The University of North Carolina Press, 1966), p. 16.
[24]John Lawson, *A New Voyage to Carolina* (Ann Arbor: University Microfilms, Inc., 1966; first printed in London, 1709), pp. 2–3.

for Savannah seems to have been based in part on Ulster towns such as Londonderry and Coleraine.[25] It was laid out in sections with squares, and with "a Common round the Town for convenience of Air," five-acre garden lots outside it, and forty-four-acre farms beyond; persons able to come to the colony at their own expense could have five-hundred-acre grants. The settlers were thus to be limited as to where they could live and how much land they could have. Slavery and liquor were prohibited. The silk industry was expected to form the economic base of the colony, supplemented by production of other items that England had to buy abroad, but South Carolinians were influential in the spread of rice cultivation along the coast and in getting the ban on slavery lifted, and in the 1740's indigo became a major crop in inland areas. By the end of the term of Georgia's charter (1752), the plantation form of community was spreading with these crops.

There were family-sized farms as well as large plantations in the southern colonies, thousands more of them in fact. Where indentured servants had the prospect of becoming freeholders at the end of their terms of service, and were able to lease or rent land or to farm on shares, small sections of large estates came to be farmed by individuals seeking conveniently worked land. The result in terms of community form was scattered homesteads, open-country neighborhoods, some with and some without a focus in manor house, chapel, or county court compound. The great estates themselves, as owners continued to add to their holdings, were often made up of scattered parcels, variously farmed, variously managed. This is to say that a unitary image of a plantation South does not reflect the actual scene. Yet the plantation form did characterize political and economic power in Tidewater regions by the end of the colonial period, and then spread with the westward movement.

The term originally referred to a clearing, then to a settlement "planted" overseas. In the southern colonies it came to mean a unit of land on which staple crops were produced by the labor of a resident, dependent class. The area was dominated by the residence, the sometimes grand manor house, of the master. Set apart from it, as a physical expression of status ranking, were servants' and slaves' quarters, and workshops, barns, and warehouses. The form, associations, and activities of the plantation were determined by the planter and his family, who were in turn— the peculiarity of such relationships—dependent on the support of the laborers. Gradually, through the seventeenth century, indentured servants who by definition made for transitoriness were replaced by a more stable

[25]The plans and subsequent changes are described in John W. Reps, *Town Planning in Frontier America* (Princeton, N.J.: Princeton University Press, 1969), pp. 238–60.

population of slaves who were legally bound to the plantation community across generations. Southern colonial legislation from the 1660's on established servitude for life, black servitude for life, and inheritance of slave status—in short, it created stable *dependent communities.*

Parish and county constituted another community framework, in a sense overlaying the first, bringing some of its members together in another network of associations. The parish vestry was at first elected by parishioners, but replacements came to be chosen by the vestrymen themselves. The established Church of England was not represented by a bishop, and parsons were hired by the vestry and subject to its will. Vacancies were frequent, and parishes were large, some so large that "chapels of ease" were built for the convenience of the scattered population. Under such conditions it may be assumed that religious observance was more an individual or family than a community function. Farms and plantations set aside their own burial grounds, and weddings often took place at home. As in England, the parish became more than a religious unit; it had civil functions too, in tithing, poor relief, and upkeep of roads, even when the county superseded it as an administrative district (often with the same boundaries). County government was conducted mainly through the county court, where justices of the peace met regularly to draw up ordinances and to handle judicial matters. At first the justices were appointed by the colonial governor, but later, through their power of recommendation, courts (like the vestries) became self-perpetuating. Often the same persons were members of both. As the area of settlement expanded, new administrative districts were required in order to minimize travel problems. Chapel and courthouse were the visible expressions of these districts, whether or not there was any population clustering around them. They brought people together regularly, temporarily. In Virginia, for example, court compounds —courthouse, jail, lawyers' offices, caretaker's residence, all surrounded by a wall—were built in central locations and often fulfilled their functions without benefit of town amenities. Dispersal of population gave General Court sessions new significance, too, since most people could no longer get to them readily and it was a special occasion when they did. Beverley describes a sheriff making morning rounds to rouse out whoever happened to be in town in order to impanel them as a jury; whoever happened to be in town was whoever could afford to be and was there to enjoy the "fashions."[26]

---

[26]*History and Present State*, pp. 257–58. Dispersal also brought about a basic change in the jury system: for the traditional requirement that jurors be men of the vicinity the rule was substituted that only six members had to be neighbors of the accused and the rest might be drawn from the town (*Ibid.*, p. 258, and Craven, *Southern Colonies*, pp. 270–71).

VILLAGE AND TOWNSHIP

"No sure fishing place in the land is fit for planting nor any good place for planting found fit for fishing, at least neere the Shoare. And . . . rarely any Fisher-men will work at Land, neither are Husband-men fit for Fisher-men but with long use and experience," wrote John White in his *Planters Plea* in the 1620's.[27] Settlement northward along the Atlantic coast entailed its own problems and community forms. The Virginia Company of Plymouth thought of settling planters to supply the fishermen in the area, but its early ventures were unsuccessful. The New England shores seemed inhospitable, a permanent living uncertain, and not until the well-financed Massachusetts Bay Company appeared in 1630 was English settlement something more than attempts at survival by individuals and small groups.

The story of one of these, the people of Plymouth colony, has been overtold if one considers its small practical influence on other communities, but some of it is worth recounting here because its first chronicler, William Bradford (governor every year but five from 1621 until his death in 1657), was intensely interested in a close community. He found his hopes of it dissolving, and, instead of recognizing them then as only hopes, he began to imagine that that community had existed at some time in the past. What happened to him is still happening, and Bradford might be astonished to know the importance of his New England village among our imaginary communities of the past.[28]

Bradford had gone to Holland in the early 1600's with a few Separatists from England. In his account, they had been "used to a plaine countrie life, and the innocent trade of husbandry," and not to the handicrafts and commerce that were the means of livelihood in Holland. The walled cities, the fashions, and the language were strange to them after their "plaine countrie villages (wherein they were bred and had so longe lived) as it seemed they were come into a new world." Then too, "contention" split their congregations and some thought of moving on, not, Bradford insisted, "out of any newfangleness, or other such like giddie humor, by which men are oftentimes transported to their great hurt and danger, but for sundrie weightie and solid reasons"—mainly, the hardships in making a living in Holland. But when members of the congregation at Leyden had made arrangements to settle in America, only a minority of their brethren

[27]Quoted in C. M. Andrews, *The Colonial Period of American History: The Settlements*, 3 vols. (New Haven: Yale University Press, 1934), I, 351.

[28]The account that follows is drawn from Bradford's *Of Plimouth Plantation*, ed. William T. Davis, Original Narratives of Early American History (New York: Charles Scribner's Sons, 1908; reprinted by Barnes & Noble, Inc., 1964).

elected to join them and the group had to be filled out in England. Of the 102 Mayflower passengers, 41 were "saints" from Leyden and the rest were "strangers," most of them from London and southeastern England, who held to the Church of England, to the Puritan wing of the Church, or perhaps to no religious body at all. The potential for dissent was realized even before they landed; the Mayflower Compact was "occasioned partly by the discontented and mutinous speeches that some of the strangers amongst them had let fall from them in the ship." That compact, of course, is generally looked to as the first charter of community government in English North America, the first agreement made among the settlers themselves rather than a set of conditions imposed by sponsors of a colony. They would be hearing from the sponsors later. And they would continue to have disagreements, then and later, compact or not.

When, for example, newcomers arrived, they were considered to be, on the one hand, reinforcements, and on the other, mouths to feed. On the arrival of the ship *Anne* in the summer of 1623, "the old planters were affraid that their corne, when it was ripe, should be imparted to the newcomers, whose provissions which they brought with them they feared would fall short before the year wente aboute (as indeed it did)," and the newcomers, for their part, were afraid that the old planters would want what they had brought. The underlying conflict had to do with the common stores of the community as against the individual "perticuler," as Bradford put it. The Pilgrim leaders had left England without signing the contract proposed by their merchant sponsors that would put all profits from the venture into a common stock and allow no division of property or proceeds until the contract period had ended (seven years). The sponsors intended to hold them to it; the colonists, once arrived, did not agree that this would be to their benefit. Bradford stood for individual property:

> The experience that was had in this commone course and condition, tried sundrie years, and that amongst godly and sober men, may well evince the vanitie of that conceite of Platos and other ancients, applauded by some of later times;—that the taking away of propertie, and bringing in communitie into a comone wealth, would make them happy and florishing; as if they were wiser then God. For this comunitie (so farr as it was) was found to breed much confusion and discontent, and retard much imployment that would have been to their benefite and comforte.

But this should not be construed as a struggle between communism and private enterprise any more than was the case at Jamestown. The difference was between what company and colonists thought would best assure the success of their venture.

Requests for land allotments focused the issue. At first, house lots had been assigned (the amount of land depending on the size of the household) and crops were to be grown in common fields. In 1623, on demand, temporary allotments of land were made and households were allowed to keep the produce from their assigned lands but were taxed to maintain the common store of provisions for the support of those "who could not be freed from their Calling"—public officials, fishermen, and the like. In 1627 the community leaders decided to buy out the company enterprise, and the first major division of property was made. The common lands that remained were soon demanded as well, and in 1632 thousands of acres were distributed.

By this time Massachusetts Bay was being settled; the "Great Migration" was on. Some twenty thousand arrived in the 1630's, as against less than five hundred in the 1620's. The new villages affected the old, economically and otherwise. The Plymouth people were encouraged to increase farm production (they had not been very successful at fur trading and fishing) to supply the newcomers' needs until they could support themselves, and this meant putting more land under cultivation and finding more pasture for cattle. In Bradford's view, "this benefite turned to their hurte," in that the people began to move away from the village. A few years later (1638) he wrote that an earthquake had shown the Lord's "displeasure, in their shaking a peeces and removalls one from an other." The warning seems not to have been heeded; in 1641 he had occasion to write that even "those of the cheefe sort" were leaving, so that "it did greatly weaken the place" and caused many others to think of moving.

The course of events is understandable in retrospect, painful though it may have been to men like Bradford at the time. Villagers had been granted "great lots" a few miles away with the expectation that they would use them only as farmlands. For the place that became Marshfield, for example, landholders had promised that they would continue to live in the village and let their servants take care of their farms, but they soon moved their families to them, and the next step was to request permission to form a new church congregation—in effect, a new community. The settlers spread out all around the initial settlement, in small family groups and individually.[29] New immigrants were also clearing farms and building villages around Plymouth. Although Massachusetts Bay Colony did not formally absorb Plymouth until 1691, the little community had lost some of its lands, its autonomy, and many of its residents long before. At some point later in his life Bradford turned to the page of his journal on which he had recorded the application of 1617 for permission to settle in America: "We are knite together as a body in a most stricte and sacred bond

[29]See John Demos, "Notes on Life in Plymouth Colony," *William and Mary Quarterly*, 3rd Ser., 22 (1965), 264–86, on "fluidity" in the early settlement. Nine towns in addition to Plymouth are named by Bradford in his account for 1639 and 1640.

and covenante of the Lord," he had written then. Now he added, "O sacred bond, whilst inviollably preserved! . . . But (alass) that subtill serprente hath slylie wound in himselfe under faire pretences of necessitie and the like, to untwiste these sacred bonds and tyes, and as it were insensibly by degrees to dissolve, or in a great measure to weaken, the same." Villages throughout New England, once planted, were subject to such changes. Spread, dispersal, hiving-off are part of the histories of many places in the colonial period, and so is resistance to these processes. There was a basic form to the New England community, but the image of it should not be allowed to block the view of how people adopted it, used it, modified it, and moved on.

A typical early "town" or township comprised a compact village—a closely-set arrangement of residences, public buildings, and open space for public use—with fields, pastures, and woodlands in the surrounding area (see Fig. 4–1). The colonial government would grant the land to a group of proprietors, who were responsible for planning and settlement, land allotments, and management of the common-field system.[30] Each head of household in the original group would be given a house lot, a share in the fields, and access to the pastures and woodlands. Field shares were in strips, as in the old English villages. Ownership was not actually communal, since individuals retained their allotments (eventually with titles to them). But plans for planting and harvesting were made at field meetings, some work was done in common, and the fields were used by all for winter grazing. In time, residents consolidated their shares into farm units distinct from the village unit. Then too, nonproprietors and newcomers would request, and sometimes demand, land in yet-undivided and common fields. Even the central common, or village green, gave way in some places to demands for land division. The common was a mustering ground, a public park, and sometimes a pasture. The meetinghouse or church was often built to face it, and as the community developed other public buildings would be constructed around it. It was meant to be a center for the community, but it was inconsistently so. Depending on their location in a town, residents might worship and market in another one; towns split for convenience' sake; administrative jurisdictions overlapped. The number of nonresident proprietors increased in the eighteenth century, as did landholding for speculative purposes. Central house lots were larger in later-

[30]A study of land policy in practice is Roy Hidemichi Akagi's *The Town Proprietors of the New England Colonies: A Study of Their Development, Organization, Activities and Controversies, 1620–1770* (Gloucester, Mass.: Peter Smith, 1963; first published by the University of Pennsylvania Press in 1924). Akagi describes the "land community" as having been different from, and independent of, the "political community" because "The freemanship . . . implied the exercise of the franchise, while the proprietorship was exclusively a property right" (p. 5; see also pp. 288–89, 291).

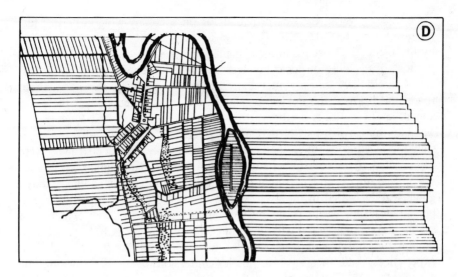

FIG. 4–1   LAYOUT OF WETHERSFIELD, CONNECTICUT, 1640–41, SHOWING
VILLAGE AND FIELD ALLOTMENTS.

Source: Charles M. Andrews, *The River Towns of Connecticut: A Study of
Wethersfield, Hartford, and Windsor,* Johns Hopkins University Studies in His-
torical and Political Science, Seventh Series, vols. VII–VIII–IX (Baltimore:
Johns Hopkins, 1889).

established towns. The close communities thus spread out. In 1831 it
could be said: "We have no villages, that is to say centers peopled by
farmers. The landowner lives on his land and the houses are all scattered
through the countryside."[31]

As for community organization, some special precepts developed
around Massachusetts Bay and were carried by migrants as the area of
settlement expanded. One was that a civil covenant might be used to bind
signers to a process of reaching mutual agreements. Another, that the
original signers or proprietors have prior rights in their township, and
property rights are basic to right community decisions. A third, church
members are best prepared to make right community decisions. Such ideas
could take shape within the colony, according to Bay Company officers,
for, having brought their charter to America, they insisted that authority
resided with them. In effect, they were creating a new central government.
New communities were expected to be bound to and by it.

[31]Albert Gallatin to Alexis de Tocqueville, quoted in Christopher Tunnard
and Henry Hope Reed, *American Skyline* (New York: The New American Library,
1956), p. 34. Edna Scofield, "The Origin of Settlement Patterns in Rural New England," *Geographical Review,* 28 (1938), 652–63, describes compact, transitional, and
isolated forms of settlement in the townships over time.

Local government was provided for on a colony-wide basis in Massachusetts in 1635–1636.[32] The new towns were then given permission by the General Court to hold town meetings several times a year for the purpose of deciding on local finances and bylaws. The town meeting generally could levy rates, direct expenditures, and make decisions about roads and bridges, the upkeep of church and school, the care of the poor, and other local needs as they arose. In its organization and functions, it was like the English parish meeting or "open vestry." It was also the occasion for electing deputies to the colonial assembly, in which towns were represented after 1634. Other rulings of the period made public office holding and voting dependent on church membership in good standing. Church going was legislated in the 1640's. But, it should be noted, church membership was not easily come by. An applicant had to show evidence of saving grace, undergoing what amounted to self-psychoanalysis plus examination by church elders of his past behavior, knowledge, and religious experiences, and then give a public confession of faith. "Owning the covenant" with God, along with his fellows, was supposed to bring him into a social covenant or compact which, although it had to be voluntarily engaged in, was similar in effect to the traditional organic community where "a family is a little common wealth, and a common wealth is a great family."[33] In light of this purpose it is interesting that, as the villages grew, the proportion of covenanters became smaller (though it varied from place to place). It has been estimated that by 1670 the proportion of church members in the Bay Colony as a whole was 20 to 25 percent. By then, too, membership requirements had been liberalized, and the requirement that a voter be a church member had been dropped.

The context for most colonial community building was a larger governmental unit with precedence in time and authority. In a few instances, such as at Plymouth and in Rhode Island and Connecticut, local controls appear to have had precedence, but sooner or later even they had to be

[32]For various aspects of local government, its relation to colonial government, and reference to carry-overs from English towns, manors, and parishes, see George Lee Haskins, *Law and Authority in Early Massachusetts: A Study in Tradition and Design* (New York: The Macmillan Company, 1960), especially pp. 66–84. Haskins emphasizes a sense of solidarity in the towns. Sumner Chilton Powell, *Puritan Village: The Formation of a New England Town* (Middletown, Conn.: Wesleyan University Press, 1963) traces the origins and early development of local institutions in Sudbury, Massachusetts. Kenneth A. Lockridge's recent study, *A New England Town: The First Hundred Years. Dedham, Massachusetts, 1636–1736* (New York: W. W. Norton and Company, 1970), applies the idea of communitarianism to early New England community building.

[33]Perry Miller, *The New England Mind: The Seventeenth Century* (Cambridge, Mass.: Harvard University Press, 1954), pp. 414–16. See also Edmund S. Morgan, *Visible Saints: The History of a Puritan Idea* (Ithaca, N.Y.: Cornell University Press, 1963).

validated by some larger unit. Bay Colony congregations who moved into the Connecticut River valley in the mid-1630's were hearing from Massachusetts Bay authorities even after they had drawn up a constitution of their own; Governor John Winthrop had worried about their going in the first place: "In point of conscience, they ought not to depart from us, being knit to us in one body, and bound by oath to seek the welfare of this commonwealth."[34] It has been suggested that magistrates thought of Massachusetts "as a single community despite its geographic dispersion,"[35] and it is frequently assumed that New England settlements were so much alike in form and organization as to give the area a unitary character and a common identity. The people in their localities, however, showed attachment to their rights and ways, and were most apt to speak of commonality when mutual support, such as for purposes of defense, seemed imperative. An example is the New England Confederation of 1643, and its preamble states, as one of the problems common to all that confederation is expected to help solve, their being "further dispersed upon the seacoasts and rivers than was at first intended, so that we cannot, according to our desire, with convenience communicate in one government and jurisdiction."[36]

The Reverend Thomas Hooker, on his way to Connecticut, had said that Massachusetts towns were set too "near each to other" to allow people to make a proper living; yet magistrates were concerned that, as it was, they could not communicate. Later in the century ministers spoke of a moral danger in people's scattering. To be at a distance from a regularly organized community and congregation was to be at a distance from God. Yet even congregations could offer surprises. Cotton Mather wrote that there had been "very fine settlements in the *northeast* regions; but what is become of them?" He had heard that a visiting Massachusetts Bay minister had urged a congregation to be "a religious people, [for] *otherwise they would contradict the main end of planting this wilderness*; whereupon a well-known person, then in the assembly, cryed out, *Sir, you are mis-*

---

[34]*Winthrop's Journal*, ed. James Kendall Hosmer, 2 vols., Original Narratives of Early American History (New York: Charles Scribner's Sons, 1908; reprinted by Barnes & Noble, Inc., 1959), I, 132. It seemed as though they were breaking a covenant. Interestingly, Reverend Thomas Hooker, who led one of these congregations, also took this position when William Pynchon withdrew Agawam (Springfield) from association with the other Connecticut valley settlements in 1638 (Perry Miller, *Errand into the Wilderness* [Cambridge, Mass.: The Belknap Press of Harvard University Press, 1956], p. 39).

[35]Michael Zuckerman, *Peaceable Kingdoms: New England Towns in the Eighteenth Century* (New York: Alfred A. Knopf, 1970), p. 12.

[36]As given in *Winthrop's Journal*, II, 100. Winthrop's reason for not inviting Sir Fernando Gorge's province of Maine to join with them is interesting: "They had lately made Acomenticus (a poor village) a corporation, and had made a taylor their mayor, and had entertained one Hull, an excommunicated person and very contentious, for their minister" (II, 99).

taken . . . ; our main end was to catch fish."[37] The wilderness was slowly being tamed, it was the people who were going wild. If they were out of sight of their elders, then Winthrop's much-quoted vision could hardly be fulfilled: "Men shall say of succeeding plantations, 'the Lord make it like that of *New England.*' For wee must consider that wee shall be as a citty upon a hill. The eies of all people are uppon us."

OPEN-COUNTRY NEIGHBORHOODS

With a great deal of land apparently available, it is not surprising that the dispersed settlement pattern took hold and spread, spread in fact across the continent, until in some areas it is hard to find any community center or focus at all. There had been scattered homesteads in parts of Europe, but in North America they came to characterize agricultural areas. Like other communities, open-country neighborhoods each have their own histories, but they have in common separate residences on—not apart from —at least enough land to support a family. During the colonial period this pattern appeared most clearly in the settlement of North Carolina, New York, and Pennsylvania.

The northern part of the Carolina grant was partly settled by independent, sporadic migration from Virginia. By 1700 a few men had taken up large tracts of land, but diversified farming on a small scale was much more common. The dominant settlement pattern became and remained one of scattered farmsteads.

Settlement in what is now New York State proceeded slowly at first. Until 1664, New Netherland was "a stepchild of the West India Company,"[38] a virtually nonplanned colony made up mainly of scattered posts for fur trading, and after 40 years of occupation by the Dutch there were only a few thousand permanent settlers. Many of them were not Dutch in origin; many, in fact, in villages and farms on the islands and along the rivers, were English—individuals and congregations, ex-servants and others from Virginia and New England, drawn, one account has it, "by the good opportunity to plant tobacco here" and "to enjoy freedom of conscience and to escape from the insupportable government of New England."[39] The Dutch had in New Amsterdam a small and diversely populated commercial center and, to the north, manorially organized estates: patroonships. Kiliaen van Rensselaer owned the only patroonship that was

---

[37]*Magnalia Christi Americana*, 2 vols. (Hartford: Silas Andrus, 1820; first published in London in 1702), I, 62.

[38]Thomas J. Condon, *New York Beginnings: The Commercial Origins of New Netherland* (New York: New York University Press, 1968), p. vii.

[39]"Journal of New Netherland, 1647" [author unknown], in *Narratives of New Netherland, 1609–1664*, ed. J. Franklin Jameson, Original Narratives of Early American History (New York: Charles Scribner's Sons, 1909; reprinted by Barnes & Noble, Inc., 1959), p. 272.

successful and lasting as such. Rensselaerwyck was a vast holding along both sides of the upper Hudson River and around Fort Orange, ruled on an absentee basis through an agent and other officers and councillors. By 1651, he had 16 leaseholders in addition to his own farmers, servants, and laborers; most of the residences were scattered along the river, away from the main house (where the agent lived).

Under English rule more manorial holdings were established, especially as governors gave land to their friends. Township settlement in the New England way was also possible then, according to the advice of Daniel Denton in 1670:

> . . . the usual way, is for a Company of people to joyn together, either enough to make a Town, or a lesser number; These go with the consent of the Governor, and view a Tract of Land, there being choice enough, and finding a place convenient for a Town, they return to the Governour, who upon their desire admits them into the Colony, and gives them a Grant or Patent for the said Land, for themselves and Associates. These persons being thus qualified, settle the place, and take in what inhabitants to themselves they shall see cause to admit of, till their Town be full. . .[40]

Otherwise, speculators acquired large amounts of land, which they would rent in small sections to individual farmers while waiting for a good time to sell, and thus settlement spread gradually, by farmsteads, along the rivers westward.

The diversity of the colony's population was persistently noted. In 1646 it was reported that eighteen different languages were being spoken on and in the environs of the island of Manhattan, among a population of four or five hundred men.[41] And the Dutch did not leave with the change in rule; in 1681 it was said that New York was still "most settled" by them. A letter dating from 1692 says "Our chiefest unhappyness here is too great a mixture of nations, and English ye least part; ye French Protestants have in ye late King's reign resorted hither in great nübers proportionably to ye other nation's inhabitants."[42]

The land granted to William Penn in 1681 attracted just as diverse a population, with a larger representation of particular groups. In accordance with beliefs of the Society of Friends, or Quakers, Penn planned a "holy experiment," with liberty in worship and a caretaker rather than a

[40]*A Brief Relation of New York: Formerly Called New-Netherlands, With the Places thereunto Adjoyning* (London: John Hancock, 1670), p. 16. This appears to be the first English account of the area. It was written to attract settlers, by one of the first settlers of the township of Jamaica.

[41]"Novum Belgium, by Father Isaac Jogues, 1646," in *Narratives of New Netherland*, p. 259.

[42]"New York in 1692: Letter from Charles Lodwick, to Mr. Francis Lodwick and Mr. Hooker, dated May 20, 1692," *Collections of the New-York Historical Society*, 2nd Ser., 2 (1848), Part I, 241–50.

coercive government. He also planned for the relation of town to country-side, and allotted town lands in proportion to farm acreage. The town, Philadelphia, was laid out in gridiron pattern with a central square, public buildings around it, and smaller squares in each quarter. Accounts of it in the 1680's and 1690's note its rapid growth and the substantial nature of the buildings. As a rhymer put it in 1692:

> *A City, and Towns were raised then,*
> *Wherein we might abide,*
> *Planters also, and Husband-men,*
> *Had Land enough beside.*
> *The best of Houses then was known,*
> *To be of Wood and Clay,*
> *But now we build of Brick and Stone,*
> *Which is a better way.*[43]

Penn had hoped for a "greene Country Towne," but Philadelphia's commercial development is the most impressive aspect of its early history. Merchants moved there from the other American colonies as well as from England. Trading first tobacco and then furs and foods, they stimulated expansion of the hinterland while they increased the wealth and importance of the town. In the surrounding area, rural settlements were supposed to take the form of townships with village centers. From Penn's description of them it appears that he considered the social implications of different layouts. In 1685 he wrote:

> We do settle in the way of Townships or Villages, each of which contains 5,000 acres, in square, and at least Ten families. . . . Many that had right to more Land were at first covetous to have their whole quantity without regard to this way of settlement, tho' by such Wilderness vacancies they had ruin'd the Country, and then our interest of course. I had in my view Society, Assistance, Busy Commerce, Instruction of Youth, Government of Peoples manners, Conveniency of Religious Assembling, Encouragement of Mechanicks, distinct and beaten roads.

There were "at least Fifty settled" townships, he said, by August 1684.[44] That there was a good deal of diversity in landholding, more, probably, than he had planned for, by the 1720's is illustrated in Figure 4–2.

[43]"A Short Description of Pennsilvania, by Richard Frame, 1692," in *Narratives of Early Pennsylvania, West New Jersey, and Delaware: 1630–1707*, ed. Albert Cook Myers, Original Narratives of Early American History (New York: Charles Scribner's Sons, 1912; reprinted by Barnes & Noble, Inc., 1959), p. 304.

[44]"A Further Account of the Province of Pennsylvania, by William Penn, 1685," in *Narratives of Early Pennsylvania*, p. 263.

Most of the early immigration was of English Quakers, but Pennsylvania soon became multicultural. Swedes and Dutch were already living along the Delaware (in small numbers), and other Europeans responded to Penn's advertisements and liberal terms of settlement. Taking up land together, or settling in the same area, some groups retained their cultural identities over long periods of time. One of these, Mennonites from the Rhineland, founded Germantown in 1683. Their agent, Francis Daniel Pastorius,

FIG. 4–2   LAYOUT OF PHILADELPHIA AND ITS ENVIRONS, ABOUT 1720,
SHOWING LARGE AND VARIED LAND DIVISIONS.

Source: From a survey map of Tho. Holme, published by Ino. Harris. Library of Congress.

wanted his settlers to have "a separate little province" in order to "feel more secure from all oppression," and Penn permitted them to have their own court, burgomaster, council, and laws. Over time, however, it was far more common for individuals to seek and take up land from the proprietors on condition of a small quitrent and statement of loyalty to them (as in other proprietary colonies). When, after Penn's death, terms of settlement became more restrictive and land more expensive, many immigrants came as indentured servants and redemptioners, serving to pay off the cost of their passage—a system much abused by the agents who shipped them. Philadelphia became a center for this kind of traffic, and appropriately miserable accommodations came into existence.

All told, more immigrants went into Pennsylvania than into any other colony in the eighteenth century. German peoples expanded an area of independent farms through the Susquehanna region, and Scots-Irish frontiersmen (from the Ulster "frontier") to the Cumberland valley. They were not always welcomed; from the 1720's come statements of fear of an "Irish" takeover, from the 1740's, of a German takeover. In 1751 Benjamin Franklin (in a passage that immediately caused controversy and still does) asked why the "Palatine Boors" should "be suffered to swarm into our Settlements, and by herding together establish their Language and Manners to the Exclusion of ours."[45]

By that time Quaker influence in Pennsylvania as a whole, considering all its various communities, was small; in the colonial Assembly it had been contested and was about to be withdrawn. One of the issues was Quaker pacifism in face of demands for funds to support England's wars and help defend other colonies and for assistance to frontiersmen in fighting Indians. Another was proprietary government as such. Quaker influence in Philadelphia was attenuated too, with growth—growth that Quaker merchants had done much to bring about.[46]

The story is, in very general terms, similar to what happened at Plymouth and Massachusetts Bay. In the beginning was the face-to-face community, and although it was not perceived in the same way by every settler, the circumstances of settlement provided a bond. In the early years civil and religious concerns were dealt with together, if only because there were neither the buildings nor the time to keep them separate; more, however, because at least the leaders held them to be part of a larger concern: right conduct. With growth in economy and population, new institutions and new communities came into being—not to destroy the old (as people closely committed to it seemed to fear) but to cast it in a special role: a repository of values that had been important to the founders, that could supply a sense of continuity or work the way memory works in an individual, as one resource for identity. This last point is clearest in the case of the New England village-and-township communities, whose form was early memorialized and substance mythicized.[47] It has a somewhat differ-

---

[45]"Observations Concerning the Increase of Mankind," *The Papers of Benjamin Franklin*, ed. Leonard W. Labaree et al., 11 vols. (New Haven: Yale University Press, 1959–), IV, 234.

[46]See Frederick B. Tolles, *Meeting House and Counting House: The Quaker Merchants of Colonial Philadelphia, 1682–1763* (New York: W. W. Norton & Company, Inc., 1963), especially ch. 10.

[47]For example, Timothy Dwight's discussion of the "village manner" of first colonial settlements in *Travels in New England and New York*, 4 vols. (New Haven, Conn.. Timothy Dwight, 1821), I, 335–38. He contrasts the village settlements of New England with individual farms elsewhere. Among the latter, "Neither schools, nor churches, can without difficulty be either built by the planters, or supported"; "persons, who live on scattered plantations, are in a great measure cut off from

ent application to Pennsylvania Quakers, who started with a conscious idea of community located not in a place or in a set of associations but, as Tolles has described it, in a "sense of fellowship" and of being a "peculiar people," a "sense of community among Friends, transcending colonial and national boundaries."[48]

---

that daily intercourse, which softens and polishes man"; "A family, thus situated, must in a great measure be confined to its own little circle of domestic objects, and wrought insensibly into an insulated character." In New England, "All the people are neighbours: social beings; converse; feel; sympathize; mingle minds; cherish sentiments; and are subjects of at least some degree of refinement." Moreover, "Even the scattered plantations in New-England have retained in a great measure the national characteristics of their country," since their habits had been formed before emigration away from the villages.

[48]*Meeting House and Counting House*, p. 89.

5

"Merchants Have No Country"

"You will find inclosed a Medal which was struck to commemorate the first American Enterprize to the Pacific Ocean. If you are a Federalist you will be pleased, but to the antifederalist, the man of Enterprize must be disgusting; nor can he wish him success, nor upon his principals is success needful, for what is property without good government?"

—LETTER FROM THE MERCHANT
JOSEPH BARRELL TO HIS
BROTHER (1787)

The movement for independence could not have gone far without urban centers. In the eighteenth century this means multifunctional places with an economic base in commerce. Their growth came mainly from the activities of merchants, who were supported in turn by their administrative and other functions (religious, informational) and by their ties of interdependency with hinterlands, other colonial centers, and overseas places. Seagoing commerce gave merchants both local and nonlocal power. They were sensitive to nonlocal changes, political and economic. Perhaps partly for this reason, Jefferson once claimed: "Merchants have no country. The mere spot they stand on does not constitute so strong an attachment as that from which they draw their gains."[1] They did have local bases of operations at the time of the English colonies' struggle for independence. Many were in positions of authority in their localities. If their localities had been simply small ports, it would have been hard to see just what advantage independence would bring (and some failed to see any advantage in any case). But beyond the colonial commercial centers were the equally needed ports of other countries. After independence had been achieved, the way to them seemed more open to men of "Enterprize."

The movement for independence developed a little later in the Spanish colonies than in the English, and in French-settled Canada not at all (until recent years, but that is quite a different story). Colonial development differed; the conditions that gave impetus to the urge for independence differed. In Spain's America, urban life had been fostered by decree and by administrative, religious, and cultural activities. A few places had the additional encouragement of being legal ports in Spain's centrally controlled commercial system (though this did not insure development: Vera Cruz, port of entry for New Spain, was beset by hurricanes, yellow fever, and pirates, and came alive when the fleet was in). The administrative centers displayed the wealth—or the facades of it (literally and figuratively) —of the Church, officialdom, and landholders. Through much of the colonial period, visitors were impressed with their pomp, with their festival occasions, with the miseries of the poor—all colorful. But most of the controls of wealth were in Spain.

Changes toward local economic development began to occur in the eighteenth century after the accession of the Bourbons to the Spanish crown and along with increased contacts with European and Anglo-American traders. Especially during the reign of Charles III (1759–1788), colonial conditions were studied and reforms instituted, some to open new ports, others to stimulate agriculture, mining, and the transportation facilities that would make productivity profitable. Intercolonial trade increased, and with it the population of ports and other distribution centers. By the end of the eighteenth century the capital of New Spain was the largest city in the western hemisphere. Though the new policies reflected attempts to solve Spain's problems in Europe, the result was colonial opportunity, including new fortunes for colonists. A sense of new opportunity was only one of the factors that made independence eventually seem possible, but it helped when people with local influence considered the question of where political authority was properly located. Their reading of the French *philosophes* on the nature of society and government led to that question, and when Napoleon invaded Spain they acted to answer it. It probably

[1] Letter to H. G. Spafford, 1814, in *Thomas Jefferson on Democracy*, ed. Saul K. Padover (New York: Mentor Book, 1946), p. 84.

helped also that traders from the new United States readily described their own War of Independence and hauled out copies of their Declaration conveniently in translation.

Yet there was no general commonality in the Spanish Empire, even within sections of it, to make up a single independence movement. Around 1800, only eight or ten years before *cabildos* began declaring independence from Bonaparte's authority in Spain, the German naturalist Alexander von Humboldt wrote from his observation of Mexico:

> No where does there exist such a fearful difference in the distribution of fortune, civilization, cultivation of the soil, and population. The interior of the country contains four cities, which are not more than one or two days' journey distant from one another, and possess a population of 35,000, 67,000, 70,000, and 135,000. The central tableland from la Puebla to Mexico, and from thence to Salamanca and Zelaya, is covered with villages and hamlets like the most cultivated part of Lombardy. To the east and west of this narrow strip succeed tracts of uncultivated ground, on which cannot be found ten or twelve persons to the square league. The capital and several other cities have scientific establishments, which will bear a comparison with those of Europe. The architecture of the public and private edifices, the elegance of the furniture, the equipages, the luxury and dress of the women, the tone of society, all announce a refinement to which the nakedness, ignorance, and vulgarity of the lower people form the most striking contrast. This immense inequality of fortune does not only exist among the cast of whites (Europeans or Creoles), it is even discoverable among the Indians.[2]

In France's America, commerce was a matter more of the vastness of the fur-trading territories than of the capacity of a commercial center. Only potentially were the hinterlands of Montreal and Quebec rich enough in various resources, and the St. Lawrence River likely enough as a shipping route, to support commercially based urban centers. One part of the potential hinterland of Montreal was the triangle formed by the Ohio, the Mississippi, and the Great Lakes. Forts were built to secure this fur-supplying area, with farm plots outside them stretching back in long strips from the rivers. Part of the area, the Illinois country, was settled for purposes of food supply for French Louisiana: Cahokia, Prairie du Rocher, Kaskaskia, and Ste. Genevieve were compact agricultural villages put together in the first third of the eighteenth century. But the English colonies had their own claims to the "northwest," based on their charters, and by mid-century land speculators were ready to act on them in the Ohio valley. Competition for beaver skins, with the threat of actual occupation of the area, led to the French and Indian War through which France lost her

---

[2]*Political Essay on the Kingdom of New Spain*, trans. John Black, 4 vols. (London: Longman, Hurst, Rees, Orme, and Brown, 1811), I, 134.

North American holdings (save for New Orleans and a couple of islands). Lands east of the Mississippi went to England, and what was left was given to Spain.

At that time the most important towns in New France were Montreal and Quebec. The site of Montreal, at the confluence of the Ottawa and St. Lawrence rivers and with access from the Richelieu and Lake Champlain, was excellent for commercial purposes. Settlement there had begun "for a testimony," when in 1642 the Sieur de Maisonneuve took a few priests, nuns, and farmers to establish a mission, planting—the legend goes —a grain of mustard seed as forecast of future achievement. It became a military post, then a trans-shipment depot for the fur trade. When English rule was established, some of the traders who had been working out of Albany and New York moved to Montreal to take advantage of its location. They brought new capital and connections with London merchants with them, and created a network of partnerships by 1783 that, as the North West Company, helped turn Montreal into a commercial center. The Constitutional Act of 1791, dividing Canada into Upper and Lower provinces, placed Montreal in the predominantly French Lower Canada (Quebec), to the anger of the predominantly English-oriented traders who saw themselves about to be ruled by French law and a French assembly. More of a threat to the Nor' Westers' position in the long run, however, was English diplomats' neglect of their interests when negotiating with the United States over boundaries, jurisdictions, and posts in the West. As the traders' accustomed territories and access routes came under American control, they turned to new ones, but the Hudson's Bay Company, with its northern oceanic access into and control of the interior, was better situated and by 1821 the Montreal traders had to choose between bankruptcy and a merger with it. As one result of the merger, Montreal was suddenly emptied of fur traders. Its growth as an urban place was also slowed by the fact that more people were now taking advantage of New York's facilities (and far more than ever after the opening of the Erie Canal in 1825) and that another potentially urban function, government, was centered in Quebec.

Quebec had been the administrative center for New France, though after 1730 the governor stayed in Montreal a few months each year. It was small; at mid-century its population was only about 5,000. It maintained its administrative importance after the conquest, however, and the provincial aristocracy continued to make its social life central to descriptions of the town. Toward the end of the eighteenth century a commercial function developed, too, when wheat and timber began to be exported through it.

Compared to Montreal and Quebec, a few towns to the south were cosmopolitan by the second half of the eighteenth century. The main ones in terms of export-import figures, population, and cultural diversity and liveliness were Boston, Newport, New York, Philadelphia, and Charleston.[3] These places, for all their distinctiveness, had in common an interdependence with other places. On one side were the agricultural, timber- and lumber-producing, mineral-producing, and labor-producing localities around them, although hinterlands were limited by lack of easily-maintained, year-round transportation. On the other were the ports and markets their ships could reach, legally or illegally.

The early development of Boston is illustrative of factors in urban development. The Massachusetts Bay Company seems initially to have intended a single, small, fortified settlement,[4] but within a few months of the first arrivals in 1630 seven separate settlements were scattered around the Bay. Boston, or the peninsula of Shawmut ("where there is a going by boat"), was probably not planned to be the central community, but then Governor Winthrop moved there, others followed, and the Court of Assistants began meeting there. It was obvious that the peninsula would not support a very large agricultural settlement, but it was centrally located in relation to the other villages and its harbor could accommodate the largest transatlantic ships. William Wood wrote in 1634 that the place was "fittest for such as can Trade into *England*, for such commodities as the Countrey wants, being the chiefe place for shipping and Merchandize."[5] Over the next few years Boston grew into a very different town from the other settlements. Its distinctiveness derived from its administrative position at first; in Wood's account: "This Towne although it be neither the greatest, nor the richest, yet it is the most noted and frequented, being the Center of the Plantations where the monthly Courts are kept. Here likewise dwells the Governour. . . ." The Company's jurisdiction, as centered at Boston, applied by 1643 to some twenty villages and more than 16,000 persons. This did not make it an "urban" center, for as yet it was not a center for other institutions nor did it have clear ties of interdependence throughout and beyond the region. Many of its residents were still small farmers, as in other New England localities. But the Bay Colony had relatively poor agricultural potential; the sea and the forests were more profitable. Boston became the center for fishing, shipbuilding and related manufacturing enterprises, shipping, and regional distribution of merchandise.

[3]The development of these towns has been examined by Carl Bridenbaugh in *Cities in the Wilderness: The First Century of Urban Life in America, 1625–1742* (New York: The Ronald Press Company, 1938), and *Cities in Revolt: Urban Life in America, 1743–1776* (New York: Alfred A. Knopf, 1955).

[4]Darrett B. Rutman, *Winthrop's Boston: Portrait of a Puritan Town, 1630–1649* (Chapel Hill, N.C.: The University of North Carolina Press, 1965), pp. 23–28 and Appendix 1.

[5]*Wood's New England Prospect* (New York: Burt Franklin, 1967; reprinted from the edition of the Prince Society, Boston: John Wilson and Son, 1865), p. 42. This was a promotional tract, first published in London in 1634.

Such activities led to alterations of the Shawmut peninsula—wharves, digging, fills—and to alterations of the alterations.[6] In 1690 it had a population of about 7,000 and in 1730, 13,000; it was the largest population center in the English colonies through much of the colonial period. Joseph Bennett, an English visitor, wrote in 1740 that Boston was the principal town of trade in all the British-American colonies and like London in many of its features. By his account it was an urban center. John Josselyn had called it a "Metropolis" in the 1660's, with its shops, wharves, and fairs and its being "much frequented by strangers."[7] Between these dates, it was growing in power in relation to distant places as well as to its neighbors. With sea-going commerce a major part of its economic base, people who had power at home also had power abroad. Their power derived not only from success in their activities as merchants; it was just as important that their home location was an urban place.

Peter Kalm, a Swedish naturalist who travelled in North America at mid-century, found fine buildings, opulence, and extensive commerce in Philadelphia, New York, and Boston, and described the interconnections of these places. He also noted differences and discords between the colonies.

> For it is to be observed, that each *English* colony in *North America* is independent of the other, and that each has its proper laws and coin, and may be looked upon in several lights as a state by itself. From hence it happens, that in time of war, things go on very slowly and irregularly here: for not only the sense of one province is sometimes directly opposite to that of another; but frequently the views of the governor, and those of the assembly, of the same province are quite different.... They have frequently taken up two or three years in considering whether they should give assistance to an oppressed sister colony, and sometimes they have expressly declared themselves against it. There are instances of provinces who were not only neuter in these circumstances, but who even carried on a great trade with the power which at that very time was attacking and laying waste some other provinces.[8]

Twenty-five years later, colonists were recognizing their common condition in relation to England, and, in Bridenbaugh's view, the communication brought about by commercial contacts was an "essential prelude."[9]

It was a long prelude, and had begun with England's version of mercantilism. Economic policies intended to build up national self-sufficiency and wealth had developed gradually in England, and not so much admin-

---

[6] Walter Muir Whitehill, *Boston: A Topographical History* (Cambridge, Mass.: The Belknap Press of Harvard University Press, 1959).

[7] *An Account of Two Voyages to New-England, Made During the Years 1638, 1663* (Boston: William Veazie, 1865; first published in London in 1675), pp. 124, 125.

[8] Peter Kalm, *Travels into North America*, trans. John Reinhold Forster, 2 vols. (London: T. Lowndes, 1772), I, 205.

[9] *Cities in Revolt*, pp. 418–25.

istratively as by private persons—landholders and landseekers, merchants, manufacturers—wanting and obtaining governmental benefits. The underlying assumption was that private and public interests supported each other (an idea that was retained in the colonies through the Independence period and applied in the new nation by Alexander Hamilton as Secretary of the Treasury). English regulations generally did not initiate, but rather were meant to protect or control economic endeavors after they were started. In shipbuilding and shipping, this worked to the benefit of colonists, for the navigation acts included them. Limitations on manufacturing in the colonies were another story, and it took the War of Independence and a new consciousness of the potentials of local resources to make up for this colonial disability.

Many points in the customary story of events leading up to the War reveal not simply merchants' reactions to England's mercantile policies but also their importance in focusing attention on issues and in getting groups together. The Sugar Act first roused widespread resentment when announced in 1764, and a movement to buy less English goods got under way. News of the passage of the Stamp Act (1765) aggravated some merchants, led by those of New York, into making nonimportation agreements. Colonists found they could get around the law by threatening to take mob action. "Sons of Liberty" associations were organized in towns and villages to enforce the boycott, colonial assemblies passed resolutions against Parliament's taxing the colonies, and a congress was called to discuss the issue on an intercolonial basis. With that, commonality began to be fostered, a commonality in reaction to what now appeared to be an outside agency: England, or England's Parliament. If Englishmen looking out across the Atlantic believed they saw an imperial community, the people in the colonies were not so sure. In working out ideas about their relation to a government centered in England, the colonial assemblies asserted their own rights as governmental bodies, assertions that became the more defiant when some of them were dissolved. The Stamp Act was repealed in 1766 (at least partly because of an economic recession in England that made the American boycott of English goods seem hard to bear), but then Parliament, in the Declaratory Act (1766) so similar to that for Ireland a half-century earlier, claimed its authority to legislate "in all cases whatsoever." Resistance to subsequent Acts again took the form of nonimportation agreements among merchants, and also encouragement of local production and manufactures,[10] but some of the sense of grievance among

[10]The value of colonial exports to and imports from England fell by almost one-third between 1768 and 1769 as a result of nonimportation agreements, with the greatest drop in imports at New York, and then rose again until 1772. It is interesting that exports to London from places other than in New England were at their highest value ever in 1775. The data are in Series Z 21–34 and 35–42, *The Statistical History of the United States from Colonial Times to the Present* (Stamford, Conn.: Fairfield Publishers, Inc., 1965), pp. 757, 758.

colonists began to be turned against the merchants who supported the boy-cotts; they were overcharging now, it was said—goods being scarce as they were—and with the repeal of most of the Townshend duties of 1767 many of the merchants responded to the complaints about them by ceasing to complain about England.

Toward the end of 1772 Massachusetts town meetings began to em-power "Committees of Correspondence" to exchange information about their problems with English officials. The idea spread, and in March 1773 the Virginia House of Burgesses suggested that the committees be organ-ized intercolonially. The first important news spread through them was of the Tea Act, whereby the East India Company was to distribute tea directly to retailers. Merchants responded once more, saying that this constituted monopoly. Sam Adams said the Act marked the end of liberty, and physicians said tea rusted the teeth anyway. The next major act was the Boston Tea Party. When Parliament reacted with the Coercive Acts, one of which was to close the port of Boston, it did not take long for a Continental Congress to form, reject them, and agree on nonimportation, nonexportation, and nonconsumption of English goods. Even so, the dele-gates admitted Parliament's right to regulate trade—as long as no taxes were imposed for the purpose of raising revenue. Economic measures were discussed together with the question of the colonists' political status, not only in the Congress at Philadelphia but throughout the colonies that au-tumn and winter of 1774 and 1775. But there was never total agreement on what should be done—the commonality newly called into being did not go that far—even when the Second Continental Congress decided to raise an army or, the next year, to advise the colonies to establish separate gov-ernments while they adopted a Declaration of Independence.

The War for Independence was not fought by a "national commu-nity" or by a society prepared, in the social contract theory of the time, to constitute a government for itself; it was more like an uprising of scattered tenants of a large manor, some of whose village officers, elders, tradesmen, and richer peasants decided to flee with the lord, others to fight it out, and others to watch it happen. The war was waged partly by local militia serv-ing in their localities, almost as the men thought proper before going home to supper. The wider war of the Continental Congress and the Continental Army was more organized but subject, too, to men's loyalties to home and crops and—perhaps a more serious portent—the haphazard support of civil authorities. In the course of the war, however, men other than mer-chants and old-family political representatives turned their attention out-ward from their local communities and from the provinces or states that the first concerns for independence had brought into being. Their doing so made it possible to lay the foundations of a larger political unit.

Trade between the rebellious colonies and England was interdicted by Congress, but it did not simply stop. Much trade was indirect, by way of Nova Scotia and the West Indies or through Amsterdam. Some of the direct trade relationships were maintained too. Robert A. East quotes a London correspondent of New York merchants in 1775, a year when Boston was occupied by British troops: "However extraordinary it may appear, yet we find there is now shipping from this place [London] for Boston nearly as much goods as ever for the Merchants there . . . O Worthy Boston."[11] In mid-1776, merchants for the first time were able legally to make business arrangements in the ports of the world and did so especially with the French, Spanish, and Dutch. The gains of Philadelphia merchants are perhaps best known; Robert Morris, for example, important in local, national, and international trading arrangements before, during, and after the war, is said to have lost one hundred and fifty ships during the war and still to have come out about even. Privateering was a profitable business during the war, as was marine insurance, military shipping, army provisioning, and speculation in Continental currency and foreign bills and drafts. Successful merchants invested their capital in several ways (as would be true after the war, too)—land, buildings, manufacturing, money lending —and thereby increased not just their own fortunes but also the productive activities of towns and regions. In both primary and secondary centers, economic changes were followed by increased public identification of what was important to the town and region. Trading activities are threads in local histories in the Independence period, just as they are the cross-stitching on the larger scene of a new nation facing the Atlantic.

To what extent the identities of the commercial centers changed during the war is difficult to determine. There were some abrupt population changes as a result of British occupation and the closing of ports.[12] Boston, for example, had a population of 15,520 in 1765; in 1776, after the closing of the port, 2,719 whites were counted; in the mid-1780's there were again about 15,000 inhabitants. Newport lost nearly half its population between 1774 and 1776, though Providence gained slightly. Figures for Philadelphia and New York also show great fluctuation. There were popular expressions of revolutionary spirit that must have put a new edge on local life, when people were released from debtors' prisons, for example, or when storehouses were stormed, or crowds gathered at merchants' houses to protest prices.[13]

[11]*Business Enterprise in the American Revolutionary Era* (New York: AMS Press, Inc., 1969; first published 1938), p. 50.

[12]The population figures in this paragraph are from Evart B. Greene and Virginia D. Harrington, *American Population Before the Federal Census of 1790* (Gloucester, Mass.: Peter Smith, 1966; first published 1932).

[13]See Jesse Lemisch, "The American Revolution Seen from the Bottom Up," in Barton J. Bernstein, ed., *Towards a New Past: Dissenting Essays in American History* (New York: Random House, Inc., 1968), pp. 3–45, for questions of both traditional and recent interpretations that ignore the lower classes; his questions are especially provocative when applied to what is known (or, rather, not known) of life in the towns during this period.

For all that business opportunities increased, at least for some, the towns that were centers of business enterprise appear to have had little lasting growth until after the Independence period. But surrounding areas should be considered too. For example, a variety of economic activities important to Philadelphia were located around and not in the city: iron forges, corn mills, sawmills, fulling mills, paper mills, and an oil mill.[14] With road building and expansion of settlement in this period, Philadelphia had an ever-wider hinterland, though Baltimore sought some of the same supporting region. Baltimore was one of the towns that grew significantly during the war years. In 1775 its population was 5,934; in 1782 it was 8,000 or more (an estimate of 1783 is 12,000–15,000); the 1790 census gave it 13,503. But more significance lies in its having only 25 houses in 1752 and 1,950 in 1786. It was in a favorable position away from British sea raids during the war, and with the end of British restrictions it was able to develop into a leading port for the tobacco trade and trade with the West Indies. Having begun to build mills in the 1750's, local merchants also engaged in the flour trade. John Adams wrote from Baltimore in 1777, "The object of the men of property here, the planters, & etc., is universally wealth. Every way in the world is sought to get and save money. Landjobbers, speculators in land; little generosity to the public, little public spirit."[15] "Public spirit?"—manufactures were established, marshlands reclaimed, and Baltimore's regional functions increased.

The proportion of the population occupied in business was, actually, very small. Even in the North it may not have been more than two or three percent. In the South it was not nonexistent, but business was less likely to be a person's main concern. A study of the northern Chesapeake region has shown the wealthiest men to have engaged in agriculture and various forms of business at the same time, including land speculation, trade, moneylending, and manufacturing. "The secret of their success was business enterprise, though almost to a man they lived as planters separated from the kind of urban community in which their more conspicuously entrepreneurial counterparts to the north had their residences and places of business."[16] It appears that although business may have been essential

---

[14]Stella H. Sutherland, *Population Distribution in Colonial America* (New York: Columbia University Press, 1936), pp. 167–68.

[15]*The Works of John Adams*, ed. Charles Francis Adams, 10 vols. (Boston: Little, Brown and Co., (1852–1865), II, 436.

[16]Aubrey C. Land, "Economic Base and Social Structure: The Northern Chesapeake in the Eighteenth Century," *Journal of Economic History*, 25, No. 4 (December, 1965), 639–54. Some of the planter's activities would have fostered self-containment of the local community: "Hardly a parish lacked one or more country stores, often no more than a tiny hut or part of a building on the grounds of a planter who could supply, usually on credit, the basic needs of neighboring small producers—drygoods, hoes and other small implements, salt, sugar, spices, tea, and almost always liquor" (p. 649). Manufacturing also was related at least in part to local needs—cooperage, for example, and milling.

to an urban place in the eighteenth century, an urban place was not essential to business.

It should also be noticed that "merchant" was a broad term in the eighteenth century, and that occupational categories in general are less useful in study of nonindustrial than industrial societies. More to the point is status in the community, as derived from family background, length of residence, role in decision making, and property. Transient and propertyless persons had low community status throughout the English colonies. People whose first gains came from commerce, and who increased the importance of their localities through their commercial activities, had high status—but in many places these very activities were mistrusted. In the Puritan ethic as transplanted to New England was the idea that it was wrong to make profits at the expense of the community. There were visibly successful businessmen among the saints, to be sure (now and then an example was made of them—Robert Keaynes is well known for that reason), and men who already had property were favored in land distribution, but wealth that could not be directly related to land and labor was a little suspect. Some merchants shared the traditional doubts about business activity; perhaps it was to deal with these contradictions in their consciences that they so readily invested in land and sought political and social position. In any case, merchants' ambivalence before the war, and the success of some of them during it, reinspired the old mistrust. A New Hampshire delegate to Congress wrote in 1779: "He who increases in wealth in such times as the present, must be an enemy to his Country, be his pretensions what they may." And Henry Laurens of South Carolina called commerce "that bane of patriotism" and asked ". . . how hard is it for a rich or covetous Man to enter heartily into the Kingdom of Patriotism?"[17]

When currency depreciated and prices rose, protests were directed against merchants as "monopolizers" and demands were made in a number of towns and states for price regulation. The successful merchants, lawyers, and large landholders who had dominated the local governments and colonial assemblies began to worry about a "popular spirit" let loose by the war. Newly settled areas were electing more representatives than before the war, and a larger portion of the legislators were farmers, artisans, and the less well-to-do.[18] The special association—community?—that existed among longtime members of the assemblies threatened to change radically as these new representatives of agricultural localities talked of prices, debts, profiteering, and the like. Merchants responded by emphasizing the invi-

[17]Quoted in East, *Business Enterprise*, pp. 35 and 196.
[18]Jackson Turner Main, "Government by the People: The American Revolution and the Democratization of the Legislatures," *William and Mary Quarterly*, 3rd Ser., 23, No. 3 (July, 1966), 391–407.

olability of private property and the need for sound credit and free trade and a government capable of protecting these goals. A stronger central government, they thought, would stabilize the currency and prevent trade barriers from being erected by individual states—and thus solve financial problems as well as maintain order. This is not to say that merchants everywhere took a single position based on a conscious class interest. Where they were situated made a difference, as studies of merchants in their localities show.[19]

There were difficult times in some commercial centers beginning around 1781. The smaller merchants of secondary ones were most apt to be ruined by the costs of war in ships, cargoes, and British markets, and after the war it took time to build up new trade. Business did improve, however, in Boston, New York, Philadelphia, Baltimore, and a number of lesser towns by the late 1780's. The credit facilities provided by new commercial banks helped, as did the incorporation of business enterprises. Merchants were also urging the incorporation of municipalities during the 1780's, so as to be better able to make improvements in local commercial and transportation facilities, proposals that were sometimes resisted when government was by town meeting. Manufacturing possibilities—textiles and glass, for example—began to be investigated in New England localities, and the paper industry was expanded in Pennsylvania. Manufacturing had been promoted during the war as a means of patriotic self-sufficiency, and now protective tariffs were demanded of the state legislatures in order to keep home production in a favorable position against imports. But there were questions of interstate trade, protection of shipping, and governmental indebtedness that individual states were not able to answer.

A need for a stronger central government than the Articles of Confederation provided for was discussed as early as 1780, before the Articles had even been ratified by all the states, and the idea was given point in 1785 and 1786 in connection with commerce in the Chesapeake Bay area. Several states recommended that "important defects in the System of the Federal Government" be considered in a general convention, and Congress agreed to this in February 1787—after, it might be noted, a revolt by indebted farmers in Massachusetts (Shays' Rebellion) had roused fears in other states and in Congress of popular uprisings that might end in violent seizures of property unless some stronger force than state militias could be used to check them.

The debates over the Articles and the new Constitution did not stop with the Philadelphia Convention of 1787. They continue: What did the

---

[19]A full-length example is Benjamin W. Labaree's *Patriots and Partisans: The Merchants of Newburyport, 1764–1815* (Cambridge, Mass.: Harvard University Press, 1962).

writers intend with this or that phrase or clause? What were they trying to accomplish and why? The debates seem often to be about interests, whether political, personal, local, sectional, national, or universal. When they do, it is a question of who has what in common and who has what in conflict. Nineteenth-century historians led by George Bancroft, themselves interested in nation building, saw a group of nation builders when they looked at the period in which independence was won and the United States Constitution was written and ratified. They saw, indeed, the creation of "national community." In the early twentieth century a few began to examine other characteristics of the founding fathers; notably and controversially, Charles Beard sought evidence of commonality in what kind of property they owned and concluded that the Constitution was the work of a small minority with interests in credit and financing, commerce, and manufacturing. Another view has been that the growth of local American loyalties led to the break with the distant central government of the British Empire, allowing the growth of commercial and financial concerns which in turn required a new central government. In the past twenty years, studies (especially by critics of Beard) have shown that great complexity in attitudes and conditions existed in this period. One way out of this evident complexity has been to assume a compatible "pluralism," with different groups going in the same direction. Another has been to apply the concept of "consensus," by means of which diverse groups agree to seek agreements, or convergence. Such views emphasize continuity in American history, from the first plantation on, and from them it does not take long to reach, again, the idea of national community, or "the genuine community of our values."[20]

There is no question but that community forms and identities, social relations, economic relations, and the derivations of authority differed in the colonies, sometimes between one valley and the next, and that the differences were not always tolerated. The struggle for independence did, however, bring people together in new ways. David Ramsey, a physician and politician who published a history of the revolution in 1789, was interested in just such changes:

> The Americans knew but little of one another, previous to the revolution. Trade and business had brought the inhabitants of their seaports acquainted with each other, but the bulk of the people in the interior country were unacquainted with their fellow citizens. A continental army, and Congress composed of men from all the States, by freely mixing together, were assimilated into one mass. Individuals of both,

---

[20]Daniel Boorstin, *The Genius of American Politics* (Chicago: The University of Chicago Press, 1953), p. 162. David W. Noble has explored the influence of the idea of covenant in such formulations in *Historians Against History: The Frontier Thesis and the National Covenant in American Historical Writing since 1830* (Minneapolis: University of Minnesota Press, 1965).

mingling with the citizens, disseminated principles of union among them. Local prejudices abated. By frequent collision asperities were worn off, and a foundation was laid for the establishment of a nation, out of discordant materials.[21]

The struggle appears also to have changed relationships within some localities. The confiscation of loyalist lands, for example, especially the large estates, was an opportunity for redistribution of property; in some instances tenants and small farmers were able to buy small amounts, thus increasing the number of freeholders,[22] but in others the land went to speculators who were not part of the locality. Increased political activity by settlers at a distance from the centers of government, such as in county conventions, and by "the humble," affected individuals' ideas of themselves as well as of their localities and states. In some instances, of course, it brought them into collision with each other. For the struggle made differences stand out, too—at no time more clearly than when a new structure for unity was proposed: the Constitution.

Those who wrote it and those who participated in state ratification conventions were not debating the nature of community but, primarily, whether or not there should be a stronger central government. In the course of the debates, however, contrasting ideas were presented about what should constitute a political community. Some wanted to see a unitary government established in place of the state governments. For most the issue was how governmental authority should be distributed, assuming it would be on more than one level. That people were attached to the smaller units was an argument repeated many times before the Constitution was ratified. It was vehemently opposed by "nationalists," such as Gouverneur Morris of Philadelphia, who called himself "a representative of America" and said that "State attachments, and State importance have been the bane of this Country. We cannot annihilate; but we can perhaps take out the teeth of the serpents." But if the state governments were not to be annihilated as such, it was still feared that the "interests" of one might be annihilated by the "common interests" of others. James Madison argued that there was not, and was not likely to be, any such common interest, mentioning differences in manners, religion, and economic production; even counties of similar size in a state did not so combine themselves. Yet he finally admitted a way in which "States were divided into different interests . . . principally from the effects of their having or not

[21]Excerpted in *American Issues: The Social Record*, eds. Merle Curti, Willard Thorp, and Carlos Baker, 4th ed. (Philadelphia: J. B. Lippincott Company, 1960), I, 112.

[22]Staughton Lynd has studied the opportunity and the action in the context of longstanding discontent in one locality, in "Who Should Rule at Home? Dutchess County, New York, in the American Revolution," *William and Mary Quarterly*, 3rd Ser., 18, No. 3 (July, 1961), 330–59.

having slaves." Hamilton said that "the only considerable distinction of interests lay between the carrying and noncarrying States," raising the issue of commerce, which was precisely what farmers in some of the states —including the "carrying" states—feared. The problem of the place of the states in the national government was, of course, handled through the "great compromise" of equal representation in the Senate and proportional representation by population in the House of Representatives. But this did not resolve the matter of sovereignty. Several times in the ratification conventions delegates spoke of the danger of taxation by two governments at once. George Mason of Virginia asked, "Will the people of this great community submit to be individually taxed by two different and distinct powers? . . . the one will destroy the other; the general government being paramount to, and in every respect more powerful than the state governments, the latter must give way to the former." Mason was a delegate at Philadelphia but refused to sign the finished document. He thought it should include a bill of rights, a point that was insisted on at several ratification conventions. He also thought it opened the way for commercial regulations to be imposed that would hurt the South, and that the clause allowing slaves to be imported for another twenty years was wrong. Another problem was size of jurisdiction: "Popular governments can only exist in small territories."

The proper size for a political community was a recurring subject in these debates. Mason was all but quoting the French political philosopher Montesquieu on republican government (as did others who worked on the Constitution), but there may well have been other sources for the feeling for smallness. The colonies had been parts of a large empire, and most of the colonists' experience of it had been of just that: parts. Still, the colonies were large in territory. They were much larger than Montesquieu envisaged successful republics to be, and the states they became remained relatively large even when they ceded lands to the general government. Most of their territory at the time of independence, however, was sparsely settled; the population was generally close to the seaboard, and "backcountry" people—in North Carolina and in Massachusetts, for prominent examples—suspected they were too far from their governments to be heard. To create a stronger one even farther away was intolerable from this point of view. Some feared that the federal district would become a bastion of tyranny over the rest of the land and a sanctuary for those who broke state laws. Others feared loss of contact with their representatives:

> The Senate will be a small Body, distant from ye people in a situation not to be observed by them—Men are apt in this condn. to forget their dependence—to lose their sympathy—to contract selfish habets. . . . A Senator will be most of his time from home—will associate with none

but his own class—will become a stranger to the condn. of the people— He should return and be obliged to live with the people. . . [23]

The entire new government might become a collection of strangers. Madison had once said, "Of the affairs of Georgia I know as little as those of Kamskatska," and to Antifederalists the differences between the states seemed so significant that they could not imagine their coming together in a general government without the liberties of all being destroyed.

It has been said that the Constitution makers were men with Continental experience and a Continental vision, while their opponents were parochial or more involved with the affairs of particular states (Continental Congressmen as against state officers during the war, for example). While the Constitution was being debated, however, both Federalists and Antifederalists used the term "community" to refer to its jurisdiction, seldom to a particular state's jurisdiction. They meant, of course, political community in the classic sense. A definition for it can be taken from one of Alexander Hamilton's contributions to *The Federalist* (newspaper articles written for reluctant New Yorkers as propaganda for the Constitution); in No. 15 the phrase "bodies politic, or communities, or States" appears in contrast to "men" as individuals. The usage here and elsewhere in *The Federalist* comes straight from John Locke. "Community" depends on the social compact, that binding civil covenant which for seventeenth-century Puritan leaders had been based on men making contracts with each other as they made a contract with God. "Of the Beginning of Political Societies," Locke wrote:

> 95. Men being, as has been said, by nature all free, equal, and independent, no one can be put out of this estate, and subjected to the political power of another, without his own consent, which is done by agreeing with other men to join and unite into a community for their comfortable, safe, and peaceable living one amongst another, in a secure enjoyment of their properties, and a greater security against any that are not of it. . . . When any number of men have so consented to make one community or government, they are thereby presently incorporated, and make one body politic, wherein the majority have a right to act and conclude the rest.[24]

Madison's concern about a potential "tyranny of the majority" led him to see an advantage in the very size and diversity that troubled Antifederalists when asked to join in the community-building compact. In *The Federalist* No. 10, he contends that "factions" and "distinct interests"

[23]From notes of Melancton Smith for a speech at the New York ratification convention, quoted in Lynd, "Who Should Rule at Home?" (footnote on p. 357).
[24]*Of Civil Government, Second Treatise* (Chicago: Henry Regnery Company, 1955), p. 78.

(based most commonly, he says, on the "unequal distribution of property") would be so numerous and widespread that it would be difficult for them to discover a common strength or act adversely to "the rights of other citizens or to the permanent and aggregate interests of the community."

The federal system that was adopted with the Constitution in 1789 was a community in terms of such principles. A quick survey of the *Annals of Congress* for the first twenty-five years shows members of several political views, some initially Antifederalist, using the term most often to mean the body politic of the United States as a whole. Sometimes the phrase "the whole community" appears, and "the whole American community." In only a few instances is the member's home state the referent, though in some contexts any kind of political unit might be meant. For other kinds of units there are other terms: village, county, society, the people, the public. But there is also the phrase "community of interests." A striking use of it is in Washington's "Farewell Address," when to show "motives" for "preserving the union of the whole" he describes the economic interdependency of the sections—North, South, East, West—as "an indissoluble community of interest as one nation."

Not everyone perceived it that way. During Washington's administration there were strong objections to Hamilton's national economic policies as benefiting "mercantilist interests only." Representatives of agricultural areas began to organize themselves around Jefferson for the expression of agrarian interests, and these "Republicans" and the "Federalists" proceeded to accuse each other of the evils of factionalism. Then as foreign problems intensified domestic discontent with the Federalists, Jeffersonian Republicans put an increasing amount of emphasis on states' rights. By the end of the century the Constitution appeared to be at best a potential community maker, not a community already made.

And at the end of the century its territory was about to be enlarged, and the national government would reach in different ways to different parts of it. New places, new interconnections were being formed. Merchants were expanding inland as well as out from the shores. If they had "no country" to a Jeffersonian farmer, maybe it was because they had several.

6

The Search For Frontiers

"[They] remove as their avidity and restlessness incite them. They acquire no attachment to Place: but wandering about Seems engrafted in their Nature; and it is a weakness incident to it that they Should forever imagine the Lands further off, are Still better than those upon which they are already Settled."

—BRITISH COLONIAL OFFICIAL

British officers at Ft. Pitt in the early 1760's despaired of keeping settlers and Indians apart. Miles from any regularly established settlements, the ex-French fort was an outpost, a holding post; it was not meant for farmers, traders, and drifters to occupy. The Indian uprising led by Pontiac (1763–1764) helped turn them back, but only briefly. Dozens of land companies formed in the pre-Independence period, apparently as easily as men met at an inn, to seek tracts in the transmontane valleys for resale to land-eager people; and land-eager people did not always check whether a company, a person, or a state had prior claim to the land they found. It was not that the seaboard areas were too closely packed for people to be able to move (though some said they were). An interest in land pervaded the settled parts of the country, and jurisdictions were not always clear.

Jurisdiction over the western lands was one of the first problems of the newly independent states and their Continental Congress. Maryland delayed ratification of the Articles of Confederation for nearly four years over the question of who. had a right to what. If the war against England was a common effort, and the lands had been "wrested from the common enemy by the blood and treasure of the thirteen states," then the territories should be "considered as common property, subject to be parceled by Congress into free, convenient, and independent governments." Besides, states with large land claims would have potential advantages in revenues, they would draw people from the small states, and likely enough they would refuse to recognize the "foreign" land companies already at work in the west.

In addition to the jealousies of the states was the problem of bringing new political units into being. The states formally established their own governments in the Independence period by means of old charters and new constitutions, many of them sketchy, with much (including the disposition of lands) left up to the legislatures for which they provided. The Articles of Confederation set up procedures for the settlement of boundary and jurisdictional disputes between states but assumed equal sovereignty of the states within their own boundaries. Land cessions by the states would create a new kind of domain, a "public domain." To encourage the cessions, Congress passed a resolution in 1780 that the lands be settled and formed into distinct states, but south of the Ohio both state and private speculative actions and intrigues complicated the problem. Washington visited his own western claims in 1784 and found some troublesome squatters[1]; on his return he told Congress that there were claimants all over the Ohio valley and recommended the New England system of orderly survey and purchase. A clear policy for land disposal, settlement, and state-formation was, many thought, badly needed.

Jefferson headed a committee that worked out the first land ordinance in 1784. It outlined the setting up of temporary governments by settlers in the territory between the Ohio and Mississippi rivers (Jefferson proposed such names as Assenisippia and Metropotamia, but Congress said no) and methods of admission to Congress as states. The land policy as such dates from 1785. Lands were to be divided into regular rectangular townships (six square miles) and sections (one square mile, or 640 acres) and sold at auction at a minimum price of one dollar an acre.

For layout and some aspects of ecological organization, the significant part of the Ordinance of 1785 is the rectangular survey. Once instituted, it imposed a gridiron on the land: regularly divided farmlands, a mile-road system, spaced farmhouses (see Fig 6–1). Thus the dispersed, open-country neighborhood was carried across the continent. The Ordinance also reinforced the idea of gridiron towns, whatever a landscape might suggest to town planners.

---

[1]James Thomas Flexner, *George Washington and the New Nation (1783–1793)*, (Boston: Little, Brown and Company, 1969), pp. 54–62.

FIG. 6–1   FARM LOCATIONS ON A SECTION OF LAND IN WEBSTER COUNTY, IOWA.

Source: *Land: The Yearbook of Agriculture 1958* (Washington, D.C.: U.S. Government Printing Office, 1958).

As for terms of settlement, the sale of land in large units is significant. This was an opening for speculators, since, as Billington puts it, "no frontiersman needed such a large tract nor could he afford to buy on those terms."[2] In time, the terms for acquiring land were eased so that family farmers could move independently. In the meantime, government surveyors and land companies showed the way west. The New England-based Ohio Company of Associates was early and aggressive in obtaining land from Congress and also played a part in the legislation for territorial government. Its land had been located by a man who had gone with the first government surveying party for that purpose. The first surveys were of the "Seven Ranges," ranges of townships parallel to the western boundary of Pennsylvania; the Ohio Company, funded through the certificates issued to soldiers in lieu of pay, acquired some one and three-quarter million acres to the southwest of them, along the Ohio River, for what amounted to eight or nine cents an acre. The Continental Congress needed the

[2]Ray Allen Billington, *Westward Expansion: A History of the American Frontier*, 3rd ed. (New York: The Macmillan Company, 1967), p. 209. For single-volume coverage of settlement region by region, see this source and Ralph H. Brown, *Historical Geography of the United States* (New York: Harcourt, Brace & World, Inc., 1948).

money, even at that rate. Its agent to Congress—by no means the first lobbyist but an extraordinarily successful one—was Manasseh Cutler, a minister, merchant, doctor, and lawyer (never an Indian chief, so far as is known). He appears to have hoped that the Ohio Company's lands would be a model for settlements in the west. Therefore he urged committee action on a governmental system for the west at the same time that he arranged for the purchase outside the terms of the Ordinance of 1785. A clear plan for political development would, obviously, encourage immigration.

The new governmental system, the American colonial system that was adopted with the Ordinance of 1787, created a single administrative unit within which other units could be formed. The first officials of the "Northwest Territory" would be appointed by Congress. When the population reached 5,000 "free male inhabitants of full age in the district," those with a fifty-acre freehold could elect representatives from their counties or townships to a general assembly.[3] This assembly could then send a delegate to Congress, with the right to debate but not to vote. "Not less than three nor more than five States" were envisaged in the Ordinance of 1787, to be constituted when specified areas had a population of 60,000. Religious and civil rights were promised, provision was made for schools, Indians were to be left alone "unless in just and lawful wars authorized by Congress," and slavery was forbidden. As for local government prior to statehood, magistrates and other civil officers were to be appointed by the assembly once it was formed. The line of authority thus proceeded from Congress to territorial officers to localities; only after a period of settlement could authority be said to flow in the other direction, and even then only on the terms laid down by the federal government.

Settlement of the Ohio Company's lands began with a preplanned town, Marietta, on a site with Indian earth mounds. Streets ninety feet wide were laid out, and areas were reserved for public use. The first settlers had a right to a town lot, an eight-acre field outside the village, pasturage along the Ohio, and a half-pint of whiskey on the first Fourth of July. An early nineteenth-century visitor called the place "New England in miniature." Although the population became more diverse as immigrants arrived from other parts of the United States and Europe, the town remained small and in the 1820's the New England minister Timothy Flint could

---

[3]Property qualifications for the right of suffrage and for office holding were general during this period, as they were thought to be "sufficient evidence of permanent common interest with, and attachment to the community" (from the Virginia Bill of Rights, adopted in 1776). Only Pennsylvania allowed anyone who paid taxes to vote and to be elected. Restrictions were gradually lifted in the older states in the first part of the nineteenth century, and most of the new states were admitted with only small taxpaying qualifications or none at all—that is, with white manhood suffrage.

still write, "In the forms of the houses and the arrangements about them, you discover that this is an establishment from New England."[4] Residents developed a modest industry in river-boat building, but the goal of settlement in the area was, and remained, the land. Even that seemed to improve further westward, and after a series of Indian wars the Treaty of Greenville (1795) opened southern Ohio to hordes of farmers and townsmen, mostly from the southern states. Other areas between the Ohio and Lake Erie attracted settlers at the same time: military bounty lands, lands reserved by the state of Connecticut from its cession and made over to a group of speculators in order to get them settled, and other speculative purchases. Especially in the northern section settlers brought with them their ideas of village and township settlement, but there were also dispersed farmsteads and large estates. By the end of the century, Ohioans were talking of statehood and some of them were pushing against the Greenville treaty line.

At that time the territory between the Appalachians and the Mississippi was still largely unknown to most Americans. The population clusters were still along the Atlantic seaboard, and a good deal of the current migration was within the states. Yet in 1803 the area of the country was more than doubled. Opponents of the Louisiana Purchase noticed that townships were being depopulated as people moved, especially from New England into western New York state. In view of their claims, it is interesting that a French visitor, Jean Pierre Brissot, observed that not one-third of the land of Massachusetts was under cultivation. Many areas did lose population during this period, and though some life went on in most of them, ghost towns began to appear. Fearing the potential power of the west in the national government, some New England Federalists talked of secession to form a sectional confederacy (which would call into question that political community supposedly represented by the Constitution).

The westward movement proceeded without any given area being "filled up" in the sense that land and other opportunities were no longer available in it. The acquisition of new territories by the United States, as urged by men with a variety of motives, set the scene; land promoters, town boosters, innovations in transportation, and discoveries of animal, vegetable, and mineral resources filled the scene. Indian presence and rights were dealt with as the occasion arose or the nerve thresholds of the settlers lowered.

Ventures and wishes together showed the direction expansion would take. New England merchants joined Spanish, British, and Russian fur

---

[4]*Recollections of the Last Ten Years* (Boston: Cummings, Hilliard, and Company, 1826), p. 29.

traders on the Pacific coast in the 1790's, and Congress approved Jefferson's plan for Lewis and Clark to check land routes months before the Louisiana Purchase was made. Before the War of 1812 there was talk of expansion in all directions; one Congressman, for instance, announced: "The Author of Nature has marked our limits in the south, by the Gulf of Mexico; and on the north, by the regions of eternal frost." Traders and trappers scattered through the Rocky Mountains with their special way of life, long periods of isolated camping broken by a more or less explosive "rendezvous" at a temporary mountain market. They moved also deep into the Spanish Southwest in the early nineteenth century, and when Mexico became independent of Spain (1821) their trade was legalized and Santa Fe became the goal of annual treks from Missouri.

Settlers followed explorers and traders outside the bounds of the United States. Moses and Stephen Austin received land grants in Mexico for the purpose of bringing colonists into her northern province; the Mexican government then encouraged more colonization by passage of a law that would allow provincial governments to make such contracts. The result was both group and individual settlement, in the form of family farms and slave-worked cotton plantations along East Texas rivers. By 1830 a campaign for annexation of the Texas part of the Coahuila-Texas province had begun in the United States. Alarmed Mexican officials cast about for ways of limiting American immigration, including outright exclusion. Anglo-Texans, for their part, objected to Mexican religious laws (most of these settlers were Protestant) and a new prohibition on slavery, and began to agitate for separate statehood. Power struggles within the Mexican government added to the confusion about their future, and the great distance between Mexico's administrative center and Texas did not help matters. Yet a visitor to one of the Texas settlements was able to write:

> All are happy, because busy; and none meddle with the affairs of their neighbours, because they have enough to do to take care of their own. They are bound together by a common interest, by sameness of purpose, and hopes. As far as I could learn, they have no envyings, no jealousies, no bickerings, through politics or fanaticism.[5]

With the division of the far northwest between Great Britain and the United States, the annexation of Texas, and the outcome of the war with Mexico, by 1848 the United States had come into possession of the con-

---

[5]Mary A. Holley, *Texas* (1833), excerpted in Ray Allen Billington, *The Westward Movement in the United States* (Princeton, N.J.: D. Van Nostrand Company, Inc., 1959), p. 135.

tinent from the 49th parallel to the Rio Grande and the promise of the blind colonial charters, land "from sea to sea," was fulfilled.

Easterners thought it was a "manifest destiny" to cover the continent, some were curious about the western lands and peoples, and few knew anything about them. There was news of rich land from migrants who had followed the Oregon and California trails in the early 1840's; otherwise, there were reports of deserts, wild Indians, bandits, and barrenness on the one hand, and on the other the wonderment of Francis Parkman: "One season on the prairies will teach a man more than half a dozen in the settlements." The population was widely scattered and diverse: hundreds of different Native American communities, Spanish mission communities, Spanish and Mexican estates, Spanish, Mexican, European, and Anglo-American trading places and camps, and American military camps. Land jobbers and town jobbers would soon be on the road, or at home in an eastern town drawing maps and writing advertisements, and discoveries of precious metals were about to be made, the rushes to them creating their own kinds of camps and towns.

Much of nineteenth-century settlement west of about the 95th meridian began either along main-traveled routes or at convenient locations for purposes of supplying people who were deliberately searching for quickly profitable new resources, such as gold. These were—as will be discussed below—stable places for people in transit. Some of them never got much beyond the print shop (see Fig. 6–1). Some of them grew into towns when another function developed at or around them, such as administration (e.g., county) or surplus-producing agriculture. Others remained as crossroads, a few became photogenically ghostly groups of shacks, and many were literally plowed under. From the perspective of the present, the main community forms that survived in the new areas were of the same sort that survived in the old: agricultural village, open-country neighborhood, and plantation; market town or commercial center; administrative center; the districts and neighborhoods of these centers; and of course translocal political units such as territory and state. The predominant form was the open-country neighborhood, with an accessible crossroads town or market town. Since means of transportation and communication improved at the same time that these places were being planted and transplanted, areas within which localities could be in contact grew larger and networks of interdependence became more extensive throughout the period of territorial expansion.

Before going on to these connections, it should be noted that, in the most general ways, expansion of settlement was similar in Canada, although obviously the means of acquiring territory do not compare. The most important governmental change in Canada occurred in 1867, when

Fig. 6–2   Advertisement for a town in the late 1850's. With such a firm foundation in hope, how could the place fail?

Source: *Land: The Yearbook of Agriculture 1958* (Washington, D.C.: U.S. Government Printing Office, 1958).

the British North America Act established the Dominion of Canada, a confederation of the provinces of Quebec, Ontario, Nova Scotia, and New Brunswick which, it was hoped, would eventually include the other British colonies and lands to the Pacific. Areas not previously organized as colonies were to be governed as territories, with an appointed lieutenant governor and council. They were to be opened to settlement from the east and from Europe, and one way to open them was with rails. Advocates of Confederation had long foreseen both economic and political advantages in railways, and the Act of 1867 specified one to connect the St. Lawrence with Halifax, Nova Scotia in order to bring the interior and coastal regions together. A railway across the continent was the next move. The first Prime Minister, Sir John Macdonald, made the railway an essential part of his national program. He expected it to stimulate trade and migration and thereby unite all Canada with a common interest.

While track was being laid, westward migration increased, but the government at Ottawa had not taken into account a possible conflict between its land policies and the landholding traditions of people already living in the west. It instituted the rectangular survey system, modeled after that in the United States, its "primary consideration, the rapid and accurate division of the prairie region into farm holdings"[6] (Fig. 6–3 illustrates narrow-lot and rectangular systems next to each other). The *Métis*, descendants of French traders and Indians of the area, had a sense of rights to the land based on Indian traditions and had occupied narrow river-lot farms in the French Canadian tradition. Many did not have recorded title to their land. When surveyors appeared in the area of the Red and Assiniboine rivers in 1869, running their lines across *Méti* lands, these settlers attempted a rebellion. Louis Riel proclaimed himself head of a provisional government and negotiated to bypass territorial status and bring Manitoba into the Confederation as a province, with assurance of preservation of local customs. But the troops sent in support of the new provincial government included volunteers who were hostile to the French. Some of the *Métis* moved on to the upper Saskatchewan, and when Anglo-Canadian settlement again approached, a second uprising occurred (1885), this time with the assistance of local Indian groups. Differing ideas about land division and settlement were only part of the problem, but they imply

[6]"Report of the Department of the Interior, 1892," quoted in J. Friesen, "Expansion of Settlement in Manitoba, 1870–1900," *Papers*, Historical and Scientific Society of Manitoba, Ser. III, No. 20 (1963–1964), 36. There follows the same complaint as has been voiced by some rural sociologists in the United States: "The survey proceeded well ahead of settlement as it rapidly superimposed a rigid stereotyped pattern without any regard to the physical characteristics of the land. No attempt was made to conform to topography, soils, drainage, and vegetation, and this system has been criticized by rural sociologists for the isolated life which it induced."

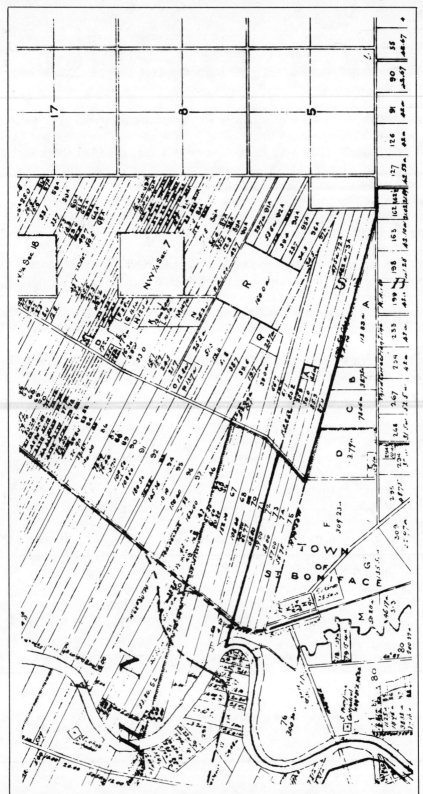

FIG. 6–3 PART OF PARISH LOT SURVEY IN MANITOBA, SHOWING BOTH RIVER LOTS AND RECTANGULAR TOWNSHIP AND SECTION DIVISIONS.

Source: From a survey map published by C. S. Lott, Winnipeg, 1894.

the more general conflict in the application of distant government policies (and force) to independently built communities. Also, the rebellions came to symbolize French and English differences, to be causes around which the differences could be argued.

Indians were placed on reservations, *Métis* were promised certain lands and then scrip for land, railroad companies were given large grants of land, and others could apply for free homesteads of one hundred and sixty acres. Individuals who followed the transportation lines west settled in dispersed, open-country neighborhoods or market towns. Some group settlement took place as well—colonies of Icelanders, for example, and Mennonites from German colonies in ·South Russia, who first established compact agricultural villages (at Steinbach and Gretna in Manitoba) and then, with the success of their farming, spread into surrounding lands. Mixed farming and large-scale wheat growing, and cattle raising to the west (as in the United States), provided the economic base.

By the 1860's, trade and communication between the Red River and St. Paul were such that eastern Canadians feared (with reason) United States designs on their western lands. To strengthen the Canadian hold was one reason for Confederation. Settlers from both sides of the border and from coast to coast continued to cross back and forth, however, some for permanent residence and some for more or less temporary work. The ease and frequency of migration has troubled authorities from time to time, but since about 1870 it has not put the border in question nor has it produced more than superficial similarities. Parts of western Canada and the western United States have ecological factors and settlement patterns in common; they also have in common residents' beliefs in the distinctiveness of their own communities and of their community ties within a region and to a national government and economy. A Canadian geographer has described the situation in the ninteenth century this way:

> ... The same general pattern of development and level of technology prevailed on both sides of the 49th parallel not as the result of the direct movement of ideas across the border, as is sometimes believed, but by the movement of these ideas through a few key channels, many of which were in the Eastern United States and Canada, and then from higher to lower levels within each country, via the existing structure of government agencies and newspapers.[7]

In both Canada and the United States, some developments in transportation were locally inspired, encouraged in order to increase the importance of a particular place. After the 1820's more became nonlocal in that their objective was to provide connections between places. In the colonial

---

[7]John H. Warkentin, "Western Canada in 1886," *Papers*, Historical and Scientific Society of Manitoba, Ser. III, No. 20 (1963–1964), 115.

period, the few and limited links between places had not formed a network in the sense of connections between a number of like and unlike places. Within small regions, localities not otherwise connected to each other depended on some major or minor commercial center. This pattern can be described with the term "hinterland" from the point of view of the dominant place. When the technology for establishing true networks became available in the nineteenth century, commercial centers competed strenuously to maintain the pattern and to extend their hinterlands. They sought and sponsored road building, then canal building, then the early railroad building. In time the net effect would be networks, but first it was a matter of local advantage.

The Lancaster Turnpike built in 1794 between Philadelphia and Lancaster, Pennsylvania, was a privately built toll road which stimulated other such enterprises. By 1825 private companies had completed more than ten thousand miles of roadway in New England and the middle Atlantic states, mostly in short segments and with high toll rates that left farmers dependent on their old rough and muddy tracks. More ambitious was the federally funded National Highway, chartered in 1806 and destined to become a major highway of the westward movement. Between 1811 and 1818 it was extended from the upper Potomac River, at Cumberland, Maryland, to the Ohio River, at Wheeling, West Virginia; it reached Vandalia, Illinois, in mid-century.

But whether privately or publicly inspired, overland transportation before the railroad age was inadequate to tie the country together. Water transportation began to seem more promising, though there were problems with it, too: floods, droughts, winter freezing in the north, and high freight rates. The first commercial centers of the interior had their start from the advantages of water travel. On the Great Lakes, the Ohio River, and the Mississippi River, towns developed that sought hinterlands for themselves and new road as well as river connections to other centers. When the steamboat was introduced (1807 on the Hudson River and 1811 on the Ohio and the Mississippi), they became more important, for within a few years traffic of all kinds was quicker and cheaper. Also, litigation rising out of competition among steamboat companies helped prepare the way for an open national market. In Gibbons *vs.* Ogden (1824), the Supreme Court denied the constitutionality of a monopoly where interstate commerce was involved. With the steamboat, New Orleans became the most important commercial center for the West and South, a main trans-shipment point and also a center of social activity and entertainment, all the more interesting because of its cultural diversity (partly from its French and Spanish backgrounds). Other western commercial-route towns—St. Louis, Cincinnati, Pittsburgh, Buffalo, Albany—were provincial by comparison. But canal building gave impetus to their growth. If turnpikes were not adequate and if river traffic tended, in the Mississippi system, toward New Orleans, then canals, for all the difficulty and expense of their construction, could connect the lakes, rivers, roads, and towns to each other and thus draw western trade eastward—or so local boosters said. The boom in canal building began after the Erie Canal was completed (1825), though the idea was current some fifteen years earlier. The success of that project was almost immediate. Freight rates between Buffalo and Albany were reduced from $100 to $15 a ton, and travel time from twenty to eight days.

Many of the canal projects were never completed and remain only as testimonies to ambition. In the late 1820's a transportation innovation was made that was to outdo, outdistance, and outlast all plans for canals. The railroad was at first a sort of toy for imaginative entrepreneurs who were looking for new investments. But in 1828 the Baltimore and Ohio Railroad was begun, a diversion from Baltimore's canal plans; by 1840 there were almost as many miles of railroad as of canals, though canal transport was still cheaper; and by 1850 the main towns east of the Mississippi, both North and South but especially north of Baltimore, were connected by railroads and growing by means of their connections. In a speech in Nashville in 1851, J. D. B. DeBow (editor of *DeBow's Review*, a journal promoting southern economic nationalism) said that northern enterprise had "rolled back the mighty tide of the Mississippi and its ten thousand tributary streams until their mouth, practically and commercially, is more at New York and Boston than at New Orleans."[8] Until after the Civil War railroads were concentrated in the Northeast and Old Northwest, with lines scattered through the mid-Atlantic states and the South; then they extended into and along the Far West. They stimulated dispersed agricultural settlement on the Plains and away from the market towns on waterways; their depots turned into market towns, some into commercial centers; and they also made it possible to exploit more of the resources of long-settled regions, such as coal in West Virginia. Older commercial centers, both ocean ports and inland places, vied for their favors. That rail connections could make or break a town was more obvious than it ever had been with roads, rivers, lakes, or canals.

But railroad companies quickly became nonlocal, and there were objections. "The prospect that outsiders might control the enterprise could hinder seriously [the promoter's] efforts to raise funds locally. One Ohio railroad organizer, for example, argued with his fellow promoters in 1851 that it was inadvisable to employ an engineer from the East to locate the line. Local people would, he said, suspect 'that this Eastern man would

---

[8]Quoted in Harry J. Carman and Samuel McKee, Jr., *A History of the United States*, 2 vols. (Boston: D. C. Heath and Company, 1931), I, 611.

come here with Eastern habits, feelings, associations and *interests*, the effect of which must be, to give everything an Eastern aspect.' "[9] Local and regional self-consciousness appears frequently in this period of incipient interdependency. Given the diverse origins of nineteenth-century settlers west of the Appalachians—French villagers next to German farmers, Irish and Russian farmers across the stream from each other and hoping to remain quite separate—and the frequency with which many of them migrated, it is surprising that they should have developed loyalties within any extensive region of the country. Yet the men they elected to office identified common interests and acted to strengthen regional ties, especially in votes on the issues, such as internal improvements, that came before Congress. Reinforcing regional or "sectional" identifications were the perceptions of outsiders—westerners believing that there was such a thing as "Eastern habits," for example, and vice versa. The tendency to make such references in the political sphere (and to act on them) can be traced back to the Constitutional Convention, when concerns were expressed about the potential strength of the western territories. In 1820 it was apparently easier to consider a "compromise" admission of a western state on southern terms (Missouri), along with a northeastern state on northern terms (Maine), than to face the issue of slavery on its own terms. For that matter, regional identity came to be expressed with special intensity in the South and became, eventually, indistinguishable from nationalism. In 1850, at a convention in Nashville called to consider "southern rights" while the status of the territories obtained from Mexico was being debated in Congress, a delegation from South Carolina called for secession from the Union, and Langdon Cheeves promised glory: "Unite and you shall form one of the most splendid empires on which the sun ever shone." The connections, the ties of interdependency among regions, were not yet clear. It was easier to react to a threat to one's feeling for a locality, and it was more comfortable to consider local advantages, than to try to participate in the nonlocal forces for change. People were on the move, but they appear to have expected the landscape to stay still, and to have been puzzled by the changes that their movement itself produced.

One little-understood aspect of change was that migration routes and settled places support each other. The Ohio River, for instance, was a natural highway, and from it come early examples of a particular type of community. Points of access to it became points of supply for migrants, and, thus, stable places whose existence depended on an ability to provide services for people in transit. Commercial centers generally have had at least districts for transients, but the westward movement produced towns

[9]Harry N. Scheiber, "Urban Rivalry and Internal Improvements in the Old Northwest, 1820–1860," *Ohio History*, 71, No. 3 (October, 1962), 227–39.

whose sole function, for a time, was to help people move further. We might call such places *transit centers*. Some survived by developing other commercial functions, and some simply disappeared when the jumping-off places themselves moved west or the routes to the west changed.

Pittsburgh was, at first, a transit center. At the Forks of the Ohio (Monongahela and Allegheny rivers), it was one of the three main portals to the west in the late eighteenth and early nineteenth centuries. People and merchandise were carted to it from Philadelphia and other points in the east, and there transferred to river boats. Layover facilities were needed and, along with them, commercial and manufacturing enterprises for purposes of supply. In 1787 the local newspaper (established in 1786) printed the comment: "They take this for a resting place or halfway house and think it vain to waste their labor making improvements . . . because, next year they shall go down the river."[10] The first census (1790) listed only 376 inhabitants for Pittsburgh. Twelve years later a French visitor wrote that there were four hundred houses, "principally of brick," clustered along the Monongahela and that the town had become the "market place" for near as well as distant settlements. Most of the merchants, he said, were associated with Philadelphia firms. Boat building and related manufactures were becoming important to residents—as was true in many river places, some quite close to Pittsburgh.[11] A few years later the town appeared to visitors to be going into a decline, at least relative to what was happening in newer towns further down the river. Transit towns generally were subject to oscillations of fortune in their early years, as now one area and now another attracted farmers and before networks of commerce and manufacturing were established. But there was no science of urban economics to guide the observers, nor, for all their visions of local and regional growth, could they have perceived the westward movement as a whole. Timothy Flint's account of what was happening at Pittsburgh in the second decade of the nineteenth century illustrates how change in a growth rate could be viewed at that time:

> . . . the wealth, business, and glory of this place are fast passing away, transferred to Cincinnati, to Louisville, and other places on the Ohio. Various causes have concurred to this result; but especially the multiplication of steamboats, and the consequent facility of communication with the Atlantic ports by the Mississippi. There is little prospect of the reverse of this order of things. The national road, terminating at Wheeling, contributes to this decay of Pittsburgh. Her decline is not much

[10]Quoted in Richard C. Wade, *The Urban Frontier* (Chicago: The University of Chicago Press, 1964), p. 11.

[11]François André Michaux, *Voyage à l'ouest des monts alléghanys . . .* (1804), excerpted in Oscar Handlin, *This Was America* (New York: Harper & Row, Publishers, 1964), pp. 109–12.

regretted, for she used to fatten on the spoils of the poor emigrants that swarmed to this place. Accustomed to scenes of parsimony, misery, and beggary, and to transient and unprincipled men, occupied in the hardening pursuits of manufactures, she had been brought to think all men rogues, misery the natural order of things, and of course little entitled to commiseration, and every way of getting money fair game. The traveller was too apt to think of her as immersed in "sin and sea-coal;" for the constant use of fossil coal, both for culinary and manufacturing purposes, has given a sooty and funereal aspect even to the buildings; of course much hospitality could not be expected here.

He adds that hotel charges were twice what they were in Boston, and hopes that the decay of business in Pittsburgh will be accompanied by improvement in "moral and humane institutions."[12]

Transients and the places established for them were disturbing to many. As the proportion of long-term residents increased in the successful river towns, they seem increasingly to have complained of those who came and went. As such towns grew, transients became a people apart, physically apart in blocks devoted to transport and stopover facilities. As the pioneering edge of settlement moved on, these sections were maintained for the workingmen of transportation and migration, the men who drove the wagons and worked the flatboats, keelboats and packet boats, ferryboats, pirogues, scows, and later the steamboats. Respectable residents were sure that the boatmen came on shore for the purpose of destroying the place, or short of that to destroy themselves in boozing, wenching, fighting, gambling, and rioting. It was, of course, profitable to supply their needs for food, shelter, and entertainment, but sooner or later townspeople would speak of the waterfront districts for transients mostly in terms of their vices. Somehow, none of the towns boosted as commercial metropolises escaped the vices. Yet, of course, a closer look at any one of these towns would show a complex history and equally complex attitudes toward change. For an example, consider the growth of St. Louis:

In 1764, after France's defeat by the English but before the cession of Louisiana to Spain was known, a new French post was built at the western edge of the Illinois country under the supervision of a fourteen-year-old boy. Auguste Chouteau had gone along on the first expedition of Pierre LaClède of Maxent, LaClède and Company, which had just obtained a monopoly charter from the French governor at New Orleans for trade on the Missouri and the upper Mississippi rivers.[13] At this time there were three small villages and a garrison on the banks of the Mississippi; the new post drew some of their population when the east bank was turned

---

[12]*Recollections*, pp. 17–18.

[13]Chouteau's account is in *The Early Histories of St. Louis*, ed. John Francis McDermott (St. Louis: St. Louis Historical Documents Foundation, 1952), pp. 45–59, 89–97.

over to the British. In 1766, a lieutenant at the fort noted that St. Louis had a large company house and "about forty private houses and as many families," with a garrison of several officers and twenty men.[14] The plan drawn by Chouteau in 1780 shows an elongated gridiron, three streets parallel to the river and twenty perpendicular to it. The regular lines along the river are like those laid out by the French at Montreal, Mobile, and New Orleans. There were common fields near the village, and it was intended to leave a space between the river and the private lots, but such places were sold when the town began to grow (after acquisition by the United States).[15]

For nearly forty years St. Louis was a military post and the residence of the lieutenant governor of the Illinois district of New Spain, but it did not lose its French character. Except for the Spanish officials and a few fur traders who used it as a base, people from other parts of New Spain did not settle at St. Louis. Rather, settlers and traders came to it from Illinois, Canada, and lower Louisiana. When the United States took possession, St. Louis was essentially a trading center, as LaClède had planned.

Congress established the Louisiana Territory in 1805 and made St. Louis its capital. In September 1806 Lewis and Clark arrived back in St. Louis from their expedition to the west, with tales that were immediately to draw traders to the town to get ready to do some exploring of their own. It continued to be the capital when the Missouri Territory was created in 1812 but was denied that status when the State of Missouri was admitted in 1821. It thus lost an administrative function, but by then its commercial and transit facilities had grown. It also acquired an institutional function in 1826 when a new Roman Catholic diocese was established with St. Louis as the cathedral city. One almost immediate result was the opening of a hospital and new schools. But it was still a small town; its most rapid growth occurred after 1840.

In 1799 the settled population was 925, including 268 slaves; in 1810 it was still only about 1,000. When John A. Paxton made a study of the town in 1821 for *The St. Louis Directory and Register*, he found 155

---

[14]Philip Pittman, *The Present State of the European Settlements on the Mississippi*, ed. Frank H. Hodder (Cleveland: Arthur H. Clark Co., 1906), p. 94.

[15]These sales did not please Chouteau, who, late in his life (1825), was a witness before the recorder of land titles. On the town square: "This deponent does hereby declare that this square belongs to the Inhabitants of the Town of S' Louis for their Use as a Public Place, and if any persons should contend that it does not . . . . He having been the first in possession of the same, will contend for His right to the same, He only relinquishing it for the benefit of the Mayor, Alderman and Citizens of the Town of Saint Louis as a Place Public" (*Early Histories*, pp. 96–97).

For an interesting account of French building practices at St. Louis and possible relations to Normandy, French Canada, the lower Mississippi, and the West Indies, see Charles E. Peterson, "The Houses of French St. Louis," in *The French in the Mississippi Valley*, ed. John Francis McDermott (Urbana: University of Illinois Press, 1965), pp. 17–40.

French families in a population that he estimated at "about 5,500."[16] By this time an upper part, "The Hill," had been added to the town, and Paxton could count a total of 651 dwelling houses, 46 "Mercantile establishments," and a few manufactures. St. Louis had become an outfitting place for traders, army officers on their way to more distant points, and surveyors. It was also the location of a government land office, the "emporium" for trade along the Mississippi, Missouri, and Illinois rivers, and the main shipping port for lead from the Missouri and Wisconsin mines.

A few years later, writers who told the story of the early days were endowing them with the simplicity and intimacy often associated with small communities, far different from usual descriptions of a garrison and traders' base. A local resident, for example, wrote in 1831 of the earliest years:

> The soldiers had, by degrees, become amalgamated with the inhabitants; comfortable dwellings were erected; and small fields in the neighborhood, now called *common fields*, had been opened and improved. The government was in a manner patriarchal; the whole community seemed to compose one family, under the guidance of a common father, and enjoying a common patrimony.[17]

And a French visitor in the 1830's learned of an "isolated and simplified" life before 1805, all purposes "embraced within the domestic circle,"

> ... and it is asserted that, during upwards of thirty years, there was not a solitary instance of civil delinquency, or of crime. Bargains were sealed by a grasp of the hand, and the currency of the country consisted of deer-skins.[18]

About the same time, Washington Irving, working from the papers of John Jacob Astor and his company (which had competed with the St. Louis-

---

[16]In *Early Histories*, p. 71. This seems high. Wade uses Paxton's figure of 3,500 for 1818 and then says, "Though the pace slackened during the depression, the figure passed 5,000 in 1828." But he adds in a footnote, "Population figures for St. Louis, no matter how official, are unsatisfactory because a large number of its residents spent most of their time in the mountains or mines" (*Urban Frontier*, p. 201).

[17]William Primm, "History of St. Louis," in *Early Histories*, p. 116. Compare the tone of this with the following statement about Pittsburgh (written in 1826): "We cannot help looking back, with sorrowful heart, on that time of unaffected content and gaiety, when the unambitious people ... in the village of 'Fort Pitt' in the yet unchartered town of Pittsburgh were ignorant and careless of all the invidious distinctions, which distract and divide the inhabitants of overgrown cities" (quoted in Wade, *Urban Frontier*, p. 203).

[18]Joseph N. Nicollet, "Sketch of the Early History of St. Louis," in *Early Histories*, p. 158.

based Missouri Fur Company), attempted a description of the town for 1811:

> St. Louis ... possessed a motley population. ... Here were to be seen about the river banks, the hectoring, extravagant, bragging boatmen of the Mississippi, with the gay, grimacing, singing, good-humored Canadian voyageurs. ... Here and there were new brick houses and shops, just set up by bustling, driving, and eager men of traffic, from the Atlantic states; while, on the other hand, the old French mansions, with open casements, still retained the easy, indolent air of the original colonists...[19]

In looking at any community record, it is necessary to consider the describer as well as the description, and sometimes also the audience. Paxton, for example, aimed his *Directory* toward the residents of St. Louis, and it is interesting that he offered them an explanation for what may have been serious problems from their point of view. When he mentioned the 155 French families of 1821, he was in the midst of saying that the population was mixed. Most were "Americans, from every part of the Union," and there were also "foreigners of various nations." He went on:

> Consequently the Society is much diversified, and has no *general* fixed character.—This, the reader will perceive, arises from the situation of the country in itself new, flourishing, & changing: still that class who compose the respectable part of the community, are hospitable, polite, and well informed. And here, I must take occasion, in justice to the town and country, to protest against the many calumnies circulated abroad to the prejudice of St. Louis, respecting the manners, and dispositions of the inhabitants. Persons meet here with dissimilar habits, of a different education, and possessing various localities. It is not therefore surprising, that, in a place, composed of such discordant materials, there should be occasional differences and difficulties.—But the reader may be assured that old-established inhabitants have little participation in transactions which have so far so much injured the town.[20]

Thus, residents, calm yourselves, there are likely to be difficulties in a diverse population. The implication is that dissimilarity and change make problems. This theme builds into a fair crescendo in the United States by the end of the nineteenth century. Meanwhile more cultures and life styles were being represented in more and more places, and the places grew and changed apace.

There were, however, tangible evidences of well-being accompanying growth, and tangible, physical difficulties that could be overcome. Num-

---

[19] *Astoria, or Anecdotes of an Enterprise Beyond the Rocky Mountain*, 2 vols. (Philadelphia: J. B. Lippincott Company, 1961; first published 1836), I, 106–107.
[20] In *Early Histories*, pp. 71–72.

bers and kinds of businesses and buildings, transportation and trading connections, newspapers, lyceums, libraries, schools, churches—these provided the first and called attention to the second. Paxton was optimistic, for example, about the problem of muddy streets. He noted that the Trustees of the town had passed an ordinance for paving the sidewalks of Main Street, "a very wholesome regulation," and that they ought now to pave the middle of the street and other streets. Two years later, however, a not-so-optimistic writer in the *Missouri Republican* was caustically telling the Mayor and Aldermen: "*By all means prevent the paving of Main Street. That street is the only navigable water-course through the city for craft of the larger size.*"[21] The underlying difficulty was lack of agreement on the financing of such improvements, that is, on whether the city or the property owners should pay for them.

However one interprets different views of a town and its problems, St. Louis was changing. Begun as a trading post, it became a secondary administrative center for Spain and then the United States but continued to serve primarily as a transit place. Then, from the 1840's on, as the "gateway to the west" it attracted not only people in transit but also increasing numbers of European immigrants—tradesmen, craftsmen, and laborers—and farm and small-town people from the eastern states, some of whom saw the opportunities of a growing urban place and some of whom had originally intended to move further but stayed. By 1850, when railroad connections were beginning to be built, the population was more than 77,000. By 1870 it was the third largest city in the United States, with a population of 310,864. During these years manufactures increased (farm equipment, for example) and the construction industry expanded, though it could not come close to providing adequate housing for all the newcomers. It also competed with Chicago to be the railroad center for the west, but by the end of the century Kansas City was drawing some of the trade away from both.

Generally speaking, commercial centers moved west throughout the nineteenth century, and unless local resources could be developed the potential for growth of small commercial centers along the eastern routes was limited. In some instances, the security that might have resulted from their having another, noneconomic reason for being was precluded by mistrust of them. For example, sites for the capital cities of new states were deliberately chosen away from commercial centers (in the case of Kentucky, away even from the established cultural and educational center of Lexington). Increasingly productive agriculture around them, with the technological advances of the 1840's and 1850's, helped; nearby coal and iron deposits were still more important for long-range growth. In the

[21]Quoted in Wade, *Urban Frontier*, p. 283.

second half of the nineteenth century, industrial successes in New England led city leaders in the Ohio and Mississippi valleys and on the Great Lakes to believe that their best chance of countering potential decline was to encourage manufacturing. In the Cleveland *Leader* in 1856 it was said that "no thinking man with capital will stop here when we have only commerce to sustain us. A manufacturing town gives a man full scope for his ambitions." According to Bayrd Still, the idea was being echoed in Milwaukee in the late 1860's, by which time Cleveland had become a manufacturing center, and within a few years one-third to one-half the local labor force was engaged in manufacturing.[22]

As early as 1859 an advocate of urbanism wrote that there was a "steady and rapidly increasing tendency of the people of the plain to seek a home in cities and villages, notwithstanding the great temptation which fertile, cheap and easily improved lands hold out to become tillers of the soil and growers of cattle."[23] Other observers of the 1850's and 1860's were distressed by the prospect, but it was evident that cities were growing not only because of European immigration to them but also because of migration from rural areas. The city was becoming, in the imagery of later historians and sociologists, the "frontier."

The frontier has been, more than anything else, an image. The U.S. Census report for 1890 defined it as "the limit of settlement—the frontier line of population," and depicted it on colored maps by population density, the line being that between less than two and more than two persons per square mile. This is the Census report that inspired Frederick Jackson Turner and historians who followed him to study the influence of the frontier, or of available land and resources, on American institutions:

> Up to and including 1880 the country had a frontier of settlement, but at present the unsettled area has been so broken into by isolated bodies of settlement that there can hardly be said to be a frontier line. In the discussion of its extent and its westward movement it can not, therefore, any longer have a place in the census reports.[24]

In studies of the westward movement the frontier was taken to mean much more than a demographic line. Turner changed it into a line that distinguished European traditions from the American way of life, a line just beyond which energetic and resourceful people wrested a living from

---

[22]"Patterns of Mid-Nineteenth Century Urbanization in the Middle West," *Mississippi Valley Historical Review*, 28, No. 2 (September, 1941), 187–206.

[23]Jesup W. Scott, "Westward the Star of Empire," excerpted in Charles N. Glaab, *The American City: A Documentary History* (Homewood, Ill.: The Dorsey Press, Inc., 1963), p. 166.

[24]*Report on Population of the United States at the Eleventh Census: 1890*, Part I, Department of the Interior, Census Office (Washington, D.C.: Government Printing Office, 1895), p. xxxiv.

untried land and built, again and again as the frontier moved on, individualistically democratic institutions along with their homes, barns, and meetinghouses. His students, including some who studied Canada, have redefined it many times, until the concept has become as controversial as any in American historiography—the adage "everyman his own historian" might be turned into "every historian his own frontiersman."

There is an underlying problem of identifying the American institutions whose origins are being sought. Then too, the evident variety of resources, customs, and activities in newly settled areas must be considered. To comprehend this variety, Harry N. Scheiber finds the frontier in "the site, bordering unsettled areas, in which new communities are founded," and the pioneer to be the "builder of new communities."[25] So far, however, not enough thorough studies have been done of particular localities to bear out generalizations about a "frontier experience." The investigation conducted by Merle Curti in Trempealeau County, Wisconsin, is an excellent example of what needs to be done, but such work should be done in many regions and among communities that took different forms.[26] More detailed studies should also be made of geographic mobility, both of people who acquired land and of people who did not. In this regard, it would be interesting to compare specific townships, sections, and neighborhoods in Canada and the United States. For all the general evidence of mobility in both countries (such as in census reports), many accounts leave the impression that Canadians have more of an "attachment to Place," as the British officer put it in the 1760's, than do Americans.

The implication in many works on the "West" (beginning at the Atlantic seaboard) has been that society was formed on a *tabula rasa*, an open landscape, a countryside that was first to be turned into farms. Some revision occurred after 1959, when Wade's *The Urban Frontier* was published. He began the book, "The towns were the spearheads of the frontier. Planted far in advance of the line of settlement, they held the West for the approaching population." Other town studies are now being made in a context of general processes in American history rather than only as local histories. Social scientists have fostered this kind of interest by their urban studies. If it is a question of how American institutions were formed, some have said, then cities have been the frontier, with their diverse cultures in close contact, with residents working out ways of solving practical problems (as in providing municipal services) and making agreements to

---

[25]*The Old Northwest: Studies in Regional History, 1787–1910*, ed. Harry N. Scheiber (Lincoln, Nebr.: University of Nebraska Press, 1969), pp. xviii, xix.

[26]*The Making of an American Community: A Case Study of Democracy in a Frontier County* (Stanford, Calif.: Stanford University Press, 1959). See also Stephen Thernstrom, *Poverty and Progress: Social Mobility in a Nineteenth Century City* (Cambridge, Mass.: Harvard University Press, 1964) on the working class.

resolve conflicts, and with their expanding opportunities for economic, political, and social improvement. "The City as Frontier of Social Control" reads a subheading in an outline-textbook of sociology; and Charles Abrams entitled his contemporary urban analysis, *The City Is the Frontier.*

The image of the frontier is still strong, and keeps reappearing as one way of trying to understand change. Another way is to imagine a past more simple than the present, with amply spaced small communities of people who got along well together. Somehow, people in that past also thought the good community was in the past. It keeps receding, just as frontiers move on as soon as they are approached.

7

Nineteenth-Century Planning For Heavenly And Unheavenly Places

*"For here have we no continuing city,
But we seek one to come."*

—HEBREWS 13:14

Urbanization began in some localities in North America long before boundaries and frontiers were sought, as did the building of communities to try to realize an ideal. Native Americans had a few expanding cities, and some communities' forms indicate careful preplanning. European settlers from the sixteenth century on built places with hopes of growth and development of several functions and of ties of interdependency—thus, "urban" places as defined in this study. They also tried to "build in Brick and Stone" the ideals they thought were being neglected or distorted in both Old World and New World urban centers—thus, utopian places.

This does not mean that urbanism and utopianism are necessarily related to each other. It is possible to find direct responses of utopianists to urban problems in the mid-nineteenth century, at the turn of the century, and at present, but ideals like theirs are often expressed in other ways. Furthermore, those who perceive and are concerned about urban problems do not always (or even very often) go off and build new communities. If one counts ideal, preplanned, intentional, or utopian communities over time, slow waves of them appear which do not correspond neatly with periods either of rapid urban growth or of awareness of urban problems. Responses to commercial cities were different from responses to industrial cities. And some utopian ventures were attempts to rationalize community life around manufacturing—Lowell, Massachusetts, was one, and Robert Owen's New Harmony, Indiana, another. Others, of course, were intended to be self-contained and self-sufficient refuges for people who had in common their rejection of the society around them. Yet the economic developments that gave rise to industrial cities in the nineteenth century also reinforced utopian efforts. In some ways they made them possible. That is, a place can survive only if certain economic demands are met, either through self-sufficiency or through some relationship with the "outside," and at certain periods the conditions of the society at large have made ideal communities economically possible. Another reinforcement came from the convenience with which industrial centers could be attacked when utopianists reasoned through their urges to reject established society.

The colonial industry that had the most effect on town growth was shipbuilding and enterprises related to it: sail making, ropewalks, anchor forges, cooperage, cabinetmaking, and foundries for making nails and other hardware. The work of such establishments, outside the home, helped give Boston, Newport, Philadelphia, and to a lesser extent New York and Charleston their urban appearance. Food processing, distilling, candle making, ironworks, and paper mills were additional specializations in some areas (Philadelphia, for example). But as long as most of the business of making and selling was domestic—whether a sideline or a main part of life in a household—industrial change was slow. Shoemaking became a highly skilled craft for some New Englanders but could not account for community growth. The various facets of woolen cloth making, from sheep raising to sewing, also developed in New England, but each facet was domestic and many steps were required, each removed in time and locality from the previous one.

People who were involved in cottage industries often worked part time at such a job and divided the rest of their time and energies among other activities. A farmer or a shopkeeper could be a part-time craftsman and thereby supplement his income and perhaps satisfy his urge to make things. The women of a household could do the work of the household and its garden and in addition spin, dye, weave cloth, and sew. But the factory system drew to itself all the work energies of landless and otherwise unoccupied persons. The first textile mills depended on the labor of girls or women and children, presumably on a temporary basis. As the factory system spread and manufacturing became more and more centralized and central to the life of particular places, migrants and immigrants were drawn into factories who might have had no plan to spend their lives in them—but then usually did, since there were few alternatives in *manufacturing centers.*

Some attempts were made before 1800 to foster manufactures in a particular place with the idea that the community itself would depend on them; they were unsuccessful, but still interesting as attempts. One was at Paterson, New Jersey, at the Passaic River Great Falls, where "The Society for Establishing Useful Manufactures" hoped—with a corporation charter from New Jersey—to manufacture cotton yarn and other goods. Alexander Hamilton supported the project; in the same year, 1791, he delivered to the Congress a "Report on the Subject of Manufactures" in which he argued that governmental support of industry would increase the independence of the new nation. The spirit of enterprise, he said, would be expanded in a nation that fostered manufacturing along with agriculture and commerce. Encouragement of immigration and the use of women and children in the factories would solve the problem of a too-small labor force.[1] Some yarn, cloth, and other items were produced at Paterson, but by 1796 the venture was failing. Industry at Paterson was not successful until about 1840, when locomotives began to be built there. In 1832 Philip Hone, a New Yorker, wrote in his diary that it was a "cotton spinning dirty village. . . . Green trees have given place to brown stone walls, and the singing of birds to the everlasting noise of spinning jennies and power looms."

Specialization in manufacturing as central to the economic life of a place depended on rational methods of mass production. These developed most quickly in association with technological inventions in the second half of the eighteenth and the early nineteenth centuries. The steam engine and textile machinery, such as Arkwright's spinning jenny, were the fulcrums of England's industrial revolution. Transported to America (Samuel Slater slipping out of England in 1789 with jenny plans—transmittal of which were forbidden—in his head is the textbook example), such inventions inspired new manufacturing enterprises and further experimentation.

The key American invention in terms of its economic effects in this period was Eli Whitney's cotton gin. This device for separating fibers from seeds made it possible to process large amounts of a hardy, short-staple cotton, the "upland cotton" that could be grown on many kinds of soil where the warm season was long. With it, short-staple cotton production expanded in the South, and, as the Tidewater and Piedmont lands were "mined" and fresh soil was sought, producers carried the plantation form

---

[1]"It is worthy of particular remark that, in general, women and children are rendered more useful, and the latter more early useful, by manufacturing establishments, than they would otherwise be. Of the number of persons employed in the cotton manufactories of Great Britain, it is computed that four sevenths, nearly, are women and children, of whom the greatest proportion are children, and many of them of a very tender age. . ." Secretary of the Treasury to the House of Representatives, "Report on the Subject of Manufactures," excerpted in *The Basic Ideas of Alexander Hamilton*, ed. Richard B. Morris (New York: Pocket Library, 1957), p. 279.

of community westward to and beyond the Mississippi River. Farmers and planters devoted more and more attention to cotton and less and less to other agricultural products, and thus formed a growing market for western farmers. Much of the cotton was exported to England from Charleston, Savannah, Mobile, and New Orleans, and this new business helped these centers grow. Some was shipped to New England, where spinning mills began to change the character of the older towns and bring new ones into being. Textile manufacturing was not the only concern of these towns. Tool making developed too, partly as an adjunct of the textile industry and partly in connection with other enterprises. Eli Whitney, again, was responsible for a far-reaching change in techniques of production. In the factory he set up at New Haven, Connecticut in 1798, he began to experiment with making interchangeable, readily assembled parts for muskets, and with a factory division of labor—the beginning of assembly-line production.

The materials and processes of production had yet to be brought together, however, and this required more than just the idea of doing it. It required capital that could be risked over a period of time, markets and sure means of getting to them, and a constant or expanding, localized labor supply. These needs were not met all at once but the means of meeting them were found in the same period of time, in the years after the War of 1812.

The circumstances surrounding the war played a part. The problem of a neutral country's shipping rights while Britain and France were at war had led to a number of proposals and measures to restrict trade with these countries but also strengthened the idea that the United States could become more independent of Europe and its problems by producing its own cotton and woolen goods and other previously imported manufactures. In 1808 the soldier, diplomat, and Connecticut mill owner David Humphreys proposed a toast at a Philadelphia dinner: "The Best Mode of Warfare for our Country—the artillery of carding and spinning machinery, and the musketry of shuttles and sledges." In the same year Henry Clay introduced a resolution in the Kentucky legislature that members should wear home-made clothes; in 1810 he proposed to the U.S. Senate that supplies for the navy be purchased from home-grown and home-made products. Textile production did increase. Then during the war, with its further dislocations of shipping and with new military needs, American manufacturing establishments multiplied.

This did not in itself raise manufacturing to a position of community eminence. For a long time to come, much of the capital for transportation and manufacturing developments that would make centers grow had to be obtained from English and European financiers, since there was little in the ex-colonies. But one way of gathering what there was together was through incorporation. A corporation could draw on many investors without necessarily risking the fortune of any one of them. Over a period of time, the corporation itself—at least on the managerial level—became a significant form of association, sometimes referred to as a "community." In the beginning, however, a corporation charter was often a way of securing a legal monopoly, especially for purposes of acquiring land for speculation and of undertaking transportation developments.

The best-known of all who discovered the advantages of corporate enterprise in the first half of the nineteenth century were the "Boston Associates." They were not the first; three hundred charters had been granted in the United States by 1800. But these few families made use of the corporate form to establish and direct a variety of businesses. Their first industrial enterprise (1813) was the Boston Manufacturing Company of Waltham, Massachusetts. By 1816 they were ready to begin production in the first procedurally complete cotton-manufacturing plant in the world, all operations under one roof and company-built housing for workers nearby. This was the year, too, when British goods poured into the United States after the wars had kept them out, and many of the small, recently established mills went under. Henry Clay helped put the country's first protective tariff bill through Congress to try to make American manufacturers more competitive with the cheaper foreign imports. The Waltham plant was successful, and by 1822 the original investors had received dividends totaling 104.5 percent. In the meantime they had also founded an insurance company, and later they established banks, real estate companies, other factories, and transportation enterprises.[2] In addition to drawing competitors and businessmen in other fields into their control through these enterprises, they showed the way to separation of ownership from management and supervision of industrial operations. They ruled from a distance; the workers whose lives their decisions affected had only the most indirect, and much-mediated, relationship to them. Of all the features of corporate enterprise, this had the most impact on the nature of community in nineteenth-century America.

Yet manufacturing communities did not develop—the manufacturing center did not become a lasting form of community—until the potential of widespread markets had been realized by means of transportation links. It was primarily railroads that made this possible. Summarizing the situation prior to 1860, Cochran and Miller say, "Communication, not production, was the key to industrialism in the United States. Settled haphazardly to suit real estate speculators rather than farmers or manufacturers, America was made up of separate economic areas . . . until knit by railroad and

---

[2]Vera Shlakman, "Economic History of a Factory Town," *Smith College Studies in History*, 20, Nos. 1–4 (1935), 37–45.

telegraph into a cohesive Union. By 1860, east of the Mississippi this cohesion had been achieved" and local self-sufficiency was disappearing.[3]

As for a labor force, it could be supplied in part by this nation of farmers; more immigration would be needed too. Easterners continued to be concerned that the open lands of the west would draw people away at the expense of their region. Yet migration to the commercial and manu-facturing centers increased throughout the nineteenth century in relation to that to western farmlands, just as the proportion of nonfarm workers in the labor force increased (from less than one-third in 1820 to almost half in 1870).

The burst of growth of *industrial centers* in the United States came after the Civil War, but the necessary foundation of a national economy had been laid before. The technological developments that led to the mechanization of production, the accumulation of capital for purposes of production and for purposes of accumulating more capital, the linking of places as sources of raw materials, production centers, and markets, and the growth of a labor force took a century. In this time, a number of places that first existed as trans-shipment points, commercial centers, and market towns added manufacturing and, with it, continued to grow into complex urban centers. Most of these were in the Northeast and Old Northwest. In all regions, administrative and institutional centers were less likely to add manufacturing. Industrial urbanization was a special kind of urbaniza-tion; it occurred most readily where capital was available from on-going commercially based urbanization.

An example of growth through the addition of industry to a com-mercial center is Cincinnati. Laid out by speculators in 1788, at a pro-tected site on the river 450 miles from Pittsburgh, by 1800 it was supply-ing westward-bound farmers and shipping out the produce of settlers in the surrounding area. Daniel Drake's *Picture of Cincinnati*, written in 1815, forecast the development of manufactures to support commerce, and Michael Chevalier's description in 1835 makes it seem that the boosting was not just into the air. Chevalier, interestingly, made an effort to show that the industries of the place were comfortably apart from it:

> The foundries for casting steam engines, the yards for building steam-boats, the noisy, unwholesome, or unpleasant workshops are in the adjoining village of Fulton, in Covington or Newport on the Kentucky bank of the river, or in the country. As for the enormous slaughter of hogs, about 150,000 annually, and the preparation of the lard which follows, the town is not in the least incommoded by it; the whole process takes place on the banks of a little stream called Deer Creek ... or near the basins of the great canal.

[3]*The Age of Enterprise: A Social History of Industrial America*, rev. ed. (New York: Harper & Row, Publishers, 1961), p. 57.

He believed Cincinnati to have been built out of its own resources—"the city is its own creation"—and the main resource, for him, was "their New England patrimony" of "sharp-sighted, wakeful, untiring industry," but there was also "the manufacture of certain articles which, though of little value separately considered, form an important aggregate when taken together." The many small manufacturing establishments were to the city's advantage, he said, for they were "republican" in structure and thus the place could escape "industrial feudalism."[4] The "pork trade" was at that time its only large-scale industry. It continued to grow, as did trade, and by the time Chevalier visited Cincinnati, Eastern investors were turning it into less of a self-made place than he thought it was. In the 1850's railroads began to supplement the river route and steamboats, and after the Civil War they helped keep the city commercially and industrially important.

When an industry was the initiating factor in the development of a place, survival usually depended on adding other activities, both economic and noneconomic. Without them, the growth period, if not survival itself, of a mining or manufacturing center would be limited. Mining towns show this very well, especially since they have existed in more than one form. Some have been company towns; others, open "boom" towns.

Dependent communities developed at the early coal and iron fields of New Jersey and Pennsylvania. An individual or company would acquire a tract of mineral land and employ hundreds of families to work in their mines and mills under the supervision of managers. Accommodations were not generally provided, but stores were, and though, theoretically, money wages were paid, the workers were often continuously in debt to the company. The Duke of Saxe-Weimar Eisenach described one such place in Pennsylvania in 1826:

> [Mauch Chunk] has only existed four years, and owes its origin to the neighbouring mines, which, with all the surrounding country, belongs to the Lehigh Coal Company; a company which possesses a large capital, has existed longer than its rival in Pottsville, and conducts its operations more systematically. . . .
> . . . The company employs about one thousand eight hundred workmen, who live partly near the mine, but generally in small houses in the place belonging to the company. Their habitations form a street along Mauch Chunk creek, nearly half a mile long. A great number of them are married and have their families with them. The company has given them a clergyman, and a school with a good teacher, to instruct their children. A massive mill is also erected near the creek, in which all the flour necessary for the place is ground; the country is too rough for culture; the company exchanges in a very profitable manner coal for grain. . . .

[4]*Society, Manners, and Politics in the United States: Letters on North America*, ed. John William Ward (Gloucester, Mass.: Peter Smith, 1967), pp. 188–200.

A store belonging to the society, and furnished with all the necessary articles is also kept here. In this the workmen and their families receive the necessary articles, the price of which is deducted from their wages. . . . The company makes a great profit in this manner, and the greater part of the money expended flows back again into its treasury. The ground three miles up and down Lehigh, belongs to the company, so that no one can dispute with them the monopoly of keeping a store.[5]

In retrospect, the "company town" seems an obvious way to organize a community around a particular industry. Just as in agriculture, where there was single or centralized ownership of an extensive operation that required a large number of workers, the workers formed a dependent community. Manor, plantation, and company town are three expressions of a particular type of community. In all three, members had small amounts of private property—personal possessions, sometimes domestic animals and/or land (except on the plantations of the South, where a slave might have land for private use, as for growing vegetables, but never private property, and where he himself was legal property)—but essentially no independent means and no alternatives in the kinds of relationships he could establish in the community.

In some regions mineral resources could be obtained (at first) without large outlays of capital; individuals and partnerships could lay claims and do the work themselves. Their camp sites and the people who supplied them made up the beginnings of a town. Boom-town stories about mining are well known, and instances of a boom followed by stagnation or disappearance have occurred in every mining region. Descriptions of such places in the West outdo each other in liveliness, unless one can believe that all the residents were trying to outdo each other. Virginia City, Nevada, one of the best known, was seen in 1860 (a few months after prospectors were attracted to the Comstock area) as "Frame shanties, pitched together as if by accident; tents of canvas, of blankets, of brush, of potato sacks, and old shirts, with empty whisky barrels for chimneys; smoke hovels of mud and stone. . ." The observer describes a busy scene full of roughnecks, speculators, traders, arguers, and drunks, and then mentions the most prevalent boom-town problem: "At this period there were no laws of any kind in the district for the preservation of order." A man digging a cellar found "rich indications" and immediately laid claim to the whole street, and suddenly hundreds were digging under their own and their neighbors' tents until the whole town threatened to be undermined. "The mining laws were paramount where there was no law at all. There was no security to personal property, or even to persons. He who turned in

[5]*Travels Through North America, During the Years 1825 and 1826,* 2 vols. (Philadelphia: Carey, Lea & Carey, 1828), II, 187, 190–91.

to sleep at night might find himself in a pit of silver by morning."[6] In 1865 Virginia City and Gold Hill had a population of about 15,000—half that of Nevada as a whole, and the biggest "bonanzas" were yet to come. Need for wood and water created other jobs, but without mining the place had no basis for existence. Its decline began in the early 1880's, when the main silver veins had been worked out and, in addition, the price of silver was falling.

The naturalist John Muir wrote in 1879 that Nevada was

> already strewn with ruins that seem as gray and silent and timeworn as if the civilization to which they belonged had perished centuries ago. Yet strange to say, all these ruins are results of mining efforts made within the last few years. Wander where you may throughout the length and breadth of this mountain-barred wilderness, you everywhere come upon these dead mining towns, with their tall chimney stacks, standing forlorn amid broken walls and furnaces, and machinery half buried in same, the very names of many of them already forgotten amid the excitements of later discoveries, and now known only through tradition—tradition ten years old. . . . Some of them were probably only camps built by bands of prospectors, and inhabited for a few months or years, while some specially interesting canyon was being explored, and then carelessly abandoned for more promising fields. But many were real towns, regularly laid out and incorporated, containing well-built hotels, churches, schoolhouses, post-offices and jails, as well as the mills on which they all depended; and those whose well graded streets were filled with lawyers, doctors, brokers, hangmen, and real estate agents, etc., the whole population numbering several thousand.[7]

Muir called this "misdirected enterprise," and wished people would deliberate more about the use of their energies.

Perhaps they tried to in Central City, Colorado. With its neighbor Black Hawk, it formed a continuous settlement along the sides of a gulch and near a number of camps. Although, obviously, a mining population is a transitory one, within a few years of the original find (1859) it had brick and stone buildings. Its central location kept its population up, and then it added another attraction: an opera house. Becoming a small-scale cultural center was not enough, however, to last out the depression of the nineties or, especially, the abandonment by the federal government of the silver purchase policy.

Short-lived mining communities helped other places, their supply centers, grow to the point that they could survive temporary adversities. Galena, Illinois, an old trading post, was laid out as an access town to the lead-mining region in 1826. San Francisco was a village with a nearby

[6]J. Ross Browne, "A Peep at Washoe," *Harper's New Monthly Magazine*, 22, No. 127 (January, 1861), 154–55, 161.
[7]"Nevada's Dead Towns," *San Francisco Evening Bulletin*, January 15, 1879.

mission and presidio when the Gold Rush began. Denver, with its beginnings in the rush to Cherry Creek, quickly became more than an accessible supply base; the energies of its promoters turned it into a regional commercial center, a territorial and state capital, and a home base for other development projects in Colorado. Its main work was in freighting for the mines; smelting was added when a railway was constructed to reach coal fields at Pueblo (1872). Silver-processing developments led to the establishment of a mint, which the U.S. Treasury acquired. Stock raising and both irrigation farming and dry farming developed through the 1870's to add to the city's business. By the end of the century there were sugar refineries and small factories. The city had yet to become self-conscious about its appearance, but its importance to the West was assured.[8]

Nineteenth-century Denver illustrates the general idea that several functions reinforcing each other were most likely to keep a place growing. Yet, often, it seemed to be poverty that grew. Fear of a relation between industrial working conditions and poor living conditions had led Jefferson and others in the late eighteenth and early nineteenth centuries to hope that the United States would never become a manufacturing nation. Jefferson did change his mind to some extent about the necessity for manufacturing after the War of 1812, but fear of social effects of industrialization as based on English and European examples remained. Morton and Lucia White have written that eighteenth-century American cities "had not become large enough or unattractive enough to stir men into passionate ideological argument about the virtues and vices of urbanization, or into identification with the country or the city as *the* place in which the good life was to be lived."[9] These cities, commercial centers, had sometimes been indicted for vice, but fear of them as places seems to have grown as they grew in the first half of the nineteenth century. Their growth, of course, depended in part on the development of manufacturing, and even small manufacturing centers came under attack. Herman Melville approaches the "Tartarus of Maids," an isolated New England factory village, like Dante descending into the Inferno, and there,

> Not far from the bottom of the Dungeon stands a large whitewashed building, relieved, like some great white sepulchre, against the sullen background of mountainside firs, and other hardy evergreens, inaccessibly rising in grim terraces for some two thousand feet.
> The building is a paper-mill.

[8]Denver's development is described in a regional context in Constance McLaughlin Green, *American Cities in the Growth of the Nation* (New York: Harper & Row, Publishers, 1965), pp. 129–48.

[9]*The Intellectual Versus the City: From Thomas Jefferson to Frank Lloyd Wright* (New York: Mentor Books, 1964), p. 18.

Out of concern for social conditions, the first manufacturing centers as such were preplanned communities. They have in their planning a kind of idealism that cannot be ignored, for all that its outcome appears to be pervaded by self-interest. Perhaps the beginning is with Samuel Slater who, as manager of Almy and Brown's mill at Providence, Rhode Island, in 1799, established one of the first Sunday schools in the United States for the edification of the children who were working for him. Industrial community planning as such, however, begins with one of the Boston Associates. Francis Cabot Lowell had visited English and Scottish manufacturing centers to study their methods before he helped set up Waltham, Massachusetts, in 1813. He hoped to avoid the unhealthful conditions he had observed and thought through the social, as well as the economic, problems of centralized cotton manufacturing. The so-called Waltham system (see p. 138) turned the main point of a company town—control of the labor force—into a plan for a virtuous local community. Instead of children, who had been used in the early mills, women and girls from the farms of New England were hired, with the expectation that they would work for a year or so, living in carefully supervised boarding houses, and then go home again. With the success of Waltham even when business conditions were poor (until about 1821), the system spread through northern New England, wherever there was good potential for water power.[10]

The most-described example of a preplanned mill town is Lowell, Massachusetts, at the falls of the Merrimac River. Set up in 1823, it became the Boston Associates' most successful manufacturing center and several other textile companies established themselves there. For many years it was maintained as a showplace; visitors were welcome, from Davy Crockett to Charles Dickens. Almost all were impressed with its cleanliness and orderliness, especially those from across the Atlantic, who carried with them images of quite different factory conditions. Dickens' description in *American Notes* reads like a public-relations brochure for the place. Since he saw it on a one-day excursion from Boston (in 1842), perhaps he did not have time to become aware that it had its detractors. Two years before his visit, the reformer Orestes Brownson had written that the mortality rate was low because "the poor girls when they can toil no longer go home to die." The girls were not supposed to or expected to strike, but they did, because of working conditions (nailed-down windows, for example), wage cuts, and arbitrary dismissals, and then the names of troublemakers were sent around to other local companies. Boarding-house regulations were also objected to on occasion, and regulations

[10]See Caroline F. Ware, *The Early New England Cotton Manufacture: A Study in Industrial Beginnings* (New York: Russell & Russell, 1966).

in general in this age of the philosophy of individual choice. Yet a well-regulated life was the whole idea: to provide for every aspect of life, to provide a complete community in that all the social institutions its organizers thought were desirable were represented in it. In this it was not so far from the communalistic experiments of the time. In 1846, when the system had already begun to break down, a Unitarian minister wrote a history of Lowell with its ideals at heart. After describing the origins, growth, and facilities of the town, he notes that it has been commended by some as a model community and condemned by others as a hotbed of corruption. He wished to show the exact facts, because "We are destined to be a great manufacturing people. The influences that go forth from Lowell, will go forth from many other manufacturing villages and cities." Therefore, he describes typical establishments:

> On the banks of the river, or of a canal, stands a row of mills, numbering, on different corporations, from two to five. A few rods from these, are long blocks of brick boarding-houses, containing a sufficient number of tenements to accommodate the most of the operatives employed by the Corporation. Between the boarding-houses and the mills is a line of a one story brick building, containing the counting room, superintendent's room, clerk's and store rooms. The mill yard is so surrounded by enclosures, that the only access is through the counting room, in full view of those whose business it is to see that no improper persons intrude themselves upon the premises. . . .
> Each of the long blocks of boarding-houses is divided into six or eight tenements, and are generally three stories high. These tenements are finished off in a style much above the common farm-houses of the country, and more nearly resemble the abodes of respectable mechanics in rural villages. . . . The front room is usually the common eating-room of the house, and the kitchen is in the rear. The keeper of the house, (commonly a widow, with her family of children,) has her parlor in some part of the establishment and in some houses there is a sitting-room for the use of the boarders. The remainder of the apartments are sleeping-rooms.

He gives some of the rules of the houses, including restriction of residence to persons employed by the company, prohibition of "improper conduct," and accountability of the housekeeper for boarders' conduct, including "whether they are in the habit of attending public worship." The result, in his view, was an influence toward "good order and good morals." He uses the term "moral police," and implies that only through its maintenance of virtuous lives can the evils of manufacturing cities be avoided. Another factor he emphasizes, however, is the temporary nature of the girls' employment. Where English operatives "are operatives for life, and constitute a permanent, dependent factory caste," the American "come from distant homes, to which in a few years they return, to be the wives of the farmers and mechanics of the country towns and villages."[11]

But the labor force in New England was already changing. In the 1830's and 1840's it was shifting to immigrants from French Canada (many of whom also expected to work temporarily and then go home) and from Ireland. These workers were Catholic, and the older residents of the villages and towns expressed their reactions to them in anti-Catholic terms. At the moment, there was no room for the community institutions and ideals they brought with them, although the expansion of manufacturing enterprises meant that there was room for their labor.

The impulse to plan for community ideals[12] has had its most lasting expression in associations based on religious commonality. Most religious communities have been agricultural, though crafts and machine skills have been developed as needed locally. Communities based on other commonalities of belief—including beliefs about the nature of community—have sometimes been agricultural, sometimes diversified, and sometimes specialized along the lines of one or a few manufacturing enterprises. It is interesting that manufacturing has seldom succeeded in making these places last. Evidently they cannot compete successfully; competition, for that matter, is not usually their reason for being. There are built-in limitations to their search for markets, and problems of dealing with inflation and depression. But economic conditions are only part of the story. Each place has its own history and hopes.

Some religious communities have been communistic with regard to property and work, and some have not. Both kinds have a long history; both have existed in many parts of the world. Monasteries and convents are special instances of community. Missions are communitarian in some ways but may also be considered as dependent communities. In Europe, several communalistic groups developed out of reaction to the power of overlords, princes, states, or the Church and to struggles for power among them. The searches for change usually lumped under the term "Reformation" included attempts to restore, in a practical way, what was believed to be the discipleship and brotherhood—that is, community—of the early Christian church. Since one tenet of this restoration was entry into the

---

[11]Henry A. Miles, *Lowell, As It Was, and As It Is,* in Charles N. Glaab, *The American City: A Documentary History* (Homewood, Ill.: The Dorsey Press, Inc., 1963), pp. 130–42.

[12]Terms for such communities are many and vague. In these pages, however, note the following usages: *Communalistic* ideas emphasize local autonomy. *Communistic* refers to common ownership of property. *Communitarian* is a more inclusive term for attempts to achieve social goals within local communities; communitarian places may or may not be communalistic and may or may not be communistic. *Utopianism* is the envisioning of such goals in such a way as to produce plans to realize them.

group by a voluntary, maturely considered act of belief, these "primitive Christians" rejected infant baptism. The name for them was therefore Anabaptists. Three main groups from this period still exist; named after regional leaders, they are the Mennonites (Holland), Amish (dissenters from the Swiss Brethren in the late seventeenth century), and Hutterites (Austria). Anabaptists tended to withdraw from open conflict and therefore, under persecution, to migrate. Generally avoiding the trappings of the world, they tried to establish separate communities as self-sufficient agricultural villages and sought simplicity in their households (close-knit patriarchal families), appearance, worship, methods of work, and economic relations. Among these "plain-sect" peoples, Hutterites went to the extent of community ownership of property.

Dutch Mennonites first reached North America just before the English conquest of New Netherland. Their village was destroyed in that conquest, but others were established in the eighteenth century. The Mennonites and Hutterites who settled on the plains and prairies of the United States and Canada crossed the Atlantic much later, in the 1870's, after having built a number of successful farming communities in Europe and South Russia until forced to move on by restrictive government policies. Amish from the Canton of Bern in Switzerland arrived in Pennsylvania beginning in 1727. Others came later in the century.[13] Several Pietist communities were also established in Pennsylvania, the best known of which is the Ephrata Cloister (beginning in the 1730's as a semi-monastic community and lasting, with modifications in the monasticism, until reorganized as an incorporated body, the Seventh Day Baptists, in 1814). The Moravian Brethren adopted a system called General Economy in 1741 at Bethlehem, Pennsylvania, with the church as the property-holding unit; it was adopted at several other Moravian communities but finally dissolved in 1762.[14]

[13]John A. Hostetler describes the Amish in terms of Redfield's idea of "little community" in *Amish Society* (Baltimore: The Johns Hopkins' Press, 1968).

[14]Arthur Bestor says of the Moravians that their communitarian organization had its beginnings before migration from Europe but took shape under American conditions. He develops the idea that the experience of migration caused "social yearnings to crystallize in communitarian form": "Migration, after all, was a search for a new and better society, and it involved, in colonial America particularly, the temporary creation of new social institutions. To a certain extent every group settlement possessed some characteristics of a communitarian experiment," and sectarian groups had a stronger sense of "unity and separateness" to begin with than did other immigrants (*Backwoods Utopias: The Sectarian Origins and the Owenite Phase of Communitarian Socialism in America: 1663–1829*, 2nd ed. [Philadelphia: University of Pennsylvania Press, 1970], pp. 22–24).

There were practical factors as well: an "economy" for all in sharing the work and its results in a little-known environment; and the foundations in religious belief, nurtured over centuries until they seemed to impel rather than explain action, cannot be ignored. There was, for example, the Biblical basis for not selling land: "The land shall not be sold for ever: for the land is mine; for ye are strangers and so-

Shaker villages became the most widespread of the religious communities, obtaining converts from New England to the Ohio Valley in the mood of religious revival in the early 1800's. By the 1820's a Shaker village was a standard stop for tourists, who were generally more interested in observing the Shaker form of worship than the community organization (eventually the Shakers, for this reason, closed their services to outsiders). A small band of English immigrants led by Ann Lee Stanley had arrived in New York in 1774 and purchased land for a settlement in the township of Watervliet, a few miles from Albany, two years later. As members of an especially fervent religious society whose worship included a ritualistic dance, they had been abused and often jailed in England, and now, during the American War for Independence, persecution of them took the form of suspicion that they were British spies. Yet they did attract converts in this period of unrest—the only way the number of believers could increase, since they believed that celibacy was essential to a perfect life. Community organization began in 1787 with the founding of the New Lebanon Society at New Lebanon (Columbia County), New York, which became the "Mother-Church" and model for other places in which converts were gathered. Property was communally held, except for that of new converts, who were not admitted to full membership until after a preparatory period. For that matter, though Shakers believed that perfection could be attained only in the chaste, disciplined life of their communities, they did not insist that the whole world had to join them in order to be saved; much of the work of redemption was expected to go on in the next world. Thus the Shaker villages remained small, and there was less chance of their being sullied by individualistic and worldly innovators.

---

journers with me" (Leviticus 25:23). Church ownership of property was one expression of this.

Early Christian teachings could also be interpreted along communitarian lines. The writings of Paul emphasize mutual sympathy and support (I Corinthians 12:24–26 and 16:1–2); the churches (congregations) are told to "come out from among" unbelievers and be separate (II Corinthians 6:17); and sharing is for the purpose of equality (II Corinthians 8:12–15). The best-known texts are in the Acts of the Apostles: "And all that believed were together, and had all things common; And sold their possessions and goods, and parted them to all men, as every man had need" (Acts 2:44–45); "And the multitude of them that believed were of one heart and of one soul: neither said any of them that ought of the things which he possessed was his own; but they had all things common.... Neither was there any among them that lacked: for as many as were possessors of lands or houses sold them, and brought the prices of the things that were sold, And laid them down at the apostles' feet: and distribution was made unto every man according as he had need" (Acts 4:32, 34–35).

William A. Hinds, one of the committed early students of American community ventures, wrote that the hope of the Second Coming of Christ had brought into being, as practical beginnings of heaven on earth, "more social experiments than any other event, actual or anticipated, in the world's history, save his first coming" (*American Communities and Cooperative Colonies*, 2nd ed., rev. [Chicago: Charles H. Kerr, 1908], p. 563).

Religious belief united also a group of German immigrants under the leadership of George Rapp. They bought land in western Pennsylvania in 1803 and organized a "community of equality" at a place they called Harmonie, holding property in common and encouraging celibacy without making it an absolute rule. In addition to farming, they built a tannery, mills, a woolen factory, and a distillery. By 1810, all were producing well, but they decided to move to Indiana, to a site better suited to diversified agriculture and closer to a river for purposes of marketing. The second Harmonie was built near the mouth of the Wabash River in 1815 and, again, became an economic success very quickly. They established manufacturing facilities and raised a variety of crops for themselves and for sale, but illness and unfriendly neighbors made them decide to go back to Pennsylvania. In 1824 they sold their holdings, through an agent, to the English industrialist-reformer Robert Owen, and began a new town, Economy, a few miles from their first one. They were hardly settled there, however, before a newcomer appeared who persuaded some of the members that their lives there were too restricted and they should come over to his place. George Rapp held together those who were left until his death in 1847, but productivity was declining along with population. Few children had been born in the community and its numbers had been maintained by further immigration from Germany. When these were no longer attracted to it, and the young people moved away from it, it could not maintain its earlier economic level. Nor could it keep up with other businesses in the area which had more capital to invest in equipment.[15]

The communalism of a number of nineteenth-century communities was based only partly on religious principles. Other social ideas and economic practices related to them were equally important to the founders and their following (or some of it). John Humphrey Noyes, one of the first students of the American experiments and himself a founder (Oneida), distinguished between religious and nonreligious "socialisms," and many subsequent writers have maintained these categories, sometimes with the addition of a transcendentalist one. There are differences in origins and goals; membership, however, is not so easily categorized. People would wander from one community to another; during their stays, short or long, they would share their ideas with each other; and there were many who became members of a community without any commitment to its founders'

---

[15]Charles Nordhoff visited Economy in 1874 and described its neatness, the loveliness of its situation on the Ohio River, its silent streets, and a hotel whose main guests were tramps. Of the 1,000 or so inhabitants in the 1820's, the population then was 110, "most of whom are aged, and none, I think, under forty." "The society does not seek new members, though I am told it would not refuse any who seemed to have a true vocation. As to its future, little is said. The people look for the coming of the Lord. . ." (*The Communistic Societies of the United States* [New York: Schocken Books, 1965; first published 1875], pp. 63–95).

ideas. The proportion of the latter seems to have increased as the communitarian movement spread, especially in the 1840's.

Whatever their bases in principle were, the distinctive characteristic of communitarian places was their emphasis on the community as a social unit. Founders were trying deliberately to institute a local primary group, to use the sociological term, in the midst of an expanding, industrializing nation. In the population at large the small family appears to have been the essential unit, and among communitarians the family idea was essential. The relation of a family to the community differed in the various places they planned, but where the nuclear family was considered the basic unit, the community was considered an extension of it, and where it was not, the community was itself to be the family. For example, note the "social principles" of William Kiel, founder of Bethel, Missouri (1844) and Aurora, Oregon (1856):

> All government should be parental, to imitate, as they say, the parental government of God.
>
> That therefore societies should be formed upon the model of the family, having all interests and all property absolutely in common; all the members laboring faithfully for the general welfare and support, and drawing the means of living from the general treasury.
>
> That, however, neither religion nor the harmony of nature teaches community in any thing further than property and labor. Hence the family life is strictly maintained. . .[16]

The idea that the family is a model for society is found in the writings of many communitarians. Noyes thought that, however much the followers of Robert Owen and Charles Fourier tried to maintain their opposition to each other, they shared the main idea of an "enlargement of home—the extension of family union beyond the little man-and-wife circle to large corporations. . ."[17] The image of the family implies a structure and emotional attachments that were often carefully worked on in these communities, but it also implies a continuity over generations that was more difficult to provide for. What happened at New Harmony, particularly since conditions seemed especially favorable for the community to last a long time, illustrates the problem.

When the Rappites sold their Indiana site to Robert Owen, there was already a village of regular streets and public buildings around a square, several hundred acres of improved land (out of about thirty thou-

---

[16]Quoted by Nordhoff, in his description of the Aurora and Bethel communes, in *Communistic Societies*, p. 309.

[17]*History of American Socialisms* (New York: Dover Publications, Inc., 1966; first published 1870), p. 23. Nordhoff, concluding his survey of the places he visited, suggests some conditions for "communistic living" that are based on the idea that "a commune is but a larger family" (*Communistic Societies*, pp. 409–18).

sand), orchards and vineyards, and structures and machinery for the manufacture of textiles, pottery, hats, boots, soap, candles, and glue, and also
a dyeworks and saw- and gristmills. Owen had successfully managed a
"model" factory town at New Lanark, Scotland, and was prepared to
finance the community's beginnings, envisioning it as more than an experiment. He thought that independent, compact villages that united agriculture and manufacturing would develop from one such beginning and form
a cooperative system. On promotional visits to Washington, D.C., in late
February and early March, 1825, he is reported to have described to the
House of Representatives his principles of work, play, and education:
"Make a man happy and you make him virtuous—this is the whole of my
system, to make him happy, I enlighten his mind and occupy his hands,
and I have so managed the art of instruction that individuals seek it as an
amusement."[18] And in a letter a few days after he returned to New Harmony: "The United States but particularly the States west of the Allegheny
Mountains have been prepared in the most remarkable manner for the New
System. The principle of union & cooperation for the promotion of all the
virtues & for the creation of wealth is now universally admitted to be far
superior to the individual selfish system. . . ."[19]

The immediate response was indeed encouraging—800 persons arrived within six weeks, and in October the number had increased to 900,
including "many intelligent and benevolent individuals" plus some "black
sheep."[20] Owen, in late April (before very many had arrived) decided
that a probationary period was needed, a "half-way house," before a full
"community of equality" could be instituted. He therefore drew up the
first of several constitutions, offering a "preliminary society" in which private accounts would be kept. In Bestor's view, the three-year period of this

[18]Alice Felt Tyler, *Freedom's Ferment: Phases of American Social History
from the Colonial Period to the Outbreak of the Civil War* (New York: Harper &
Row, Publishers, 1962), pp. 198–200.

[19]Quoted in Bestor, *Backwoods Utopias*, pp. 113–14. Bestor gives a detailed
account of Owenite hopes, responses to them, and confusions that beset life at New
Harmony.

Owen's ideas formed in response to conditions in England, especially among
the unemployed during the economic troubles that followed the Napoleonic wars.
By way of general principles, he hoped to build up a system of "villages of cooperation" that would keep workers self-employed and remove the distinction between
town and country and between industrial and agricultural conditions; to make it
work, social institutions would have to be changed, since they were formative of
man's nature, and religion and education both had fostered competition by convincing
individuals that failure meant faults in themselves rather than in the institutions.
Such ideas were, to put it mildly, unusual in America in the nineteenth century,
and when New Harmony failed it was widely believed that it was because of Owen's
condemnation of religion.

[20]According to Noyes, working from the notes of A. J. Macdonald, who had
interviewed those who were left in the area of New Harmony in the 1840's (*History
of American Socialisms*, p. 35).

constitution gave Owen a chance "to evolve a plan that was really a plan," including the clarification of property rights, and "to select qualified members," but he botched the chance. He returned to England, leaving his son in charge, and, over all, seems to have spent more energy publicizing the possibilities of the place than working out specific arrangements for it. Within the community, a *Gazette* and a free school were established, which might have been expected to increase commonality and a sense of the future. The school was directed by William Maclure, a scientist who saw educational reform, such as in learning through practical activities, as central to social reform. But along with the effects of the community's having to buy provisions—not producing enough for its own needs—the expenses were great, and it was up to Owen to bear them.

On his return in January 1826, the "community of equality" was constituted, but then the group began to divide. Over the next year and a half there were a number of divisions and reorganizations, secessions and a regrouping by occupations; even the school became separate from the community. Faced with dissent, disorganization, and disharmony, Owen seems at each instance to have come up with a new idea or plan rather than to have required anyone to examine what already existed. Thus, when the Agricultural Society and the Mechanic Society refused to support the School Society, it occurred to him to establish a new community school for "social education," and when the latter failed he blamed the School Society. In one of his few expressions of disappointment with his community project, he said he had wanted all the children to be "educated in similar habits and dispositions, and be brought up truly as members of one large family," but the School Society had divided them into classes and had prevented him from "amalgamating the whole into a Community."[21]

In a few planned communities, the attraction was individual self-realization or even, simply, individual advantage. Failure at New Harmony has sometimes been ascribed to the individualistic motives of members—in other words, their unwillingness to recognize the primacy of the community. One place, Brook Farm, was at first intentionally based as much on the hope of self-realization and expression as on any other principle. Its organizer, George Ripley, a clergyman and member of the Transcendentalist Club of Boston, said that what he really wanted was to be "independent of the world," but since he also wanted to farm on a scale that would require help, and to have "a society of educated friends," he would sacrifice his private feeling "in the hope of a great social good." Ripley wrote these ideas to Emerson in November 1840, hoping to enlist his support; Emerson, on his part, was writing to Carlyle: "We are all a little

[21]Bestor, *Backwoods Utopias*, p. 199.

wild here with numberless projects of social reform. Not a reading man but has a draft of a new community in his waistcoat pocket." Ripley's draft was for a joint-stock company, subsistence farming (the place obtained was an estate at West Roxbury, a few miles from Boston), and a school. Brook Farm was filled with lively people, many of them young and evidently attractive, from the beginning, and it was said that the most important activity there was talk. Emerson, though he preferred to visit than to join it, called it "a perpetual picnic." Hawthorne, who stayed at Brook Farm from April to November 1841, used it as a setting for *Blithedale Romance*; although he was generally critical of the quest for utopia, until Boston becomes a relief to the hero of the story, Hawthorne still carried away a certain amount of nostalgia.[22] Visitors were fascinated with the unconventional clothes, the "weeds scratched out of the ground to the music of Tennyson and Browning," and people sitting on the floor when they listened to lectures. The main innovations at this community were in its educational system, which was also the main source of income. Included were an "infant school" (for children under six), a primary school (six to ten), a college preparatory course, and an agricultural course. In addition to curricular changes to keep students aware of new work in the arts and sciences, an informal atmosphere was promoted: students and teachers worked, played, and studied together. As part of the background to this system, it may be significant that the faculty and students' families formed, to begin with, a kind of "community" of association and interests as intellectuals.

In 1844, members of the Brook Farm Association decided to adopt the organization of phalanxes of agricultural and mechanical arts as proposed by the French socialist, Charles Fourier, and publicized in the United States by Albert Brisbane and Horace Greeley as a means of social reform.[23] The farm had not supplied their needs; expansion to other activi-

---

[22]Perhaps it was related to his sense of village life. In *The Scarlet Letter*: "This old town of Salem—my native place, though I have dwelt much away from it both in boyhood and maturer years—possesses, or did possess, a hold on my affections, the force of which I had never realised during my seasons of actual residence here.... This long connection of a family with one spot, as its place of birth and burial, creates a kindred between the human being and the locality, quite independent of any charm in the scenery or moral circumstances that surround him." But in *The Marble Faun* he announces that all cities "should be made capable of purification by fire, or of decay, within each half-century."

[23]Fourier wrote bitterly of the irrationality and wastefulness of civilization, and especially of competition, in the early nineteenth century. To reach economy, simplicity, and arrangements suited to what he conceived of as the inborn human nature, he proposed "natural" groupings ("phalanxes"—1,620 persons in a 5,000-acre area) of people engaged in agricultural pursuits and handicrafts, with community kitchens, common living quarters, and cooperative buying. Like Owen's, his arrangements would erase the line between town and country, but the property relations he proposed were not innovative: phalanxes would be run on joint-stock terms,

ties, such as carpentry, printing, and small-scale manufacturing, and a more orderly arrangement for getting things done might help. Besides, it would be interesting to be an example to people elsewhere. They borrowed money for the new enterprises, started a socialist publication, *The Harbinger*, and began construction of a new building, their "Phalanstery." But in the Spring of 1846, before it was finished, it burned. Unable to make up that loss of investment, a few struggled on at Brook Farm for two or three years but most of the community dispersed, several because of interest in new ventures elsewhere.

Long-term economic success has been rare among the heavenly communities. Where the material foundations for perpetuation of the community have been established, as for example by the Hutterites, key factors seem to be commitment to the community as such, and self-sufficiency. Economic success has been possible also when a community has undertaken to supply a need of the "outside" society, or to find sources of support and markets in other places. Mormons established both self-sufficient village communities[24] and a city-state that became a commercial center on one of the roads west (Salt Lake City was laid out to plan in 1847, with wide streets, large lots, and farmlands outside the city; although intended to be isolated from government, it was drawn in with the acquisition of the West and the overland migration following the Gold Rush). "Perfectionists" gathered together by Noyes maintained Oneida and Wallingford, New York, on the basis of skilled work and, subsequently, manufacturing that required large numbers of hired outsiders; when criticism of its communism of persons (a "complex marriage" system) as well as of property forced a change, it turned into a successful joint-stock enterprise, Oneida Community Ltd. All the communitarian ventures in the United States had to form some relationship with the outside to maintain even relative self-sufficiency. Taxes had to be paid, tools and machinery bought to insure productivity. Searches for areas where contact with the outside could be minimized only led to further searches as the constantly

---

and there would be freedom of occupational choice and payment in wages. Of the twenty-eight Fourierist phalanxes established in the United States between 1841 and 1858 (there had been less than ten Owenite communities), the best known are the North American Phalanx (1843–1854) at Red Banks, New Jersey, organized by Brisbane and Greeley and others, and the Wisconsin Phalanx (1844–1850) at Ceresco (now Ripon).

[24] Lowry Nelson, "The Mormon Village: A Study in Social Origins," *Proceedings of the Utah Academy of Sciences*, 7 (1930), 11–37, traces influences and conditions that brought Mormons to settle in the Great Basin in compact villages in a period when the predominant form of westward-moving settlement was dispersed neighborhoods or isolated farmsteads. Among the influences he mentions are the old Jerusalem of scripture and the New England town; conditions serving to perpetuate the form were a high degree of social integration, an arid climate with limited, localized water supplies, and fear of Indian attacks.

expanding economic and political networks caught up with the new communities (part of the history of Mennonites and Doukhobors in the United States and Canada can be followed in this fashion).

When the general economy was predominantly agricultural, so were the communes. As it became more commercial and industrial, religious communities remained agricultural, some lasting if they had the resources and could maintain commitment to their social institutions, and others struggling between self-containment and a place in the economy. In some places, leadership seems to have made the difference between holding onto the original ideals and dropping them in the struggle—Kiel's communities, for example, and perhaps George Rapp's. In others, the determination of the group was more important—followers of Etienne Cabet expelled the man but practiced his ideals for more than fifty years, longer than any other nonreligiously organized group in America[25]—and the outcome of their struggle depended on changes over which they had little control. In places where socialist reformers took account of and used the technology that was changing relationships between places and between classes on the outside, commitment to the new place was hard to hold. Moreover, in practicing their ideals in a locality and hoping they would spread from there to transform all society, they were not acknowledging the impetus and energy of industrialization to make its own transformations first. An entrepreneur in Boston might send his child to school at Brook Farm and be quite comfortable about his own future. Communitarians did not have revolution in mind.

It may be that, from the one hundred or so communitarian ventures before 1850, and the score or more toward the end of the century, some principles of community form and action were transmitted to the noncommunitarian society. But these ventures must be ranged alongside thousands of other instances of community building that were occurring simultaneously. Many included some dependence on family, close associations, and cooperation. Preplanning was a part even of land-jobbers' roles. Although much of it was for the purpose of advertisement, community ideals still appeared in their setting aside of public places and their specific provisions for local government, religion, and education.

Perhaps the most significant difference between communitarian and other places was the hope in the former of making all decisions about the local community within the community itself. At the opposite extreme were completely dependent communities, such as plantations and company towns. It has sometimes been said that the communitarian and anti-urban

---

[25]The inspiration was Cabet's utopian novel, *Voyage en Icarie* (1840). See Nordhoff, *Communistic Societies*, pp. 333–39, and Robert V. Hine, *California's Utopian Colonies* (New Haven: Yale University Press, 1966), pp. 58–77.

movements in the nineteenth century were essentially conservative or reactionary, in that they reverted to traditions of agricultural villages and "little communities" long gone. But, after all, the scriptural Heaven itself was laid out as a city, as the later urban reformer Josiah Strong pointed out. Those who wanted to maintain conditions of dependency were much more tightly tied to the past than any of the communitarians and urban problem-viewers. The existence of dependent communities in an incipient urban-industrial society forms part of the background to the Civil War. At the time of and after the War, as will be described in chapters 8 and 9, the kinds of differences observed generally to exist between urban centers and rural areas complicated questions of the nature, function, and potential for autonomy of local communities.

8

Towards A Rural-Urban Dichotomy

*"The world is apt to stick close to those who
have lived and got wealth there: a country life and
estate I like best for my children."*

—WILLIAM PENN

*"Busy haunts of men, not the remote wilderness,
is the proper school of political talents."*

—GOUVERNEUR MORRIS

Here we begin to draw some new lines; we begin to delineate concepts of community as they have developed since the 1860's. We can draw the first of these lines between city and countryside, so as to separate and distinguish them, or we can draw lines to show connections between various kinds of places. If we decide to draw a line of separation (the better to categorize), then issues and conflicts that involve people on the two sides of it may be analyzed in terms of their characteristic differences from each other. Arthur M. Schlesinger, Sr., one of the first students of urban history as a major part of United States history, discussed the "widening breach between North and South" before the Civil War in terms of the growth of towns and cities in the North and West while the South was in bondage to agriculture and to the "Northern business community."[1] A Southern historian, Frank L. Owsley, thought also that the clash was the result of fundamental differences between a commercial and industrial North and an agrarian South—although he considered agrarianism to be a freedom rather than a bondage.[2] The difference between an urban-industrial and a rural-agricultural society is now commonly cited as one of the factors in the conflict of North and South. The diverse groups, activities, regions, interests, and self-identifications of the country have been drawn into the two categories more easily since business and agriculture have had spokesmen who used such terms.

From the perspective of connections between places, the issues and conflicts may be analyzed in a number of other ways. With regard to the Civil War, there was for example a question of the nature of political community, of whether the compact of the Constitution was binding on all persons or whether the states were parties to it and could independently dissociate from it. There were in this period networks of transportation and communication which were not urban or rural but were, to a large extent, regionally clustered. There were expressions of class consciousness and of class and race conflict which cut across localities and regions. There were also conflicts between cities, cities and states, religious groups, and older residents and new immigrants.

It is sometimes said that, at their roots, these were conflicts between urban and rural interests, but we should take care not to let such categories hide other issues. For, at the same time, images of what was urban and what was rural were developing, and images tend to persist long after their basis in reality has changed. The urban-rural images of the Civil War and post-War periods seem to have a regional or sectional cast to them; it should be noted, however, that such images are sometimes local interpretations of a situation and sometimes psychological frames of reference that have little to do with either localities or regions.

From any perspective, geographic regions of the United States have had distinct economic bases, and in a given period of time they can be shown to have differed in the focuses and density of their transportation and communications networks, in patterns of population distribution and migration, and in number and kind of urban places. For example, in 1860, when nearly 20 percent of the population of the United States lived in towns of 2,500 or more persons, the figure was only a little over 7 percent in the states that were to form the Southern Confederacy. Highest growth rates were in the West. East of the Mississippi, the population of the

---

[1]"The City in American History," *Mississippi Valley Historical Review*, 27, No. 1 (June; 1940), 43–66. Schlesinger defined a central problem for historians to be one of discovering the persistent interplay of town and country in the evolution of American civilization.

[2]"The Irrepressible Conflict," in *I'll Take My Stand: The South and the Agrarian Tradition* (New York: Harper & Brothers, 1930), pp. 61–91.

southern states (including slaves) was two-fifths that of the northern, and it was generally a more dispersed population. Of the eight port cities with more than 100,000 persons, only one was in the South—New Orleans, center for river traffic and especially for exporting cotton—and even it was coming to depend on New York merchants and financiers, as western farmers were using the railroads to send their produce toward the Atlantic seaboard instead of shipping it down the Mississippi. Port cities were still the largest cities (and commerce was still the source of the largest fortunes), but the fastest-growing ones were those of the western valleys and Great Lakes regions, with railroad ties to the older ocean ports and to hinter-lands, and with manufacturing as good potential for further growth. Sec-ondary centers in the Northeast and Old Northwest were more numerous, more diverse, larger, and faster growing than in the South. The importance of older southern centers, such as Charleston and Baltimore, had been steadily decreasing in relation to them, in terms of population growth rates and value of goods produced and shipped. The market towns at the heads of navigable rivers, the administrative centers, and the crossroads towns of the South were all small. Some railroad connections were being made in the interior—Atlanta, for example, was a center by the mid-1850's, with lines to Charleston, Augusta, Savannah, Montgomery, and Nashville—but there were twenty-one thousand miles of track connecting northeastern and northwestern places as against nine thousand in the South. For such reasons Hinton R. Helper (whose book, *The Impending Crisis of the South*, published in 1857, was burned for its economic indictment of slavery) thought that what the South needed was a great commercial and manu-facturing city.

Such cities were springing up and outward almost overnight in the North and West. Generally, percentage increases in regions as a whole were not as high as in the towns through most of the nineteenth century, and growth rates were greatest in the more newly settled areas and at cen-ters that provided access to them. Thus, as settlers moved down through the Ohio valley, the East-North-Central and East-South-Central census divisions had sharp population rises in the first two decades of the nine-teenth century, and Pittsburgh, Cincinnati, and Louisville grew more than apace. When people moved into Missouri, St. Louis grew. As the Lake region developed, the Lake ports developed: Rochester, Buffalo, Cleve-land, Detroit, Chicago, and Milwaukee maintained growth rates of more than 100 percent for two decades or more. Settlers moved into Iowa, and Des Moines grew; into Minnesota, and St. Paul and Minneapolis grew.

In every region, institutional changes inevitably occurred in the new and growing places. Traditional community institutions were called into question and debate about them helped give a focus to local life. New institutions were tried, including schools, promoted in the East for the West as a way of tying the country closer together; religious organizations such as those that grew out of that special and transitory community of the frontier, the camp meeting; associations based on interests, such as lecture societies, or concerns, such as the abolitionist groups. The very process of forming associations took on a pattern of its own as people moved from place to place; groups came into being almost as though they were the next month's meeting of the ones they left behind. With the multiplication of rural neighborhoods, villages, and towns in the second half of the nineteenth century, kinds of association became identifiable over wide areas. In the 1880's a Russian businessman and writer who ventured a variety of businesses in a variety of American communities described some of the main groups: churches, which he found to be competitive; Masonic lodges; literary, music, singing, reading, and debating clubs—"Every little hamlet inevitably has some such societies; in thickly populated agricultural areas every inhabitant also inevitably belongs to two or three of them"— horse races; yacht clubs; hunting and fishing societies; shooting clubs; lawn-tennis clubs; cricket clubs, and billiard and chess societies. Generalizing, he said:

> The unusual mobility of the American people and their passion for change of residence also foster in strong measure both the diffusion of knowledge and the spirit of general equality. Tens of thousands of people, artisans for the most part, constantly move around over the whole Union. On the road and in the new places, as a result of the national quality of quickness in acquaintanceship, they constantly come in contact with new people, new ideas, and new impressions, which they assimilate very rapidly.[3]

In a mobile population, multiple "voluntary associations" might give a person a sense of his existence in a place. Page Smith has suggested that their proliferation in mid-nineteenth century towns "can best be explained in terms of an effort to recapture that sense of personal involvement which had been so strong in the original covenanted community," that, indeed, "Such a plethora of organizations is obviously a disease of the body politic in communities which have lost all sense of an integrated community life."[4]

---

[3]Tverskoy, pen name for Peter A. Demens, from a travel book published in 1895, excerpted in Oscar Handlin, *This Was America* (New York: Harper & Row, Publishers, 1964), pp. 349–70.

[4]*As a City upon a Hill: The Town in American History* (New York: Alfred A. Knopf, 1966), p. 174. Smith cites Baker Brownell's *The Human Community*, pp. 249–51, for the idea that "as the community declines in significance and holding power the impulse to make formal organizations seems sometimes to go wild." It might be more accurate to say that as traditional forms of association break down, come into question, or simply have not yet been established in a place to which diverse people have migrated, new forms appear, and what they are depends on who and what is available. The old forms may or may not have provided everyone with a "sense of community"; the new forms may or may not provide everyone with a sense of community.

This is hard to substantiate, since many of the joiners had no experience of a covenanted community as established in and carried out from New England, and if such an effort was being made, was it a disease? In any case, an increasingly wide range of choice of associations was becoming available to small-town and rural people, not just to those of the growing urban places. Also, as Smith points out, many of the local clubs and societies had statewide and national affiliation, so that extensive groups were potentially in communication with each other.

Another means of local communication with nonlocal potentials was the newspaper. It extended the range of residents' knowledge about local events, municipal affairs, and regional concerns, and was increasingly important as towns became more than—or were from the beginning something other than—face-to-face associations. In addition, urban papers began to circulate beyond their localities and to distribute the news of an international press.

Politics was still another focus of activity, and national parties extended potentially translocal ties. On the one hand were local leaders dealing with local issues; on the other, state, sectional, and national alignments of groups. Town meetings, conventions, campaigns, and election days were events that could be used to reinforce localism or to bring groups together on nonlocal issues. Often it was a personality that became nationally known through publicity—Andrew Jackson, for example—rather than an issue. Parties did develop around particular issues, however, and from local beginnings sought wider support. There was a short-lived Working Man's Party in eastern towns in the early 1830's, interested in economic reforms and against Jackson. The Liberty Party, abolitionists in the early 1840's who wished to work within existing political structures to effect changes, reached out through the support of nonpolitical organizations. It formed a coalition with splinter groups from both Whigs and Democrats in the Free Soil Party of 1848, opposing extension of slavery into the territories. New alignments came out of debates on the issues of the 1850's: admission of California, territorial organization of Nebraska, rival governments in Kansas, the Dred Scott case, the business panic of 1857, John Brown and Harper's Ferry. In 1860, four parties presented presidential candidates to the electorate, and a majority in the northern states elected Lincoln. To southerners, this was an election by one party in one section, a "combination for the subversion of the Constitution," South Carolinians declared.

It has been said that the immediate cause of the breakdown of the American political system at this point was the breakdown of the party system, that party organizations ceased to play their national roles. It does appear that secession and war occurred when "national" parties failed to hold together. But it can also be argued that the major parties, strong as they were in some states and localities, and capable of maintaining nation-wide contacts, had not yet been able to develop the means of assuring themselves of nation-wide support. For example, the American, or "Know-Nothing,"[5] Party was a nativist movement which had been active in the early 1850's. Then it split over the Nebraska issue and disappeared in many parts of the country, some of its membership returning to the Democratic Party and some supporting candidates of the newly formed Republican Party. But in New Orleans, Know-Nothings succeeded in 1856 in winning the elections for mayor and a few other officers away from the Democrats and a new Whig-reform group, partly by means of terrorizing people at the polls. Before the elections of 1858, they threatened to take the entire city government, and began by lifting the voting lists from the registrar's office. In response, a "Vigilance Committee" formed, and both groups prepared for their own war. They held each other off, but then the Know-Nothings won most of the offices and went on to elect a full ticket in 1860.

Within the framework of the federal government as it worked from 1789 to 1861, politics for most people had to do more with their localities and states than with the nation. Expansion, distance, was one factor (as some Antifederalists had feared when the Constitution was ratified); another was the generally "strict" or narrow interpretation of constitutional provisions with regard to federal powers. The federal administrative machinery had not extended itself in this period, and people looked to their state and local governments for most services. Moreover, there were individuals and families with habits of office holding on the local and state levels who, whether well thought of or badly thought of, were at least known. Often, too, when decisions on the national level appeared to affect an area adversely, its representatives gave voice to state and local interests.

The most important theoretical statement of states' rights was a set of ideas developed by John C. Calhoun that eventually took on the character of a sectional ideology. The Constitution, he said in *The South Carolina Exposition and Protest* (1828), "has formed the States into a community only to the extent of their common interests; leaving them distinct and independent communities as to all other interests."[6] In the debates of 1850, he traced the problems of the country to agitation over slavery and the growth of the North at the expense of the South. These were the recurring themes of southern spokesmen from the 1830's to 1861. From their perceptions not just of sectional differences but also of the power of indus-

---

[5]Given this name from their response to questions on their beliefs: "I know nothing in our principles contrary to the Constitution." In most of the country their attack was directed against foreign-born persons and especially Catholics, but anti-Catholic policies were dropped in Louisiana localities because of the large number of Catholic voters.

[6]*The Works of John C. Calhoun*, ed. Richard K. Crallé, 6 vols. (New York: D. Appleton and Company, 1853–1855), VI, 37.

trialization in nation building, they were developing a concept of political community based on interests. Mississippi's Secession Ordinance declared that the people of the northern states claimed "the right of protection for every species of property owned by themselves" while they forced Congress to a condemnation of the property of southerners (i.e., slaves). Jefferson Davis told the Confederate Congress in 1861 that the original compact between the states for purposes of security against foreign aggression had been perverted by a "political school" in the northern states into "a machine for their control in domestic affairs." Geographic conditions having made slave labor unproductive in the North, they "consulted their own interests by selling their slaves to the South and prohibiting slavery within their limits," and when they had obtained a controlling voice in Congress they proceeded to aggress against the rights of the southern states. In his inaugural address in 1862, Davis said that the Confederacy had been formed to save the South from "despotism of numbers"; in order "to preserve in spirit, as well as in form, a system of government we believed to be peculiarly fitted to our condition, and full of promise for mankind, we determined to make a new association, composed of States homogeneous in interest, in policy and in feeling."[7]

Lincoln's first inaugural address gives the opposing argument. Since ". . . . no government proper ever had a provision in its organic law for its own termination," there was no lawful possibility of disrupting the Union. And if the United States were "an association of States in the nature of contract merely, can it as a contract be peaceably unmade by less than all the parties who made it?" In his opening message to Congress on July 4, 1861, he defined sovereignty as "a political community without a political superior," said that only Texas had ever had this status, and contended that the states had their legal status only within the Union.[8] It followed that if no state could secede from the Union, none could declare war against it—only individuals could take up arms, in an insurrection, and they could be dealt with accordingly. But it took the Fourteenth Amendment to establish the priority of the national community, in that "No State shall make or enforce any law which shall abridge the privileges or immunities of citizens of the United States."

After the Civil War, local politics continued to stimulate lively encounters, and state politics to be a means of access to power, and often of carrying out local interests. But political orientations became less and less tied to local, state, and regional concerns. The origins of the shift lie before the Civil War, in the immigration and migration, the expansion of communications, and the nonlocal associations that have already been

[7]In *Documents of American History*, ed. Henry Steele Commager, 2 vols., 7th ed. (New York: Appleton-Century-Crofts, 1963), I, 389–91, 407–10.
[8]In *Documents of American History*, I, 385–88, 393–95.

mentioned. The aftermath of the war speeded up the process. Not all of the factors contributing to this can be discussed here, but the role of businessmen must be noticed because they set the scene for the growth of urban communities in the South along with their promotion of policies in support of a national community. They also had a way of connecting the rural and the urban, of making different communities dependent on each other. Yet at the same time that ties of interdependency were increasing throughout the country, the images of rural and urban were becoming more distinct, more clearly established, more influential in various kinds of action.

First, northern businessmen relied on a mobile, competitive labor force. Southerners were well aware of this, and used it as a point of attack. The best-known such attack is that of George Fitzhugh, who insisted that wage labor was worse than slave labor because there was no protection if one was old, ill, or out of a job and no recourse for unfair treatment except, in his view, "revolution" to tear apart the social fabric. In *Sociology for the South* (1854) and *Cannibals All! or, Slaves Without Masters* (1857), he argued that only the employers were really free in a "free society." Free laborers were more dependent than slaves, being at the mercy of masters who felt no responsibility for them. He accounted for the rapid growth of northern cities by the homeless workers being driven to them, "to dwell in damp and crowded cellars" and do the menial work that capitalists demanded. The criticisms of social reformers in the North were not so very different in the antebellum period. Parke Godwin, for a time a Fourierist and editor of *The Harbinger*, wrote in *Democracy, Constructive and Pacific* (1844) that when the remains of feudalism had been swept away industry was left without organization for the protection of laborers. Where Fitzhugh would have a slave system recognized for its worth in relationships of master and slaves on a plantation, Godwin would have industry reorganized on a basis of union of interests of capital, labor, and talent, beginning in a township unit where all contributed and were rewarded in terms of their contribution. In both views, a more stable, more organized local community was wanted than industry seemed to provide. But from the point of view of the businessman, there were investments to be made and enterprises to be begun.

In the South, not all were content with a single economic base—the production of staple crops—and diversification was being proposed and tried (it is just as false to picture the antebellum South as one field of cotton or tobacco after another as it is to assume that planter society was southern society). Once new enterprises took hold in the South, their northern promoters and creditors would face the problem of an appropriate labor force. So, possibly, would southern slave owners and supporters of the slave system, for they were not agreed about the tasks to which slaves could be put. .It has been estimated that, in 1860, about half a million bondsmen (one-eighth of the total) lived in towns or were used in something other than agricultural work—in lumbering, turpentine production, sawmills, gristmills, quarries, fisheries, mining, on boats, on roads and bridges, on railroads—and some thought they could be used to build up the industries of the South. Others thought that skills and factory work endangered the "perfect dependence" of the slave; a Virginian said of his bondsmen who were working at an iron furnace that they "got a habit of roaming about and *taking care of themselves*" (italics in original), and another master said that "whenever a slave is made a mechanic, he is more than half freed. Wherever slavery has decayed, the first step . . . has been the elevation of the slaves to the rank of artisans and soldiers."[9] To clarify the matter of a labor force would clearly be to the advantage of investors in the South.

Second, many of the important businessmen of the North were tied to the South before the war and thought it necessary to maintain ties. They urged peace in 1860 and 1861. New York merchants and financiers were especially concerned, since the cotton-carrying trade was important to them and southern planters were heavily in debt to them. Producers and distributors elsewhere feared the loss of southern markets; the Boston *Post* said that they were worth $60,000,000 annually to Boston and that therefore one section could not "live and flourish without the other." Shortly after the election of 1860 a Detroit dry-goods merchant who wished that his fellows would stand on principle said harshly, "From the days of Carthage to those of James Buchanan the great mercantile centres have been peaceable—ever ready . . . to *buy* immunity but not to fight for it."[10] Business leaders attempted to use their influence on Lincoln and other government officials to offer concessions to the South, and when Senator Crittenden's proposals for compromise were being discussed they organized themselves, held mass meetings, and circulated petitions. While southern militia were training at courthouse squares, some of the businessmen advocated letting the states secede in order to avoid the war. Meanwhile, southerners were repudiating their debts, just as they feared, and businesses were failing—more than during the 1857 panic. The South was productive, a special kind of frontier, and conditions there would have to be stabilized, even if only after a war, in order for the business community to extend itself securely.

During the war some business lagged, some industries grew, credit

[9] Kenneth M. Stampp, *The Peculiar Institution: Slavery in the Ante-Bellum South* (New York: Random House, 1956), pp. 64, 147, 398.
[10] Letter from Zachariah Chandler to Lyman Trumbull, quoted in David M. Potter, *Lincoln and His Party in the Secession Crisis* (New Haven: Yale University Press, 1942), p. 116.

facilities grew, and a business-urban base for national politics developed. Commerce was most adversely affected, and would never recover its former position in the economy. The total value of exports and imports shipped in 1865 was 80 percent of what it had been, but that carried in American ships was only 33 percent of what it had been. Heavy industry and manufacturing enterprises expanded, however. Six new foundries were built in Pittsburgh, for example, and nearly two hundred new factories in Philadelphia. Some of the expansion was in response to government needs for munitions, other army equipment, and more rolling stock to carry the larger amounts of freight. Also, production of farm machinery was increased to replace farm labor. Factories began to mechanize, at least those of the firms that could afford it. Many plants were consolidated, and firms merged. Congress provided legislation to encourage industrial growth, such as protective tariffs and national banking acts. New nonlocal trade associations appeared; beginning in the 1840's and 1850's for the purpose of reaching mutually beneficial agreements on markets and prices and dealing with the threat of labor organization, they developed lobbying techniques to influence tax and labor legislation. Railroad companies received federal charters (the Union Pacific's was the first such since 1816), subsidies, and grants of land that amounted to sizeable proportions of some of the western states. The cities sent representatives to Washington seeking support for railroads that would benefit them. Merchants, manufacturers, and bankers combined their efforts in particular localities and across localities, fostering, among other growth measures, the interlocking and consolidation of separate railroad enterprises. A few men, such as Cornelius Vanderbilt, developed rail networks out of such efforts that were independent of any one or a few urban bases—transurban, in effect, though the sources lay in the urban places that had been building up their capital energies over many years. If conditions were right, the South could be included in these and other enterprises.

The third factor in the role of businessmen was their finding a not too many-toned political voice. As a coalition party, Republicans in 1860 had promised a protective tariff, free homesteads, a Pacific railroad, and immigrants' rights in order to draw the votes of both businessmen and farmers. During the war a split appeared, those who fought hardest for emancipation and new institutions for freedmen in the South being grouped as radicals. Among them was Representative Thaddeus Stevens of Pennsylvania, an ironworks owner and lawyer who, in debates over methods of land reform between 1865 and 1867, called for confiscation and redistribution of the lands of "chief rebels." "If the South is ever to be made a safe Republic let her lands be cultivated by the toil of the owners, or the free labor of intelligent citizens. This must be done even though it drive her nobility into exile."[11] But this was not the popular view, then or later. Such a change in landholding patterns would indeed have been revolutionary, whatever means might have been used to achieve it. One of its greatest effects would have been the creation of self-determining communities out of the traditionally dependent communities. Many Republicans, however, limited their attention to the prevention of a revival of agrarian power through the reelection of prewar officeholders, and to the problem of maintaining order. These, rather than basic community changes, seemed the necessary conditions for investment and economic development. That a free labor force and the extension of business connections through the South would ultimately bring about some basic community changes was not thought through; indeed, both northern businessmen and southern landholders acted to delay them.

For all the appeals of "moderate" Republicans in the 1870's, who were inclined to minimize federal intervention in the South, white southern voters felt themselves to be at a disadvantage under Republican leadership. The South did need capital for development, but federal policies just after the war did not substantiate claims of either radical or moderate Republicans that their leadership would bring about economic development. There was also the galling presence of troops, the occupation forces, to be remembered and invoked even when pressing problems had changed. They were reminders of the destruction of the war, after which it seemed impossible to begin again; only a tradition remained—and remnants of a means of staple-crop production. The obvious solution for both small and large planters was to find a way of continuing the tradition. Doing so would depend on obtaining credit, and local and nonlocal sources soon appeared. In the villages and towns, men with small amounts of capital obtained credit from northern financiers that they then extended to planters of the neighborhood. But interest rates were high at every point in the credit arrangements, and small growers ended up heavily in debt, mortgaged, and likely to become part of a spreading pattern of sharecropping and tenant farming. These were, in effect, a continuation of dependent communities.

For the newly freed population, changes in local community life derived less from economic conditions than from the spread of new institutions, including churches and schools. The movement for independent

---

[11]Quoted in Kenneth M. Stampp, *The Era of Reconstruction, 1865–1877* (New York: Vintage Books, 1967), p. 127. Some lands were redistributed toward the end of the War—the sea islands and coastal rice fields of South Carolina and Georgia, and six plantations around Davis Bend, Mississippi—but most were soon restored to their original owners. Such "experiments, orders, and systems were bound to attract and perplex the government and the nation," W. E. B. Du Bois says in his account of backgrounds to the Freedmen's Bureau—itself an experiment with means of community change (see *The Souls of Black Folk* [New York: Fawcett World Library, 1961], pp. 23–41).

churches for blacks had begun in Philadelphia in 1787. Although a number of sects and denominations were represented, Methodists and Baptists formed the main groups. According to Litwak, churches had become the center of the black community by the time of the Civil War. "Encompassing virtually every aspect of Negro life, the church provided innumerable services. In addition to being a center of religious devotion and ceremony, it was a school, a political meeting hall, a community recreation and social center, and, not too infrequently, a haven for fugitive slaves."[12] Opposition to separate churches did appear—in Frederick Douglass' paper *North Star* they were called *"negro pews, on a higher and larger scale,"* which continued the separation begun by enemies; "If there be any good reason for a colored church, the same will hold good in regard to a colored school, and indeed to every other institution founded on complexion."[13] Yet they served to make tangible the local bonds of free blacks in the northern, predominantly white and exclusionary towns and cities, and it was thus that they were carried into the South after emancipation. Along with the impulse toward church organization came mutual aid societies, the insurance and "sickness and burial" societies found mainly, to begin with, in rural areas where people with few means put together a basic form of economic cooperation for some essential aspects of life.

Schools, another potential focus for community life, also spread rapidly during the Reconstruction period. This was partly the result of a kind of missionary activity, such as through the Freedman's Bureau (the New England schoolmarm is the stereotypical image of the period), but it was strongly supported by black leaders who were convinced—as Jefferson had been for whites a century earlier—that schooling was a route toward the political understanding necessary for participation in the rights of citizenship. The Reconstruction governments instituted school systems in the southern states, which had always had far fewer schools than the northern, and the increase in school enrollment rates gives some idea of the changes taking place. In 1860, 1.9 percent of nonwhite children in the entire United States were enrolled (as against 59.6 percent of the white school-aged population); in 1870, 9.9 percent (54.4 for whites); in 1880, 33.8 percent (62.0 for whites). In some places white and black children attended the same schools. In South Carolina's Constitutional Convention in 1868, the black minister and educator, F. L. Cardozo, supporting a measure for public schools, had said in response to an objection that white families would be obliged to send their children to school with blacks: "We only compel parents to send their children to some school, not that

[12]Leon F. Litwak, *North of Slavery: The Negro in the Free States, 1790–1860* (Chicago: The University of Chicago Press, 1961), pp. 187–213 (quotation from p. 188).
[13]*Ibid.*, p. 212.

they shall send them with the colored children; we simply give those colored children who desire to go to white schools, the privilege to do so."[14] But by the end of the century the Supreme Court had extended its "separate but equal" doctrine to schools (Cumming *vs.* County Board of Education, 1899).

Among whites, a "New South" movement got under way about 1880, extending from state governments, where conservatives had gradually resumed power, to towns and villages where industrious persons promoted local enterprise as a solution to a potential unemployment problem: white youth unwilling to work the land on the same terms as the freedmen. There was a "cotton mill campaign" that resulted in more than four hundred new mills by 1900; iron and steel production increased, and southern promoters actively sought northern capital and managers. W. J. Cash compared this movement to "the passage of the great Methodist revivals of the early ninteenth century":

> At Salisbury, North Carolina, one Mr. Pearson, holding a revival meeting in an improvised tabernacle, preaches "powerfully" on the plight of the poor whites, declares that "the establishment of a cotton mill would be the most Christian act his hearers could perform"—and next evening at a great mass meeting the village's first mill is actually organized, with another minister at its head. . . .
>
> The impulse leaps from community to community . . . stirring up the old local patriotism so characteristic of the South and setting these communities to striving to outdo one another in furthering the cause, proceeding on a wave of enthusiasm so intense and so general that in many places where poverty is most rampant, where it seems almost impossible to raise sufficient money to launch a mill, it actually sets yeoman farmers, too poor as individuals to provide even so much as a single share of capital, to combining in groups of a dozen for the purpose; sets laborers to forming pools into which each man pays as little as twenty-five cents a week.

He quotes the North Carolina editor, Gerald W. Johnson, to the effect that hamlets built mills without investigating the advantages of the locality for textile manufacturing, and the community leaders—doctors, lawyers, teachers, planters, and even clergymen—were urged to run the new enterprises simply because they were community leaders. "The main thing was the salvation of the decaying community. . ."[15]

The great majority of the population of the southern states continued to be occupied with agriculture. Only a few centers became industrially

---

[14]In *The Origins of Segregation*, ed. Joel Williamson (Boston: D. C. Heath and Company, 1968), pp. 55–61.

[15]W. J. Cash, *The Mind of the South* (New York: Alfred A. Knopf, Inc., 1941), pp. 181–82. See also Broadus Mitchell, *The Rise of Cotton Mills in the South* (Baltimore: The Johns Hopkins Press, 1921).

important. Birmingham, Alabama, founded in 1871, became an iron and steel center, but until after the second world war it was a rare example of industrial centralization in the South. The cotton textile industry, according to Rudolf Heberle, "had its main period of growth in the South at a time when electrification together with a relatively ample labor supply in rural areas made concentration in large cities unnecessary and decentralization in small urban communities possible."[16] The population centers of the South were relatively small commercial and service centers, county seats and capitals, and processing centers for lumber, oil, and agricultural products. In 1880, thirty-one had more than 10,000 inhabitants, and the important ones were still essentially commercial: New Orleans, Louisville, Richmond, Atlanta, Charleston. In that census, when more than 28 percent of the population of the United States as a whole lived in places defined as urban, 9.4 percent of those in the southern states were urban residents; in 1890, proportions were about 35 percent for the United States and 13 per cent for the southern states. Inland towns began growing along railroad lines, and gradually manufacturing was added to the older commercial centers. But in 1900 only a little more than 10 percent of the labor force in the South was engaged in manufacturing enterprises, as compared with almost 30 percent in other areas, and more than 60 percent worked in agriculture, forestry, and fishing as compared to 25 percent outside the South.

Relatively slow as they seem, changes in agricultural life were occurring in the South. Yet an ideal of an "Old South" remained. Southern novelists began writing of the decay of the old aristocracy, but in 1930 a wide-ranging defense of the southern way of life appeared, *I'll Take My Stand*, put together by twelve major writers. From the introduction: "The younger Southerners, who are being converted frequently to the industrial gospel, must come back to the support of the Southern tradition. They must be persuaded to look very critically at the advantages of becoming a 'new South' which will be only an undistinguished replica of the usual industrial community."[17]

Meanwhile, the post-Civil War period was in general a time of great population movement, business expansion in all directions (including outside the country's boundaries), and complex political associations on local and nonlocal levels. Issues on the federal level after the war did not range people neatly along one or the other party line. As had happened before,

[16]"The Mainsprings of Southern Urbanization," in Rupert B. Vance and Nicholas J. Demerath, eds., *The Urban South* (Chapel Hill: The University of North Carolina Press, 1954), p. 15. This study presents a theoretical framework for the role of industry in urban development. The collection as a whole is useful for understanding urbanization in the context of recent and on-going changes in a particular region.

[17]*I'll Take My Stand* (New York: Harper & Brothers, 1930), pp. x–xi.

particular questions of program or policy stimulated formation of short-lived parties which split, merged, and split again as time passed and the questions changed or were posed in different ways.

Some of these questions appeared to divide the country into rural and urban sections. Tariffs, trusts, railroad monopolies, taxation, interest rates, the national banking system and money policies were issues on which opinions were expressed by farmers' organizations. Discontent of farmers over their poor position in relation to manufacturers and financiers resulted in local associations, regionally strong alliances, and, in the 1890's, a third-party challenge. It has been said that the farmers' movement, from Grange beginnings (1867) to the formation of the People's party (Populists, 1892) was inspired by an agrarian tradition developed in the colonial and antebellum periods; a tradition of agriculture essential to the good life and responsible political community, of "natural" land and "natural" hands working it, of antagonism to those, especially merchants and bankers, whose income seemed ultimately dependent on and yet was a step removed from the land. An interdependent development of urban and rural, and eastern and western, radical opinion in the nineteenth century has, however, been studied.[18] One issue, by way of example, is that of monopolies. Resentment against monopolistic practices of railroads was shared by western merchants, eastern importers and shippers, producers and refiners in the Pennsylvania oil region, laboring men, and western farmers. The cooperative movement also cut across regions and classes. Ideas of cooperation in one form or another had been around a long time; after the Civil War a few consumers' and producers' cooperatives were begun in eastern towns and in the Ohio Valley. Grangers then took up the plan. By the 1890's cooperative colonies had been begun in Georgia, Alabama, and Colorado, and collective enterprises were being talked about at farmers' meetings throughout the country.

Short of instituting new cooperative colonies, farmers found in local political associations a meeting ground that was not the same as either neighborhood or nation. The rallies, the conventions, the picnics began to bring them together in a yet-undefined community. Newspapers for agricultural and rural audiences acquired wide circulation. The local and state groups combined into regional organizations, and in 1889 the Northern and Southern Alliances sent delegates to a general convention at St. Louis with the Knights of Labor, the Farmers' Mutual Benefit Association, and the Colored Alliance to discuss common action. One of the issues that prevented their uniting at this time was the status of black representatives; the Southern Alliance, in some ways the strongest of these groups, insisted that even if particular states admitted them to their organ-

---

[18]Chester McArthur Destler, "Western Radicalism, 1865–1901: Concepts and Origins," *Mississippi Valley Historical Review*, 31, No. 3 (December, 1944), 335–68.

izations only white persons should serve on the national council. Despite these differences, and the ideological differences separating socialist members from the rest and labor organizations from the rest, a new national party was in the process of formation. Militants from the midwestern states called for another convention, and, in 1892, a platform for a People's party was drawn up. The planks included union of rural and urban labor forces, regulation of civil service, unlimited coinage of silver and gold, a graduated income tax, and government ownership of railroads, telegraph, and telephone. The platform committee also passed resolutions favoring the initiative and referendum system of legislation and the direct election of senators. The party organization dissolved during the fight over whether to support Bryan in 1896, but some of its ideas remained alive—and it would never again be just to say that American farmers were politically isolated.

Finally, outside the South the pace of industrial urbanization was increasing. Steam, oil, and electric power made possible a greater concentration of industry and with it a greater concentration of laborers and supporting service enterprises. This is the period of the "rise of the city" for urban historians.[19] The scene described by an Austrian diplomat in 1871 happened to be of Chicago, but it was to be described again and again, by others, elsewhere, ten, twenty, fifty years later:

> ... I stroll about the streets. The heat is intolerable and the first sight of Chicago is not encouraging to an idle man. It is closing time in the shops and factories. Streams of workmen—men, women, shop boys, merchants of all kinds—pass me on foot, in omnibuses, in trams, all going in the same direction, that is, all making their way to their little homes outside the town proper. All look sad, preoccupied, and worn out with fatigue.
>
> The streets are like all others in America. The houses are built of wood, but in imitation of brick and stone. Clouds of coal smoke issue from innumerable factory chimneys, accumulate in the streets, throw dark shadows on the brilliant shop fronts and on the gorgeous gold letters of the advertisements which cover the facades up to the garrets. The soot seems to stifle the crowds, who, with bent heads, measured steps, and arms swinging like the pendulum of a clock, fly in silence from the spots in which they have labored all day long in the sweat of their brows. In all the great thoroughfares, as far as one can see, rise the gigantic telegraph poles, placed quite close to one another, and topped by a double bishop's cross—the only kind of cross seen in this city of which the God is money.

[19]Urban history is a fairly recent field of study for United States historians, but several surveys are available. The first major one is Arthur M. Schlesinger, *The Rise of the City: 1878–1898* (New York: The Macmillan Company, 1933). More recent ones include Blake McKelvey, *The Urbanization of America (1860–1915)*, (New Brunswick, N.J.: Rutgers University Press, 1963), and *The Emergence of Metropolitan America: 1915–1966* (New Brunswick, N.J.: Rutgers University Press, 1968); Constance McLaughlin Green, *The Rise of Urban America* (New York: Harper & Row, Publishers, 1965); and Charles N. Glaab and Theodore Brown, *A History of Urban America* (New York: The Macmillan Company, 1967).

I mix with the crowd, which drags me on with it. I strive to read the faces I pass, and everywhere meet the same expression. Every man is in a hurry, if only to get a few minutes sooner to his home to make the most of the few hours of rest, after having expended the largest possible amount of work in the long hours of labor. Everyone seems to dread a rival in his neighbor. The crowd is the embodiment of isolation.[20]

Chicago's growth in population seemed phenomenal: from less than 5,000 in 1840, to nearly 300,000 in 1870 and 1,700,000 at the turn of the century. New York, Philadelphia, Pittsburgh, and the midwestern and farwestern towns grew dramatically too. In 1860 only nine cities in the United States had populations of more than 100,000; by 1910, there were fifty. Rates of growth of urban places taken together, however, were actually slower between 1870 and 1910 than they had been in the 1840's. It was the great size and the functional and social changes that drew attention to them. Although commercial and administrative centers grew too, the most-noticed places were those in which manufacturing establishments and related service activities were concentrated. Regionally, growth rates were lower in New England and the Middle Atlantic states than in more newly settled areas of the country, but an "urban hierarchy" was already observable in 1870—dominant regional metropolises supported by smaller centers which were in turn supported by a number of surrounding small cities.[21] Chicago's development from wheat exporter to railroad center to commercial-industrial-financial center, all within about fifty years, placed it in a dominant position in the midwest, a position from which other kinds of activities (including argricultural) could be stimulated and subcenters encouraged. Seen in a historical context of population concentrations in the United States, these regional clusters were nothing new except in total numbers. It was not size alone that made them different, nor their relation to other places. The old urban boosters with their talk of Athens and Rome were being countered by people who drew their images from Manchester and hell. From "busy haunts of men ... the proper school of political talents," cities had become places for "ignorant masses," "political bosses," "vicious pleasures," isolation in a crowd. At the same time, painters were exhibiting country estates, New England school children, waterfalls, mountainsides with mystical towns across the river, in the distance—or living in Europe.

[20]The Baron von Hübner, *Promenade autour du monde, 1871* (1873), as excerpted in Oscar Handlin, *This Was America* (New York: Harper & Row, Publishers, 1949), p. 302.

[21]Harvey S. Perloff, Edgar S. Dunn, Jr., Eric E. Lampard, and Richard F. Muth, *Regions, Resources, and Economic Growth* (Baltimore: The Johns Hopkins Press, 1960), pp. 15–23.

9

Community Images And Analyses

*"What language about the community
(or other human whole) conveys what kind
of understanding about it?"*

—ROBERT REDFIELD

In the periods considered up to this point, "community" was not being used as an explanatory concept. It referred to localities in which people lived and worked and to jurisdictions—an area of municipal government, for example, and the people and activities comprised within it. It was used also for the jurisdiction of the federal government, and in this regard more than one interpretation had appeared: "Community" could be either a given condition of the United States Constitution or an expression of a bonding of interests. The significance of this difference in interpretation should be clear. If political community has a specific origin in the act of constituting a government, then an explicit authority resides in that constitution and alternatives to that authority lie outside it. If, however, political community is a combination of interests, or a way of perceiving mutual interests, then the alternatives are matters of power—power to give particular interests a voice, or to make them dominate others—and the struggles proceed on the level of who has access to power. The Civil War kept the southern states in the Union, but it did not bring about an agreement on the interpretation of political community (if anything, the South won this point in the sense that, over time, more and more people have adopted views of "interests" and "power").

Beginning in the late nineteenth century, the concept of community began to be used to explain behavior. Gradually it was turned into an analytic concept, an expression of a particular dimension of human behavior that could be studied in its own right, on its own terms, distinct from (though not without the interaction and influence of) other aspects of life. As such, it showed a variety in local form and organization and suggested ways of comparing and evaluating them. Interestingly, the "scientific" statements of students of community well into the twentieth century resembled popular images of different places. Also interesting is the strengthening of type-images of places just when they were becoming more subject to nonlocal forces for change, growth, and dependence on each other. Rural and urban are the broadest categories (as vague for scientists as for laymen), then city, small town, and countryside. Each impossible without the others, each excited judgments about the others. The judgments were often a spur to local change, even reform. They also affected state legislators' decisions on local charters, finances, and taxation. In a historical context of urban processes (see pp. 8–9), the type-images were at cross-purposes. Yet in one form or another they are still with us, with the addition, now, of at least one major new one: the suburb. These images must be recognized for what they are. Their derivations are important, too, for the discovery of trends, and, although they cannot be completely traced in this kind of survey, lines of derivation will be suggested.

In the 1870's social critics turned their attention to the American city, especially to its less savory parts: its slums, obvious poverty (that of stomach equated with that of soul), wretched entertainments. At the same time, unkind things were being said about small towns and rural neighborhoods. The attention given to cities, the energy with which urban life was raked over for the next forty or so years, has obscured contemporaneous criticism of rural areas and small towns. Perhaps the very amount of writing on cities has led historians to ignore the frequency of references to backwaters, dead towns, country bumpkins, hicks, and cottonseeds, and that the word farmer was not always used in an adulatory way. In any case, it is the "anti-urban" tradition that has been most studied. David R. Weimer, in the collection *City and Country in America*,[1] identifies three main traditions that appear to have informed American attitudes toward cities: (1) devotion to nature, or agrarianism (from Crèvecoeur and Jefferson to Frank Lloyd Wright and Baker Brownell), (2) urbanism (mostly among urban planners before World War I, and then as represented by Robert Moses, Christopher Tunnard, and critics who would rebuild cities), and (3) regionalism (the Regional Planning Association of America in the 1920's, with Clarence Stein, Henry Wright, Lewis Mumford, and

[1]New York: Appleton-Century-Crofts, 1962.

Benton Mackaye) and a few other syntheses (such as in Clarence Perry's "neighborhood" idea and the Goodmans' "communitas"). Morton and Lucia White, in *The Intellectual Versus the City*, find anti-urbanism in general to be a "powerful tradition . . . in the history of American thought" and suggest that a contemporary urbanist must either ignore criticisms of the city or see some wisdom in them, the "sometimes justified, sometimes baseless, fear and anxiety about urbanization."[2] They point out that the nature of the city has changed greatly since American writers first began to respond to it; that a definition of the term is hard to come by; yet that writers have been persistently critical of specific places such as Boston, New York, Chicago. As they indicate, however, America's reaction to the city is not necessarily embodied in the works of writers. People who live and work in the cities, or in the countryside, do not always do so either out of thoughtful regard for the advantages of the place or under duress of economic or other need. Many Americans have rejected or accepted what they perceived of urbanization without any reference to a particular place. Glaab and Brown, in *A History of Urban America*, argue that "a basically anti-urban tradition does not stand the test of historical analysis." They cite the complexities of popular thought, sectional considerations, attacks on some features of the city along with defense of others (for one, the industrial machine repels but cultural opportunities attract), and anti-Europeanism. In many of their quotations of views from the first half of the nineteenth century the city appears as an expression of the best as well as the worst potentials of civilization. They say that "if the city as a place to live was viewed as inherently unhealthy, the desirability of the city as an institution for the promotion of economic activity was seldom questioned."[3]

In the nineteenth century, attacks on urban places were made in legislatures, churches, literature, and farmers' journals. Support for them sometimes appeared in the same places, as well as in travel accounts, geographic studies, and promotions of particular towns. By the early twentieth century, views could be informed by special sociological studies, but ambivalence persisted. It appears sometimes directly and sometimes obliquely in writings about small towns. Twentieth-century America wept over Sherwood Anderson's spinster librarians and elm leaves in the streets and tiny newspaper offices where someone reached for a wider world. Poets and storytellers, sociologists, and reformers looked at a small-town America while they lived in urban America, and it is hard to know which child is father to the man. There were small towns in the late nineteenth and early twentieth centuries; wholesalers, retailers, bankers, and editors hoped they would grow, busied themselves to help make them grow, and their frustrations were recorded by their sons and daughters in stories and

[2]New York: The New American Library, 1964, p. 15.
[3]New York: The Macmillan Company, 1967, pp. 53–81.

plays through the 1930's. There were cities that did grow, many of them with quiet, elm-lined streets and Sunday afternoon lemonade-drinking neighborhoods not so different from the small towns as they came to be remembered; others, and sometimes the very same ones, where carts and wagons clattered and street railways groaned on curves and people complained of the noxious fumes of coal-burning factories and the "neurasthenias" resulting from busyness and frustrations.

An image of village life was kept alive while actual villages were being described as dull, dusty of street and mind, half-empty and confining for those left in them. The stories are not without sympathy for the places and the people; Sarah Orne Jewett's *Deephaven*, Mary E. Wilkins Freeman's *Pembroke* are examples from New England. But some towns were being depopulated while some were adding new businesses and growing, and stories of growth and change and failure and abandonment of places are repeated from east to west. In 1882 Mark Twain went up the river to Minneapolis and marveled at the energy with which the land was being settled:

> From St. Louis northward there are all the enlivening signs of the presence of active, energetic, intelligent, prosperous, practical nineteenth-century populations. The people don't dream; they work. The happy result is manifest all around in the substantial outside aspect of things, and the suggestions of wholesome life and comfort that everywhere appear.[4]

Between rapidly growing river towns is a tranquil and reposeful landscape, that is, "until the unholy train comes tearing along," the train that is wreaking havoc with steamboat commerce. The same year (1882), Edgar Watson Howe published his *Story of a Country Town*, Fairview, Missouri, where people worked hard and grasped at religion and desperately sought to fill some void. In 1891 Hamlin Garland described the *Main-Travelled Roads* of Wisconsin, Iowa, and Dakota territory, beginning the collection of stories:

> The main-travelled road in the West (as everywhere) is hot and dusty in summer, and desolate and dread with mud in fall and spring, and in winter the winds sweep the snow across it; but it does sometimes cross a rich meadow where the songs of the larks and bobolinks and blackbirds are tangled. Follow it far enough, it may lead past a bend in the river where the water laughs eternally over its shallows.
>
> Mainly it is long and wearyful, and has a dull little town at one end and a home of toil at the other. Like the main-travelled road of life it is traversed by many classes of people, but the poor and the weary predominate.[5]

[4]*Life on the Mississippi* (New York: Bantam Books, 1945), p. 384.
[5]Greenwich, Conn.: Fawcett Publications, Inc., 1961, p. 12.

But, like a return to the scene of the crime, Garland does, must, go back in his mind to those dull little towns and homes of toil. Recall the British officer at Fort Pitt, who said that Americans have no attachment to place. There is attachment. It may be precisely the people who move about who take the view Howells took in his *Suburban Sketches* (1875): He "would not willingly repose upon the friendship of a man whose local attachments are weak," and as proof of his sensibility and constancy he would expect his friend to show "a sentiment for the place where one has lived two or three years, the hotel where one has spent a week, the sleeping car in which one has ridden from Albany to Buffalo."[6] A mental image of a small, close community is also an attachment, for all that it is only to a place of the mind.

The most pervasive such image in the United States has been of the New England village and township. It was a model for a few writers in the early nineteenth century, and remnants of ideals related to that model persisted when people looked at cities and countrysides later on. Jefferson's formulation sets out the political outlines as he saw them in 1816. Within federal, state, and county jurisdictions is a unit of direct participation: the township, "the vital principle of [New Englanders'] governments, [which] have proved themselves the wisest invention ever devised by the wit of man for the perfect exercise of self-government, and for its preservation.[7] Timothy Dwight's view in 1821 has already been cited (see footnote 47, pp. 92–93); it adds a feeling for social advantages in close local relationships, such advantages as shared sentiments and the support of churches and schools. Alexis de Tocqueville, visitor in 1831 and 1832, whose *Democracy in America* is still required reading in many undergraduate history and political science courses, saw the township both as a fundamental unit for the principles and practices of a wider government and as the home of acceptable private interests. Universally,

> The village or township is the only association which is so perfectly natural that, wherever a number of men are collected, it seems to constitute itself. . . . Town meetings are to liberty what primary schools are to science; they bring it within the people's reach, they teach men how to use and how to enjoy it.

Tocqueville believed that local units were prior and primary to wider governments and in New England were essentially autonomous in local affairs.

---

[6]Quoted in Morton and Lucia White, *The Intellectual Versus the City*, p. 106.
[7]Jefferson to Samuel Kercheval (July 12, 1816), *The Works of Thomas Jefferson*, ed. Paul Leicester Ford, 12 vols. (New York: G. P. Putnam's Sons, 1904–05), XII, 8–9. This is the same letter in which he asserts that every generation has "a right to choose for itself the form of government it believes most promotive of its own happiness" and should be enabled to do so "every nineteen or twenty years."

Thus a New Englander would be attached to his township not by birth so much as "because it is a free and strong community, of which he is a member, and which deserves the care spent in managing it."[8]

These three views have in common hopes of involvement in the concerns of a locality and imply a relation between involvement and the strength of the local community. That the image of the New England town included such hopes and implications does not mean that New England towns were the source of them, however—at least they were not the only source. The general conception has a long socio-philosophical history. Peter Laslett has suggested that the Greek and post-Renaissance philosophers who form the matrix of Western political thinking based their analyses on the intuitive psychology of face-to-face relationships: "The whole of Greek political thought was conditioned by the fact that the polis was a political society which was also a face to face society. . . . Its activities could be carried on by conversation between all of its citizens, who could, if need be, assemble as a whole for the purpose."[9] Since the household was the primary location of regular face-to-face contacts and implicitly understood authority, it readily presented itself to social philosophers as a model for society. Among the nineteenth-century founders of modern sociology, Comte, for example, regarded the family as the unit and model of all other forms of society. Robert A. Nisbet, in his conceptually important study *The Quest for Community*, has described the emphasis of these "philosophical conservatives" on traditional, small units of association as a reaction to what was perceived as disorganization and insecurity resulting from the French Revolution. To them, the Revolution came to represent social atomism and political power, the outcome of the rationalistic individualism of the Enlightenment and the precursor of forces "which, if unchecked, would in time disorganize the whole moral order of Christian Europe and lead to control by the masses and to despotic power without precedent." Thus they stressed "not the abstract individual and impersonal relations of contract but personality inextricably bound to the small social group." They held the family, religious association, and local community to be prior to the individual and thus "the indispensable supports of belief and conduct. Release man from the contexts of community and you get not freedom and rights but intolerable aloneness and subjection to demonic fears and passions."[10]

American social theorists of the late nineteenth and early twentieth

---

[8]Tr. Henry Reeve, ed. Phillips Bradley, 2 vols. (New York: Vintage Books, 1955), I, 62:71.

[9]"The Face to Face Society," in *Philosophy, Politics and Society* [first series], ed. Peter Laslett (New York: The Macmillan Company, 1956), pp. 162–63.

[10]New York: Oxford University Press, 1953 (republished as *Community and Power* in 1962); pp. 24–25.

centuries also assumed the essentiality of small social groups; many based their analyses of society on the workings of what they saw to be basic social units. These, they said, had only to be understood and reinforced in order to resolve society's ills. Charles Horton Cooley, one of the most important theorists of the time in terms of his influence on American sociology, found the basic unit to be the "primary group":

> Life in the primary groups gives rise to social ideals which, as they spring from similar experiences, have much in common throughout the human race. And these naturally become the motive and test of social progress. Under all systems men strive, however blindly, to realize objects suggested by the familiar experience of primary association.
>
> Where do we get our notions of love, freedom, justice, and the like which we are ever applying to social institutions? Not from abstract philosophy, surely, but from the actual life of simple and widespread forms of society, like the family or the play-group.

He called the "ideal of moral unity" the "mother" of all social ideals and said that "a congenial family life is the immemorial type" of it, being the source of such terms as "brotherhood" and "kindness" that describe it. He lamented that "the intimacy of the neighborhood has been broken up by the growth of an intricate mesh of wider contacts which leaves us strangers to people who live in the same house."[11] Studies of American society long reflected this view. From one study published just after the depression years:

> In earlier, simpler societies, the local community was equally as important as the family and religious institutions in supplying the individual with a sense of basic common values.... Each member of the community was accorded his place in the whole through the operation of accepted principles. He felt himself a member of a moral community....
>
> This type of local community has practically vanished in America. One may find it exemplified perhaps in a few isolated villages, but the great bulk of our citizens come under its influence no longer. The improvements in communication and transportation, the growth of large-scale capitalism, and increasing social differentiation have produced a type of life antithetical to this old-fashioned community. Even farmers no longer find their recreation together in a country neighborhood but come to town to enjoy the movies or the picnics provided by enterprising business men.[12]

During the westward movement, of course, picnics and celebrations were being sponsored by "enterprising" land speculators and tradesmen,

---

[11]*Social Organization: A Study of the Larger Mind* (Glencoe, Ill.: The Free Press, 1956; first published 1909), pp. 26, 32, 34, 35.
[12]Robert C. Angell, *The Integration of American Society* (New York: Mc-Graw-Hill Book Company, 1941), p. 190.

and, repeatedly, close life in a rural neighborhood or small town was discomforting to inhabitants who felt lonely or lost or bored with hard work of just one kind or who tried to resist the pressures toward conformity. The point here, however, has to do with the concept of the social unit. It involves both a judgment about society and a means to analyze it. If society is ideally made up of familial local units, and one has only to go over the hill to grandmother's house, then—for just one example of a problem perceived as such in this period—the diversity represented by immigrants, strangers in the land, is disturbing.

Physical aspects of the village and township image also had influence, apart from the social and political aspects noted above. The basic plan had a central public space, or commons, and buildings and residences within calling distance or closer. Andrew Jackson Downing, a New Yorker, described it as an ideal in the 1850's, with broad, maple- and elm-lined streets, cleanliness, no pigs and geese at large, pretty rural lanes, flower gardens, and orchards—all as in Massachusetts. He was incredulous that, given the vastness of the territory of the United States and the wonderful growth of new towns and states, there was no planning, and in the villages that were actually planned and laid out in advance by land companies, residents had little access to open space.

> The indispensable desiderata in rural villages . . . are the following: 1st, a large open space, common, or park, situated in the middle of the village—not less than twenty acres; and better, if fifty or more in extent. This should be well planted with groups of trees, and kept as a lawn. . . .
> This park would be the nucleus or *heart of the village*, and would give it an essentially rural character. Around it should be grouped all the best cottages and residences of the place; and this would be secured by selling no lots fronting upon it of less than one-fourth of an acre in extent. Wide streets, with rows of elms or maples, should diverge from the park on each side, and upon these streets smaller lots, but not smaller than one hundred feet front, should be sold for smaller cottages.[13]

Toward the end of the century social critics reiterated these themes. Henry George, for example, in *Progress and Poverty* (1879), supported his single-tax plan partly with the argument that it would dissolve the large cities and distribute the population (both urban and rural) more naturally in villages. William Dean Howells, in his utopian novels (*A Traveler from Alturia* and *Through the Eye of the Needle*), described "capitals"—administrative and cultural centers—in place of cities, one for each region and one for the whole commonwealth, but the ideal was the village. "The outlying farms have been gathered into these, and now there is not one of

---

[13]"Our Country Villages," in *Rural Essays*, ed. George William Curtis (New York: Leavitt and Allen, 1857), pp. 236–43.

those lonely places in the country, like those where our farmers toil alone outdoors and their wives alone indoors, and both go mad so often in the solitude. The villages are almost in sight of each other, and the people go to their fields in company, while the women carry on their housekeeping cooperatively. . ."[14]

Scholarly histories of the village in America were done in this end-of-century period,[15] and the first survey of urbanization appeared then too: Adna Weber's *The Growth of Cities in the Nineteenth Century*. This work was comparative and statistical and included, interestingly, an attempt to correct some of the popular impressions of urban as compared to non-urban life.

> The amount of viciousness and criminality in cities is probably exaggerated in popular estimation from the fact that the cities have long been under the blaze of an Argus-eyed press, so that the worst is known about them. They have hitherto overshadowed the evils in the moral life of villages, but several recent rural crimes of unwonted atrocity have awakened in the nation a truer realization of the actual facts. Many sociologists have also realized that the rural center is not so "idyllic" as has been imagined.[16]

A like conclusion, by the way, had been reached nearly three centuries earlier by the London dramatist, Thomas Dekker: "I have heard of no sin in the city, but I met it in the village, nor any vice in the tradesman, which was not in the ploughman."

Many active efforts to reform society in this period had inspiration from assumptions similar to those of the New England model. Urban reformers generally tried to create an integral set of associations for people and/or an institutional focus, a way of bringing people together for particular purposes. The main frameworks they used were religious organizations, settlement houses, and schools. It is significant that, for each, the urban setting as it was, with its problems of destitution, disease, and disillusionment, was the setting for the effort.

The Young Men's Christian Association was transplanted from England to America in 1851 with the purpose of converting the youth adrift

---

[14]*Through the Eye of the Needle* (New York: Harper and Brothers, 1907), p. 178.

[15]Examples: H. B. Adams, "The Germanic Origin of New England Towns," Johns Hopkins University Studies in Historical and Political Science, I (1882), 5–38; Charles M. Andrews, "The River Towns of Connecticut," Johns Hopkins University Studies in Historical and Political Science, 7th Ser., VII-VIII-IX (1889); Irving Elting, "Dutch Village Communities on the Hudson River," Johns Hopkins University Studies in Historical and Political Science, IV (1886); Anne B. MacLear, "Early New England Towns: A Comparative Study of Their Development," Columbia University Studies in History, Economics and Public Law, XXIX (1908).

[16]Ithaca, N.Y.: Cornell University Press, 1963 (first published 1899), p. 407.

in cities. The Young Women's Christian Association followed in 1858. By the 1880's, both were providing training and social facilities to supplement the religious emphasis as thought necessary in an urban environment. Protestant denominations formed youth groups with similar aims: to insure the survival of religion in what was seen as an irreligious setting by creating local social and "moral" opportunities. The extradenominational Salvation Army concentrated on regeneration of down-and-out people, and apparently the officers in this semimilitary organization could find a sense of purpose and participation—perhaps even of community—in seeking out the "low" places of the cities. The effects of the depressions of 1873 and 1893 repelled and at the same time turned others into direct-action reformers within their own church groups, as well as in these non-church organizations. Some part of heaven could be planned on earth, particularly where people were poor. A "social gospel" movement spread among both Catholics and Protestants, with influence from English Christian Socialists. Some Catholics took a new look at the precapitalistic organization of the guild, with its emphasis on the common good, justice for the whole community of members, and minimization of competition. Others followed Monsignor John A. Ryan, an economist, professor at Catholic University, and first director of the social action department of the National Catholic Welfare Conference, in promoting social work and advocating social legislation, especially a minimum wage. Protestant denominations also set up labor and welfare departments and social- and self-help programs. Some clergymen, among whom the best known is Walter Rauschenbusch, wrote and taught widely that Christian principles were cooperative, collectivist principles.

In 1908, twenty-five national Protestant denominations, representing black as well as white churches—perhaps two-thirds of the Protestants in the United States—formed the Federal Council of the Churches of Christ in America, with local and state councils that were in effect action groups, committed to work on labor relations, welfare legislation, philanthropy, and evangelism. This first major instance of interdenominationalism in America was an urban phenomenon, a product of and responsive to urban problems. In its focus on urban problems, it had been forecast in 1872 by the Congregational church leader and founder of the Children's Aid Society, Charles Loring Brace, who wrote that poverty and wretchedness in cities bred not only crime but also a potential for revolutionary violence. The remedy, he thought, would be to form a general organization, with state aid, to study and work on the evils and to spread a nonsectarian Christianity along with charity.[17] Sectarianism, characteristic of an agri-

---

[17]*The Dangerous Classes of New York and Twenty Years' Work Among Them* (New York: Wynkoop & Hallenbeck, Publishers, 1872).

cultural society and its relatively dispersed, less clearly connected communities, became less important; new small sects continued to form in various localities (urban and rural) but did not achieve the wide-ranging support that had turned earlier ones into denominations. Locally, religious groups brought people together at socio-religious centers in urban areas; the trend was not necessarily to diminish the significance of the locality, but certainly to bring local groups into association with each other.[18]

Part of the movement, in its local manifestations, became known by the term *institutional church*. This was a kind of settlement house (see below), the facilities of which were those of a church. Josiah Strong thought it would solve urban problems—the city could not be saved without religion for all the statistical and other sciences being devoted to those problems (Y.M.C.A. and church groups had been making surveys of their members and localities and thus, incidentally, helping to spread the gospel of community study through data collection and documentation). In *The Challenge of the* City (1907), he said of St. Bartholomew's of New York that there was "no better illustration of a socialized church adapting itself to the varied needs of the heterogeneous population of an American city." It was "Americanizing" people, it was running an industrial school, doing rescue mission work, sponsoring classes and clinics, an employment bureau, and a loan association.[19]

The settlement-house idea had direct origins in England and was indirectly influenced by on-going religious and charity activities in the United States. Jane Addams, who had been raised in an Illinois village, visited Toynbee Hall in London's East End in the 1880's and on her return began the Hull-House settlement in Chicago, in an old mansion on South Halsted Street, a slum district. About the same time, Stanton Coit established the Neighborhood Guild (University Settlement) in New York's East Side. Within the next fifteen years about one hundred settlement houses had come into existence in the cities of the United States. They were meant to be community centers and more. Their founders (mostly middle-class) attempted to provide the social amenities they thought were needed in the neighborhood as well as facilities requested for meetings, child care, legal aid, and the like. Bremner says that ideally the settlement house was not an institution but a home, an annex to drab tenement flats. Quoting Graham Taylor of the Chicago Commons: "Its books and pic-

---

[18]Will Herberg discusses religion in relation to society in the United States in terms of a "triple melting pot," "three great communities with religious labels, defining three great 'communions' or 'faiths' as a source of self-identification." The social-consciousness in the period discussed here was, in his view, part of the process whereby these larger "communities" of identification developed (*Protestant—Catholic—Jew: An Essay in American Religious Sociology*, rev. ed. [Garden City, N.Y.: Doubleday & Company, Inc., 1960]).

[19]New York, 1907.

tures, the nursery and play space, the lobby and the parlor, the music and flowers, the cheery fireplace and lamp, the dancing floor and place of assembly, are an extension of the all-too-scant home equipment of its neighbors."[20] The municipal reformer Frederic Howe said that women like Jane Addams reduced the questions of urban life to questions of family happiness and safety. Robert Woods, however, who spent most of his life in settlement work in Boston, phrased a theoretical rationale in 1898 that emphasized ideas of integrity of local institutions. He said that relief giving did not get at the causes of poverty but that "the really vital policy—within the lines of local action—is the one which aims to build up a better life for the district out of its own material and by means of its own reserve of vitality." Employment assistance and child care were important, but the goals of settlement work were chiefly

> to reestablish on a natural basis those social relations which modern city life has thrown into confusion, and to develop such new form of cooperative and public action as the changed situation may demand. To foster and sustain the home under tenement conditions, to rehabilitate neighborhood life and give it some of the healthy corporate vitality which a well-ordered village has; to undertake objective investigation of local conditions; to aid organized labor both in the way of inculcating higher aims and in the way of supporting its just demands; to furnish a neutral ground where separated classes, rich and poor, professional and industrial, capitalist and wage-earning, may meet each other on the basis of common humanity; to initiate local cooperation for substantial good purposes; to strive for a better type of local politics and to take part in municipal affairs as they affect the district. . .[21]

It was a poverty program, but unlike more recent ones the settlement program was centered in individual localities. Those who attacked it (Jack London, for example) sometimes did so for that reason. The organizers of these centers came from outside to help the poor, the other-language people of the working-class districts. A few, no doubt, stayed and identified themselves with the poor, and, like Woods, tried to develop from within the means of participation in the wider social and political scene, but more spent youthful months or years in an "experience" before going on to other careers. Settlement-house workers assisted individuals and families to make adjustments, but settlement-house projects could hardly change the conditions that brought immigrant, working-class, slum districts into being in urban areas.

[20]Robert H. Bremner, *From the Depths: The Discovery of Poverty in the United States* (New York: New York University Press, 1956), p. 62.

[21]Robert Woods, *The City Wilderness: A Settlement Study* (Boston: Houghton Mifflin Company, 1898), p. 274. Jane Addams' book, *Twenty Years at Hull House, with Autobiographical Notes* (New York: The Macmillan Company, 1949), is the classic biography of a settlement house.

The school was being conceived of by some educators during this period as a place from which the wider society could be studied and changed. There were hopes of its being representative of the society, a sort of testing ground for the society, and a community in itself. The movement known as "progressive education" had its origins in this period and in such ideas, though the ideas have a longer history. The "common school," as it spread in the 1830's through the work and writings of Horace Mann, was intended to be the bulwark of the republic. According to the historian of education, Lawrence A. Cremin, "Dreading the destructive possibilities of religious, political, and class difference, [Mann] sought a common value system within which diversity might flourish. His quest was for a new public philosophy, a sense of community to be shared by Americans of every background and persuasion. And his instrument in this effort would be the common school."[22] Mann told the Massachusetts Board of Education in 1846:

> ... any community, whether national or state, that ventures to organize a government, or to administer a government already organized, without making provision for the free education of all its children, dares the certain vengeance of Heaven; and in the squalid forms of poverty and destitution, in the scourges of violence and misrule, in the heart-destroying corruptions of licentiousness and debauchery, and in political profligacy and legalized perfidy, in all the blended and mutually aggravated crimes of civilization and barbarism, will be sure to feel the terrible retributions of its delinquency.[23]

Massachusetts passed the first state-wide compulsory attendance law in 1852 (Mississippi was the last of the states to do so, in 1918). By the end of the century, eight-year schooling was common, but there was a great disparity between cities and rural areas. The illiteracy rate was, in fact, twice as great in rural areas as among the foreign-born population of cities; rural teachers had, on the average, less than a high school education, while many cities required at least one year of teachers' training; and their pay rates were less than half that in cities.

It was in the cities that experimental programs were introduced toward the end of the century with regard to curriculum, school environment, and administration. Several were based on the community concept. Francis W. Parker's "Quincy system," for example, originating in Massachusetts and developed at the practice school of Cook County Normal School (Chicago), organized the school as "a model home, a complete

[22]*The Transformation of the School: Progressivism in American Education, 1876–1957* (New York: Alfred A. Knopf, 1962), p. 10.

[23]"Tenth Annual Report," in *Words That Made American History: Colonial Times to the 1870's*, eds. Richard N. Current and John A. Garraty, 2nd ed. (Boston: Little, Brown and Company, 1965), p. 430.

community and embryonic democracy," with the child at the center of the educative process. William Wirt's "Gary Plan" proposed a model, a "miniature of a community" in which members could participate. Its activities were to reflect those of the larger society; elementary and high school students remained in the same building in order to emphasize, Cremin says, "the continuity of education as well as the heterogeneity of the typical social situation." The school was to be, in addition, the "true center of the artistic and intellectual life of the neighborhood."[24] Most widely known is John Dewey's Laboratory School in Chicago, begun in 1896. In 1897 Dewey wrote: "In so far as the school represents, in its own spirit, a genuine community life . . . the school is organized on an ethical basis." He applied his conception of the school as "a social community which reflects and organizes in typical form the fundamental principles of all community life" to administrative matters and to the methods and subject matter of instruction.[25] The goal was to develop individual capacities and to free individual intelligence for action in a democratic society. The school might be its own community, but it could not be self contained. From the principle that democracy requires participation, it followed that those who are affected by social institutions should help run them. "The two facts that each one is influenced in what he does and enjoys and in what he becomes by the institutions under which he lives, and that therefore he shall have, in a democracy, a voice in shaping them, are the passive and active sides of the same fact."[26] Therefore the student should participate and share in the responsibility for his own education. Although progressive methods fell into disfavor for a time, the movement drew attention to the role of the school in the community, pointed out and increased its importance as a local institution—sometimes as a battleground for other community conflicts.

The goal of these reform efforts was to create communities. Institutions have always been a means of doing this. Their function in community building is to focus attention. They do not necessarily supply form and identity to a community, however. In the instances mentioned here, they were reactions to places and forces that seemed formless and nameless; they were additions to the urban scene, not fundamental changes in it.

The scene, the urban forms and identities, had yet to be described analytically. The community concept as it had developed during this period would provide one line of analysis. But it had limited usefulness as a com-

[24]Cremin, *Transformation of the School*, pp. 128–35 and 155–56.

[25]"Ethical Principles Underlying Education," in *John Dewey on Education: Selected Writings*, ed. Reginald D. Archambault (New York: Random House, Inc., 1964), p. 130.

[26]John Dewey, "Democracy and Educational Administration," *School and Society*, 45 (April 3, 1937), 457–59.

prehensive frame of reference for urban studies. It could not explain growth and change except by tracing "disorganization" and "loss of community," unless, that is, studies were focused on the ecological aspect of community. The so-called Chicago School of urban sociology did just that. In 1915 the *American Journal of Sociology* published Robert Ezra Park's essay, "The City: Suggestions for the Investigation of Human Behavior in the Urban Environment," and over the next twenty years he and his students sought the zones and "natural areas" or "subcommunities" of Chicago.[27] They did not assume that the city was "merely a physical mechanism and an artificial construction," but thought of it as an organic social unit, "a kind of psychophysical mechanism in and through which private and political interests find not merely a collective but a corporate expression." The problem, then, was to discover local organization by discovering spatial and temporal relations of activities and associations. Since with this approach one can not only describe a particular scene but also demonstrate patterns of change over time, it has more recently been recommended to historians who are interested in urban processes.[28] Yet the questions integral to this approach, questions of environment, technology, use of space, and population density, emphasize distinctions between "rural" and "urban" localities without having to take account of social processes and interrelations that may be common to them. Robert M. MacIver's discussion of community, dating from the same period, leads to an emphasis on common processes and interrelations by its attention to "community of interest," "coordination of localities," and "extension of community." He depicted smaller communities within greater ones, and identified as a political problem the working out of a noncontradictory "federal" relation between them.[29] The idea was not immediately taken up for its terms of analysis by sociologists, whose community interests continued to lie within localities, although some historians and political scientists saw in it a way of describing the national community. It is interesting, however, that both the MacIver and the Park approach were based on a conception of community as an organic unit. MacIver's "extension of community" results in another, larger community. Park's community

[27]Park's essay is included in the collection, *Human Communities: The City and Human Ecology* (Glencoe, Ill.: The Free Press, 1952).

[28]Amos Hawley, *Human Ecology: A Theory of Community Structure* (New York: The Ronald Press, 1950) is a basic formulation. Eric E. Lampard, "American Historians and the Study of Urbanization," *American Historical Review*, 67 (October, 1961), 49–61, suggests uses of the concept of "ecological complex."

[29]*Community: A Sociological Study* (New York: The Macmillan Company, 1928; first published in London in 1917). Two recent studies of city and nation are Daniel J. Elazar, *American Federalism* (New York: Thomas Y. Crowell Company, 1966), ch. 7, and Bert E. Swanson, *The Concern for Community in Urban America* (New York: Odyssey Press, 1970).

is a biosocial unit moving from equilibrium to disequilibrium to equilibrium again.

Meanwhile, new localities were coming into being that would eventually be looked at to see whether or not they were communities. *Suburbs* have long been held to be refuges for people removing themselves from madding crowds. In 1819 lots on Brooklyn Heights were advertised: "Families who may desire to associate in forming *a select neighborhood and circle of society, for a summer's residence, or a whole year's*, cannot anywhere obtain more desirable situations."[30] Country homes outside commercial centers were common, and, as turnpikes were built, pleasant houses for the wealthy appeared along them. Promoters emphasized the pure air, wholesome water, and peacefulness outside the city. Along with railroad building came industrial suburbs on the outskirts of commercial-industrial centers; some of them were planned company towns. The "bedroom communities," "dormitory suburbs," or simply residential districts spread with the development of electric trolley lines, bridge building, the automobile, trucks, and buses. By 1920 about one-fourth of the residents of the metropolitan districts of cities with more than 200,000 inhabitants could be called suburban. The question begins to be raised: Is the city growing, or is an urbanization occurring in which the city itself is not the significant unit? The Census of 1920 finds, for the first time, more than half the population of the United States to be "urban." It becomes appropriate to speak of an "urban nation." At the same time, the pull toward small residential units increases. House-and-yard, family, village are themes of descriptions of them.

After World War II, the pull is even stronger, new places proliferate, and already existing villages and small towns are enlarged and drawn into the urban orbit. To comprehend the result in terms of an urban region and nation, Jean Gottmann writes a book entitled *Megalopolis*. To comprehend the result statistically, a concept of "Standard Metropolitan Statistical Area" is developed (see, for illustration, Fig. 9–1). It is defined by the Bureau of the Census as "an integrated economic and social unit with a large population nucleus"[31]; counties (towns in New England) are the basis for tabulation, but an SMSA may cross state lines. This concept is a recognition of regional interdependence, for comprised within it are many localities, each with its own functions, each holding onto to its own potential with the strength obtained from its ties to the others. In the Chicago area, half the population lives outside the central city, but ten other places have populations of more than 50,000 and 1,113 local governmental juris-

---

[30]Quoted in Tunnard and Reed, *American Skyline*, p. 62.

[31]Bureau of the Census, U.S. Department of Commerce, *Statistical Abstract of the United States* (Washington, D.C.: U.S. Government Printing Office, 1971), p. 829.

dictions are represented. In an area with a very different history, Phoenix, Arizona, which has grown mainly since World War II, only about forty percent of the population is counted as living outside the central city, but the central city itself has a relatively low population density, little higher than that of some suburban areas.

The urban scene through much of North America, for that matter, is distinct from that of other parts of the world precisely in terms of population density. Although the central cities of 200,000 or more have a density of 5,976 per square mile, the figure for their outlying areas— where 55.5 percent of the SMSA population now lives—is only 242 per square mile. If you fly over the San Francisco-Oakland area, say, angling south and west from Martinez to San Jose, the landscape seems to be almost filled up—but filled up with varied patterns of closely spaced built-on bits of land. If you live on one of these bits, you wonder where and when the building will stop, and how the "population explosion" in your area can be controlled (and maybe also how you can get the air lanes to San Francisco International changed from over your house). You may think now and then about moving further out, about a new rapid transit system and widened highways (right beside it); they will make travel so much easier and, strangely, increase the numbers of persons going just where you are going.

Flying or using a moving van, finally you get to the fringes of the metropolitan areas, to what might be called "subururs"—encroached-upon places at the borders of the urbanized-suburbanized cloth; places wanted for summer homes, for second properties (for tax advantages and living and recreational purposes), and for getting away from it all (especially, still, as advertised by developers). Prior residents often resist the invasion, but although the economic dominance of the urban center may not be exerted the urban influence is there. For such reasons "urban sprawl" is said to have obliterated, finally, the line between city and countryside. That there was ever a completely clear line can be questioned. A given urban area is still composed of diverse localities and contains people with varying degrees and kinds of attachment to them.

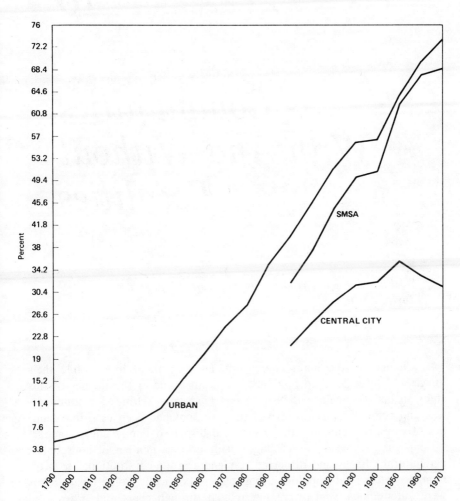

FIG. 9–1   THE URBAN POPULATION: PERCENTAGES OF THE TOTAL POP-
ULATION OF THE UNITED STATES IN URBAN PLACES, 1790–1970, AND IN
STANDARD METROPOLITAN STATISTICAL AREAS AND THEIR CENTRAL CITIES,
1900–1970. Note the increase in the proportion of the metropolitan population outside the central city. The current urban definition of the Bureau
of Census is used for 1950–1970; Alaska and Hawaii are excluded prior
to 1960. Numbers of SMSA's are as follows: 1900, 52; 1910, 71; 1920,
94; 1930, 115; 1940, 125; 1950–1970, 243 (as defined in 1970).

Source: Based on data in Bureau of the Census, U.S. Department of Commerce,
Statistical Abstract of the United States (Washington, D.C.: U.S. Government
Printing Office, 1971), tables 1, 14, 15, and 22; and Donald J. Bogue, *The Population of the United States* (Glencoe, Illinois: The Free Press, 1959), tables
3–1 and 3–2.

10

Communities With And Without Localities

"All places are one continuous space, an ultimate environment."

—W. T. HARRIS

Changes in the landscape, people moving about in it, while their images of places seem to hold still: these are some of the themes of this study so far. To begin with there was a landscape, settings for communities, and before Europeans arrived these settings had been used in a number of ways. Settlement patterns included dispersed family units, compact kinship villages, agricultural villages made up of a number of households, agricultural villages and dispersed residences around institutional or ceremonial centers, and populous urban places. Politically, some local groups were autonomous, some were interrelated through clans and tribes, and some were associated in leagues or alliances or through having been placed in a tributary position. Within and beyond some of the areas were trading networks. In the absence of written records, we can only speculate about the ways in which the locality and local group may have been significant among native Americans; in any case, obviously, there were both local and translocal ties.

European colonial settlers brought with them a history of both dispersed and compact agricultural settlement, administrative and commercial centers, and association with extensive and expansive political and religious institutions. Experience of all of these ties, local and nonlocal, was carried across the Atlantic; it is misleading to look for unitary traditions in the founding of new colonies. Colonies are, however, sponsored places, so that sponsors' plans are a major factor in their initial form. In nearly every instance, the plan was for close and not dispersed households, and the wording of instructions and regulations—and the complaints, later, of colonial leaders—makes it clear that this was not simply for purposes of mutual protection in a wilderness, as is sometimes assumed. But close settlement took more than one form: *rang* or line villages; villages with a central focus in a square or commons with a church and official buildings; similarly focused *pueblos* in the midst of large landholding units; dependent communities of laborers on large landholding units; and clusters of people at administrative and commercial centers.

As colonists enlarged the areas of settlement, some of them, in the process of acquiring more land for themselves, increased the distance between households. In other instances, particularly in the settlement of New York and Pennsylvania by German and Scots-Irish farmers, the idea of a large neighborhood of family-worked farms was brought along by the colonists, and crossroads towns for merchandizing and political-judicial purposes were established in their midst. Ties to the colonial government, and to the colonizing nation, varied with the colony and sometimes with the locality. In obtaining independence from the colonizing nation, the commercial centers where wealth was concentrated appear as a special kind of community, one capable of dominating regions, and necessary to the development of them, and, perhaps therefore, perceived as central in questions of political power.

In the new United States, as new areas were opened to settlers, colonial community forms migrated with the migrants. But there were important differences: (1) national and state governmental decisions set the framework for land acquisition and community building; (2) new ecological conditions were encountered on the plains and prairies and in mountainous and arid regions of the West; (3) commercial centers and facilities for people on the move were essential to the success of the move. The spread of settlement across the continent was predominantly a spread of dispersed settlement, but the nodal points, the major and minor commercial centers whose growth was fostered by transportation-line dominants, gave the spread its direction and at least some of its energy. The roads, canals, and railroads that connected them and provided access to agricultural and mineral resources established interdependencies within and then between regions. Manufacturing and industrial centers depended at first on local resources (water power, minerals), but with investment from outside them and with the development of transportation networks, they too became factors in regional and national economic growth. In short, the cities that took shape in the eighteenth and nineteenth centuries did not do so as separate localities, distinct though they often appeared to be in the landscape. They were essential parts of a larger expansionism.

Politically, this statement applies also to administrative centers, though their histories are less closely tied to regional development. Administrative centers were often planned to be distinct from commercial places, perhaps because of a sense of public as against private purpose, or as an expression of agrarian ideals, or perhaps because builders took the opportunity to do something they thought—and could persuade others—was grand. Capital cities and county seats were, in any case, built with visual and spatial focuses that commercial centers often lacked, and they were more apt to attract and support the educational and cultural institutions that would help characterize them. State capitals were meant to symbolize state government, and state governments were often dominated by men responsive to agricultural interests. This, of course, affected all kinds of localities, but it presented special problems to commercial-industrial places. Around the turn of the century, for example, it blocked some of the efforts of urban reform mayors where new city charters were needed to enable the municipalities to remodel their own governments, offer their own franchises, own their own public works if they wanted to, and generally increase local decision-making powers. There was a "home rule" movement in the 1890's, and by the first world war twelve states, ten of them west of the Mississippi, had freed their municipalities. Even then state legislatures, with their disproportionate representation of rural areas, had somehow to be made to pass the regulations on labor, health, and housing that would be necessary for a reform program. One instance of what could and did happen was in 1902 when the Ohio legislature passed a municipal code for places with more than 5,000 residents, taking appointive powers away from mayors and giving them to city councils or the governor. Mowry says it was aimed at Ohio's radical mayors (the "ethical anarchist" Samuel M. Jones of Toledo, for one, who had instituted a minimum wage for municipal workers and had once announced that "private ownership is a high crime against democracy"). "Since the city was the servant of the state, urban control was not enough; to reform the city one had to reform the statehouse and the governor's mansion." But urban-based reformers did carry their crusades to the state capitals, and "when this new middle-class, urban-minded reform strain was added to the older agrarian one, the existing political structure with its ideological and economic implications began to crumble."[1]

The story of a local community becomes complex when nonlocal factors are added to those that seem to be purely local. Yet the nonlocal factors cannot be ignored. Questions about their influence must at least be asked in studies of every type of place, from relatively isolated places to

[1]George E. Mowry, *The Era of Theodore Roosevelt, 1900–1912* (New York: Harper & Row, Publishers, 1958), pp. 59–68.

obviously interdependent ones. Community studies, exploring patterns and ways of life within localities, can lead to a sense of the distinctiveness and integrity and perhaps the identity of a locality within a wider context, but they can also leave a false impression of separateness. One of the reasons the Lynds' studies *Middletown* (1929) and *Middletown in Transition* (1937) are still important is that they examine change in a local community as such in a context of the nonlocal forces of industrialization and economic depression. Vidich and Bensman's *Small Town in Mass Society* (1958) is a deliberate effort to show the effects of nonlocal forces on a locality. Martindale and Hanson's *Small Town and the Nation* (1969) is a study specifically of conflict between local and translocal forces in a small Minnesota town; the authors found two distinct ways of life there, one with a local-community orientation and one with a translocal orientation.

The point needs less belaboring with regard to the parts of urban places that are referred to and studied as "communities": districts, neighborhoods, ethnic enclaves, suburbs. *Districts* correspond generally to a function (business or financial, produce, warehouse, shopping, entertainment, residential, red-light, and so on) that is part of the ecological pattern of a place as a whole. A district of a city has its own history, just as it has its own identity and conveys its own image,[2] but its history is interwoven with—inconceivable without—that of the whole city and its relations with other places. Lively examples are Gray's *Red Lights on the Prairies* (Canada's western cities) and Asbury's *Barbary Coast* (San Francisco). Yet sometimes the part is taken to characterize the whole. It was the image of districts or sections—slum and factory—that urban reformers of the late nineteenth century had in their minds when they attacked cities. Sometimes, too, a self-containment or "integrity" is sought in a district as though it were a small community. Caroline F. Ware's study of Greenwich Village in the 1920's is an important example of research in a place which has traditionally had a distinct image, but has also been subject to complex interrelations with the "outside." She spoke of it as a community, and looked for evidence of or a trend toward "community integration," social organization and order, but found the opposite. She concluded:

> No social cement bound into a social whole the fragments of old cultures—immigrant and old American—which were thrown together in this community. Nor were there any distinguishable signs that forces were at work to shape new cultural patterns out of the fragments of the old. The most diligent search brought forth no evidence that the direction of social evolution in this community was toward a social order for twen-

---

[2]See Kevin Lynch, *The Image of the City* (Cambridge, Mass.: The M.I.T. Press, 1960), on visual form and meanings. An interesting study that includes much historical information is Anselm Strauss' *Images of the American City* (The Free Press of Glencoe, 1961).

tieth-century America, but only that it was away from the social orders of the past. . . . The compelling social fact of this community was the failure of traditional controls to operate and of traditional patterns to produce a coherent social life. What new patterns may develop to replace the rampant individualism which finds few outlets in the urban life of twentieth-century America except in predatory action or escape? Whence may come organizing forces which will canalize individual energies and give them social form?[3]

"Organizing forces" have also been sought in *neighborhoods*, though most people consider these to be parts of residential districts and not self-sufficient. The significance of the neighborhood usually appears when some local institution is to be supported—an activity center, park, public service facility, school. Since this is one way of identifying a community, neighborhood and community may become interchangeable terms. They may also carry similar connotations of value. For example, what or how much should members have in common in order to be considered members? The question lies back of a number of issues. Currently, the neighborhood-school concept, developed a half-century ago, has been revived in the controversy over busing children from one part of an urban area to another as a means of desegregating school systems. Where neighborhoods are homogeneous in race and social class, advocates of the neighborhood-school concept have sometimes seemed to their opponents to be defending neighborhood values under the guise of educational values.

Ghetto assumes homogeneity, with a distinct line around it, and therefore implies a self-contained community. The line is a social line of limited access, both of outsiders to the area and of insiders to other areas. In the larger view, then, the ghetto is inconceivable without the areas that surround it and external policies and social practices to maintain it. The term appears to have had its origin in Venice, where a section near a foundry (*ghetta*) was enclosed by walls in 1516 as the only area in which Jews were allowed to live. Compulsory restriction to a particular district was, of course, much older than that (as was settlement together by choice, during the Diaspora). By extension, ghetto has come to refer to the residential districts of other distinct cultural or ethnic groups and, most commonly now, to those in which blacks live. At present it is sometimes used also in an ironic way for other local homogeneous groupings: for example, "white ghetto" when others are excluded; "old-folk's ghetto" for retirement communities. One result of this segregation, even when urban in setting, is that the included group can maintain its traditions, its culture, its identity. Anthropologically, it is an *enclave*: a group whose culture

---

[3]*Greenwich Village, 1920–1930: A Comment on American Civilization in the Post-War Years* (New York: Houghton Mifflin Company, 1935; republished as a Harper Colophon Book in 1965), pp. 422–24.

persists though it is physically surrounded by another, larger group. The federal government insured by its reservation policy that this would be the situation for Native Americans. For other reasons, it became the situation also for many European immigrant groups in both the United States and Canada, sometimes for only one generation, sometimes for more. In most instances in cities, there has been not only a cultural but also a socioeconomic class distinction from surrounding groups, neighborhoods, or districts.

A great deal has been written about enclaves, ethnic communities, and ghettos, by both members and observers. Mary Antin's *The Promised Land* (1912) describes the conflicts immigrants faced trying to hold on to something of their old culture while being expected to acquire a new one, such as in the schools. Grace Abbott's *The Immigrant and the Community* (1917) is unusual in its plea for appreciation of immigrants' special contributions to the wider community at a time when most observers demanded Americanization as rapidly as possible, and many were calling for an end to immigration. In 1927 Louis Wirth suggested that the ghetto came closer to "community" than anything the modern city had to offer and that, whatever group made it up, it was not just an ecological phenomenon but also "a state of mind."[4]

Black leaders in recent years have insisted on the integrity of, and demanded autonomy for, local community institutions. In question is not simply the location of a social group or a shared culture; the community question is also one of the location of authority, of decision making about the essentials of the life of a group. In the democratic tradition, members of a society are expected to participate in the decisions that affect them, to have a voice, as Dewey put it in the 1930's, in shaping the institutions under which they live.

Whether this is actually the case is at issue most clearly on the level of the local community. The location of authority is a crucial question, and we should not lose sight of the fact that it has been crucial—and unanswered—in the past as well as the present, among commune builders in the nineteenth century, for example, and municipal leaders of the "home rule" movement. Because the ties of interdependency have become ever more complex in nonpolitical ways, it has been perhaps too easy to leave unanswered the questions of the nature and location of political community.

To further complicate the picture, the idea of community is more and more often attached to, or spread to include, associations and group identifications whose important characteristics are unrelated either to particular localities or to any kind of locality. It is one thing to speak of places, relationships, and growth factors within them, and the development

---

[4]"The Ghetto," *American Journal of Sociology*, 33 (July, 1927), 57–71; included in Wirth's selected papers, *On Cities and Social Life*, ed. Albert J. Reiss, Jr. (Chicago: The University of Chicago Press, 1964), pp. 84–98.

of ties of interdependence between them, but quite another to speak of commonalities whose sources lie in education, occupation, interests, and the like, or even just in the urge to classify other people. Yet these two primary usages of the idea of community do share a factor: individuals identify themselves both ways.

The emphasis on community in modern America is equivalent to a search for it. But is it a search for a place? It often seems to take that form: the wish for a place in the country, a small town somewhere, a cul-de-sac in a suburban tract; the building of communes away from cities and perhaps also the organizing of communal living arrangements within towns and cities; and even attempts to rebuild cities as special communities of their own.

The wish for a place in the country is not new, but the means of fulfilling it are available to increasing numbers of persons. Credit facilities, development of recreation areas, and transportation improvements to provide greater access to them are factors. One result has been a proliferation of *recreation centers.* They are distinct in that they are generally seasonal, with a population composed partly of "regulars" and partly of transient visitors, plus a few year-round people who have or feel a special responsibility for the place. Another result has been the "subrur" phenomenon already noted, with varying lengths of stay and degrees of participation in the affairs of the pre-existing rural community or small towns of the area. If the term community is used, loosely, to mean a place with people who know or at least recognize each other, it is thus possible for an individual to have several communities, moving between them according to inclination or opportunity.

Along with actual moves, whether temporary or permanent, into the countryside goes wandering and vacation touring of backroads and places considered to be out of the way (perhaps prefaced by "Oh let's get off this awful freeway," or "Wonder where that little road leads, the one with the plum trees"). Popular interest in rural areas and small towns is increasing. From sociology to the Sunday supplement, a "different"—that is, nonurban—America is being explored. In news accounts we hear that Vernon, Vermont, population 1,060, is the site of a new nuclear generating plant; what changes will occur? Idria, California, a mercury-mining company town, population 350, is described as a "nowhere town"; "But there is entertainment at hand, an outdoor life of hunting and fishing and occasional community gatherings." Santa Cruz, a resort-retirement community, population 31,000, "finds its gaps are showing," and there is "suspicion between the old community and the new" as university students and "hippies" show up in town. Oatman, Arizona, population 48, number of saloons four, waits for "the price of gold to go up and the town to bloom again." Tudor, California, population one family plus twenty-five to thirty fruit pickers in the summertime, is "quiet, mostly, peaceful, nice for the kids here," and is to be sold. The *Wall Street Journal* reports that the Pleasant Prairie grade school near Red Cloud, Nebraska (Willa Cather country), is about to close down, the children will go to town school, and feelings are mixed. The *New York Times* reports that Brewster, New York, population 1,500, is troubled by the construction of new apartment buildings. There is human interest—and nostalgia. A recently published book, *Life in the Peace Zone*, shows some of the conflict inherent in nostalgia: Scotia, California, is a lumber-mill company town, a small and pleasant "yesterday" of the kind being sought throughout the west, and a "backwater" being abandoned by both its young and its old.[5] The very places that lose residents become attractive to outsiders. Stinking Creek, an area of scattered homes in East Kentucky, in a "land of coal and old men," has been described as beginning to have some hope, partly because of community action programs and young outsiders, such as VISTA volunteers, searching for understanding and for a helpful role. Such places can also be commercial material. Fetterman notes:

> Along Highway 80, which slashes through the saddened hills from Manchester to Hyden to Hazard to Hindman, the newsmen flock. Their purpose: "I'm here to get some poverty stuff, Mac." And the brakes of their cars squeal day after day at the same 'picturesque' spots where shabby little cabins perch and grubby children play.
> "Jesus Christ, stop and let me get a couple shots of that."
> "Boy! That's real poverty stuff there.". . .
> Many newsmen prowl the mountains of East Kentucky to "get some poverty stuff." Poverty is "hot." It is a subject rarely rejected by editors, and poverty stories and pictures are highly salable, as every free-lancer has learned. And easy to obtain.[6]

The interest in small communities sometimes takes a very practical turn. The *San Francisco Examiner* quotes the Urban Land Institute on "resurgence of small towns." A study released in May 1970 showed that 59 percent of new manufacturing plants established between 1964 and 1968 were located in nonmetropolitan areas and that 69 percent of the manufacturing dollars for employment and new plants was spent in small towns. According to the Institute, "It should be remembered that most people normally don't want to leave the area of their upbringing and their associations. Surveys have shown further that many who have left would be happy to return if there was a generally similar level of job and pay." Reasons cited for plant locations included "the desire to avoid congestion;

---

[5]Hugh Wilkerson and John van der Zee, *Life in the Peace Zone* (New York: The Macmillan Company, 1971).

[6]John Fetterman, *Stinking Creek* (New York: E. P. Dutton & Co., Inc., 1970), p. 18.

the opportunity to take advantage of untapped labor, attractive wage rates, availability of workers who can be easily trained; high productivity of labor in small towns; a desire to avoid large city competition for labor; and availability of large plant sites at reasonable costs."[7]

This kind of shift is often referred to as decentralization, as is also the movement of population out from urban centers into suburban places with their own local governments. Actually, both "centralization" and "decentralization" in the United States are aspects of a single process: the elaboration of a network of connections between places, which in itself calls new places into being.

Privately developed residential suburbs are only part of this process. In the United States and Canada suburbs have tended toward homogeneity along racial and social-class lines, because of practices of housing developers in building, pricing, and advertising and because of the image of a homogeneous neighborhood carried into them by real estate agents and residents from urban centers, rural neighborhoods, and small towns. The suburban pattern is not, however, a simple one. The form, history, identity, and image of the suburb vary; factors include the region, the nature of the dominant city, the ideas of developers and contractors, what existed at the location before people began moving to it, and the institutions established by developers and by residents. Many of them are growing at present not only with population increase but also with additions of services, other business, and industrial enterprises. Others are built around an industrial enterprise (as they have been since the late nineteenth century). And at present the "new town" idea is taking hold.

The new town idea has its origins in England, in Ebenezer Howard's "garden city" as described in his book *Tomorrow: A Peaceful Path to Real Reform* (1898). His plan was to bring town and country together—indeed, they "must be married"—by surrounding an economically diversified community with a food-producing ring that would limit its spread. Factories, warehouses, and businesses were to be just inside the green belt, and residences, shops, and public facilities in the inner circle. Work and home were to be close to each other. The first garden city was built just before the first world war: Letchworth, thirty-seven miles north of London. One was begun in the United States in 1916. Most of the development of the idea, however, has occurred since the second world war. England's postwar new towns were specifically planned to limit the growth of London by drawing population to them. In the United States, the idea of such preplanned communities has become attractive, over the past decade, to urban planners who have despaired of solving the problems of deterioration in the central city and of sprawl at its edges. The 1968 Housing Act

[7]*San Francisco Examiner*, May 3, 1970, Sunday Homes Section, Page A.

provided for guaranteed loans through the Department of Housing and Urban Development to help build new towns. The first to be started with this federal assistance is Jonathan, Minnesota, twenty miles southwest of Minneapolis. Initial plans laid out seven interconnected "villages," with their own factories, shopping centers, and schools, and projected a population of 7,000 for each. Corporations have joined in the venture, as they have in subsequently planned places, such as Park Forest South, near Chicago.

Corporations have, of course, sponsored or been the main investors in other planned communities—some sixty since the second world war, one-third of them in California. Examples are Gulf Oil's Reston, Virginia, expected to have a population of 75,000 by 1980; the "Experimental Prototype Community of Tomorrow" in Florida, organized by Walt Disney Productions with Aerojet-General, Monsanto, RCA, and U.S. Steel; Coral Springs, also in Florida, invested in mainly by Westinghouse Electric; Mission Viejo, in Orange County, California, sponsored by Philip Morris; and McCulloch Oil's Lake Havasu City in Arizona. The Irvine Company's new-town plan (Orange County, California) is the most ambitious so far: forty villages, each in an "identifiable environment," with the total population to be around 430,000. The use of the term *village* is interesting. A development area near San Jose, California, is called "The Villages"; one of its advertisements is headed: "Could you find the answer America is looking for . . . in the first rural town of the seventies?" It offers transportation by golf cart, notes that residents have vegetable gardens and General Electric kitchens, and reassures the buyer that there is an "unobtrusive but efficient 24-hour security patrol" plus municipal police. Jefferson might be a bit startled.

But the early nineteenth-century travelers would probably be interested in the fact that corporations have again, as at early Lowell, Massachusetts, become community-conscious. In 1967 E. I. Du Pont de Nemours & Company printed a handsome brochure entitled "Company and Community," raising and providing answers to the questions:

> What is the relationship today between town and factory—both institutions being very different from what they were a generation or two ago? In the wider context, what is the relationship between corporations such as Du Pont, and the whole of American society? What are the mutual interests of corporation and community, the mutual responsibilities, the problems in common? What do these institutions do for each other, and to each other? In sum, what is the social role of business?

Many corporations have provided nonwork facilities at their plant sites— athletics, movies, theater, music—in addition to provisions for off-site recreation, under company sponsorship. Their officers promote the term "our community," sometimes "our family." Again, with such interpretation, it is possible for an individual to have several communities, and to move among them not only on inclination or opportunity but also as part of his daily, weekly, and yearly routine.

The old village image does not apply at all; such communities are not a round of life. Community is no longer a group of people who participate in local life to pretty much the same degree or in the same way. If the concept of a network of associations is used for community, the difference is striking: In the self-contained village, there would be essentially one community that includes everyone. For the majority of the population of the United States today, the network of associations for an individual is shared by others in a given locality only to a limited extent, if at all; it is comprised of people in a number of locations, whose relationships comprise others in other locations, independently. Attachment and participation may be greater in one than in the others, however, so that an individual may feel something of the traditional sense of community even when the people around him do not. This is an apparent contradiction, since, traditionally, the sense of community depended on mutuality—but the search by individuals for ways of acting effectively in a society that is being publicized as "mass" or "depersonalized" brings them to behave as though there were a community role for them, as though there were "community."[8]

The search for a shared community in a locality is clearest in the contemporary commune movement. There are some general parallels with the movement of something over a century ago: The society as a whole can "afford" it (though groups must often spend a long time looking for a place they can afford); there is an urge toward "separatism" among participants who are perceived (and who perceive themselves) as different, especially when stereotyping categories are used, such as "youth culture," "hippies," and "drug culture"; and ideals of a "natural" life and of sharing are promoted in explicit reaction to the commercialism of a consumer-oriented economy, to waste in mass production, and to materialistic values. There is also a concern to organize autonomous local groups that can provide members with a sense of making their own community decisions in an interdependent society.

Many kinds of communes have appeared in the past five or six years, from independent, self-sufficient, subsistence farms, to semi-independent religious and psychedelic retreats, to ecological centers which offer instruc-

---

[8]On opportunities offered by decentralized localities within metropolitan areas, see Robert C. Wood, *Suburbia: Its People and Their Politics* (Boston: Houghton Mifflin Company, 1958), and Scott Greer, *The Emerging City: Myth and Reality* (New York: The Free Press, 1962); in the latter, especially interesting is the concept of a "community of limited liability" (pp. 97–99, 107–37).

tion to outsiders, to—simply—shared living quarters in urban settings.[9] A curious side note is that it was Fourier—not widely read by contemporary communalists—who in the early nineteenth century proposed a "food conspiracy" such as has been spreading among students and others in urban localities: cooperative buying and cooperative kitchens. How many persons are actually involved in all such arrangements, or even how many communes there are, is impossible to discover; the *New York Times* estimated about 2,000 communes (urban and rural) in December 1970, but because of curiosity about them many avoid publicity (and, of course, others seek it).

It is just as impossible to characterize them, except perhaps in terms of the main kinds of problems that different groups of the new communitarians seem especially concerned about. One is the problem of making a living. Many communes try to be self-supporting, but many more depend on some form of financing from outside (contributions, wages from jobs held outside, past savings of participants, money from home). Another problem has to do with time: how long can the commune last, and how long should it last? Many, apparently, are expected to be only temporary arrangements; a few are begun with the expectation that they will no longer be necessary when their purpose has been achieved of showing others in society how improvements in their lives can be made; and a few carry the hope of stability over the generations. Except in some instances of the latter, however, memberships tend to be transitory and there has been much visiting around—as in the nineteenth-century communes. In 1969, which *Newsweek* called the "Year of the Commune,"[10] commune leaders had cause to complain that people constantly coming and going wrecked their plans as well as their vegetable gardens. *Alternatives Newsmagazine's* Directory of Communes for 1971 cautions its readers: "This list is not published so that you will have a place to visit during your next vacation. . . . A commune is a home. Would you like curiosity seekers running through your home every day?"[11]

Probably more so than in the nineteenth century, the new communes have often been planted in what has turned out to be hostile social environments. For their part, local long-term residents especially in rural areas have considered commune building to be a kind of invasion. In one instance—the more interesting because it involves one of the longest-lasting of mid-twentieth century communes—reactions in the surrounding area expressed antagonisms that went far deeper than the existence of the commune as such.

[9]Two recent surveys are William Hedgepeth and Dennis Stock, *The Alternative: Communal Life in New America* (New York: The Macmillan Company, 1970), and Dick Fairfield, *Communes, USA* (San Francisco: Alternatives Foundation, 1971).
[10]Aug. 18, 1969, pp. 89–90.
[11]San Francisco: Alternatives Foundation, 1971, p. 42.

204 The Next Place You Come To

The place is Americus, Georgia. In 1942, Clarence L. Jordan, a young man with degrees in agriculture and theology, founded Koinonia Farm with 1,400 acres of land and a charter of incorporation. He intended to develop a bi-racial Christian community, with members "sharing their wealth and labor and 'doing business with God' "; "Koinonia," he said, was a New Testament Greek word for "togetherness."[12] His own and a half-dozen other families came to the farm in November. In December five men who identified themselves as Sumter County Ku Klux Klansmen paid their first visit.[13] Over the next few years Koinonia was accused of mixing the races, of including conscientious objectors, and, after the War, of being pro-Communist. A number of attacks on community members and property were reported. In 1956 the local White Citizens Council imposed a general boycott, covering all goods and services required by the farm, and the next year the school board voted to exclude Koinonia's children. Tension between the community and the surrounding area was at its highest in 1957, when the county grand jury investigated the farm and published a report that amplified the earlier accusations. The report also suggested that the instances of violence had been perpetrated by the community members themselves, that Koinonia was not really a religious organization as it claimed in its charter, and that white members did not really promote equality but wanted, rather, to "enrich themselves at the expense of the negro's toil."[14]

At that time there were 45 white and 15 black men, women, and children in the community,[15] and they continued to farm and to sell produce (cotton, peanuts, pecans) outside the area. According to Hedgepeth and Stock, referring apparently to a visit made in 1969, "It's only been within the past year that the local folk have loosened up at all. . . . some locals even stop by occasionally to buy muscadines, grown on 4 acres of Koinonia land that lie across the highway."[16] These authors describe the farm—"several plain wood-frame houses, a two-story wooden building, a barn, a toolshed, and a long new building, mostly completed. . . . 1,400 acres of timber, crops and cattle pasture"—and quote a member on its organization by partnerships: "Economically, we're divided into partnership units. Like two men own and raise cattle, that's their project. Two are partners for the corn and peanut program. Koinonia itself makes the

[12]Tom Lawrence, "Americus Project Survives: 26 Years Defying Klan," *Atlanta Journal and Constitution*, Jan. 26, 1969.
[13]*Ibid.*
[14]Rudy Hayes, "Grand Jury Strongly Believes that Koinonia Communist Front; 'Responsible for Violence,' " *Americus Times-Recorder*, April 5, 1957, p. 1, and "Full Text of Sumter County Jury Presentments on Koinonia," *ibid.*, p. 2.
[15]In "Koinonia to Set up Second Farm in N.J.," *ibid.*, p. 1 (a short news article with a New York dateline, next to the lead story on the grand jury report).
[16]*The Alternative*, p. 178.

loan for them to get started, then they produce, take a reasonable living standard and contribute the excess to the community." The community had also undertaken a project to provide house sites, some with houses, for poor farm families, with the idea that the urban ghetto was a product of rural displacement and that partnership farming and housing could be an "answer to the economic squeeze that's driving so many small farmers off their land."[17] The population was 35. In 1972 a reporter found "about 60 adults," half of them permanent residents and the rest "short- or long-term volunteers.[18]

Clarence Jordan died in October 1969. In the obituary that appeared in the Americus paper he was quoted as having said: "An integrated Christian community was a very practical vehicle through which to bear witness to a segregated society a decade ago, but now it is too slow, too weak, not aggressive enough. Its lack of mobility gives it the appearance of a house on the bank of a river as the rushing torrents of history swirl by, leaving it with but memories of its active past."[19]

Baltzell has written, "All too many of us are more or less nostalgic about the good-old-days of spatial cohesion in the small, local community. But modern urban man must guard his privacy precisely because he needs to have many more social relationships than in the past."[20] Thus, in his view, most relationships are maintained as "secondary," and the important "primary" ones are also based on free choice and common interests rather than on place and kinship. Stein, reviewing community studies of the twentieth century, and raising especially the question of "disorganization" of modern community life, finds that a central problem for students is "to assess the provisions which a community makes for meaningful life experiences in the context of a meaningful life cycle."[21] The community context is not now easily delimited; "communities" with which people identify themselves may or may not be related to a locality, and localities may or may not offer the range of association and experience, the "representativeness" of the culture[22] that would provide an individual with what he needs to know. From this point of view, it becomes more understandable that the term community is used for so many nonlocal associations. It is a

---

[17]*The Alternative*, pp. 175–77.

[18]Kenneth Reich, "Thirty Years for Utopia—One Commune That Lasted," *S.F. Examiner & Chronicle*, Sunday Punch, April 23, 1972, p. 5.

[19]*Americus Times-Recorder*, Oct. 28, 1969, p. 12.

[20]E. Digby Baltzell, ed., *The Search for Community in Modern America* (New York: Harper & Row, Publishers, 1968), p. 4.

[21]Maurice R. Stein, *The Eclipse of Community: An Interpretation of American Studies* (New York: Harper & Row, Publishers, 1960), p. 258.

[22]Conrad M. Arensberg, "The Community as Object and as Sample," in Conrad M. Arensberg and Solon T. Kimball, *Culutre and Community* (New York: Harcourt, Brace & World, Inc., 1965), pp. 7–27.

matter of association and identification. At the same time—to reiterate—there is increasing concern with localities and the quality of life in them. The nonlocal groupings seem not to have identities of their own; they are, rather, categories (for example, "academic community"). The associations of the one-of-a-number-of-communities kind (institutions such as colleges and hospitals and even a drug-treatment program in California called "The Family," companies, clubs, and so on) have variable identities, depending on one's relation to them. Because places imply a greater constancy of identity, locations of it, people turn to them. Places do have their own identities for the people in them, whether or not they spend all of their time there, and these identities are not arrived at by adding up all the information there is about them. A setting, a set of relationships, an image—even if carried over from someplace else—go into a sense of recognition.

They have such identity whether one is moving about, living in one place, or just ending up somewhere. An English poet put it:

> *For some, places mean coming to or going from,*
> *Comedians and singers with their suitcases*
> *Packed with signed photographs of themselves;*
>
> *Business-men in sharp suits, come to buy and sell,*
> *Still seeking their paradise of transactions,*
> *The bottomless market, where the mugs live.*
>
> *For others, places are sites for existence,*
> *Where the roads slow down and come to a stop*
> *Outside where it's good to be, particular places,*
>
> *Where the instantly recognised people live,*
> *The buses are a familiar colour and the life is*
> *Utterly civilian.*
>
> *And for a very few, places are merely the dumps*
> *They end up in, backwaters, silent places,*
> *The cheapest rooms of the cheapest towns.*[23]

[23]Douglas Dunn, "Backwaters," *New Statesman*, Oct. 3, 1969.

Index